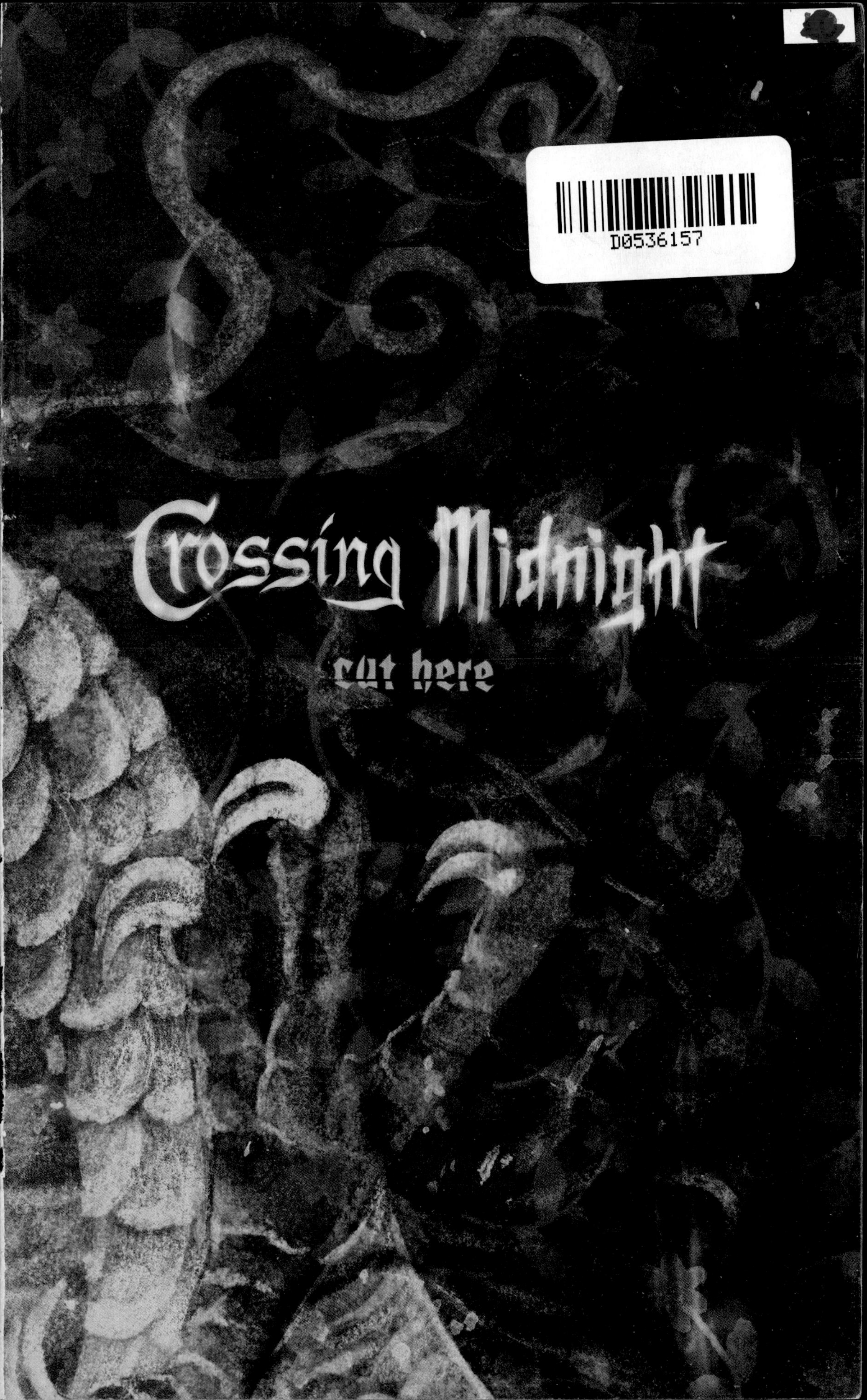
Crossing Midnight
cut here

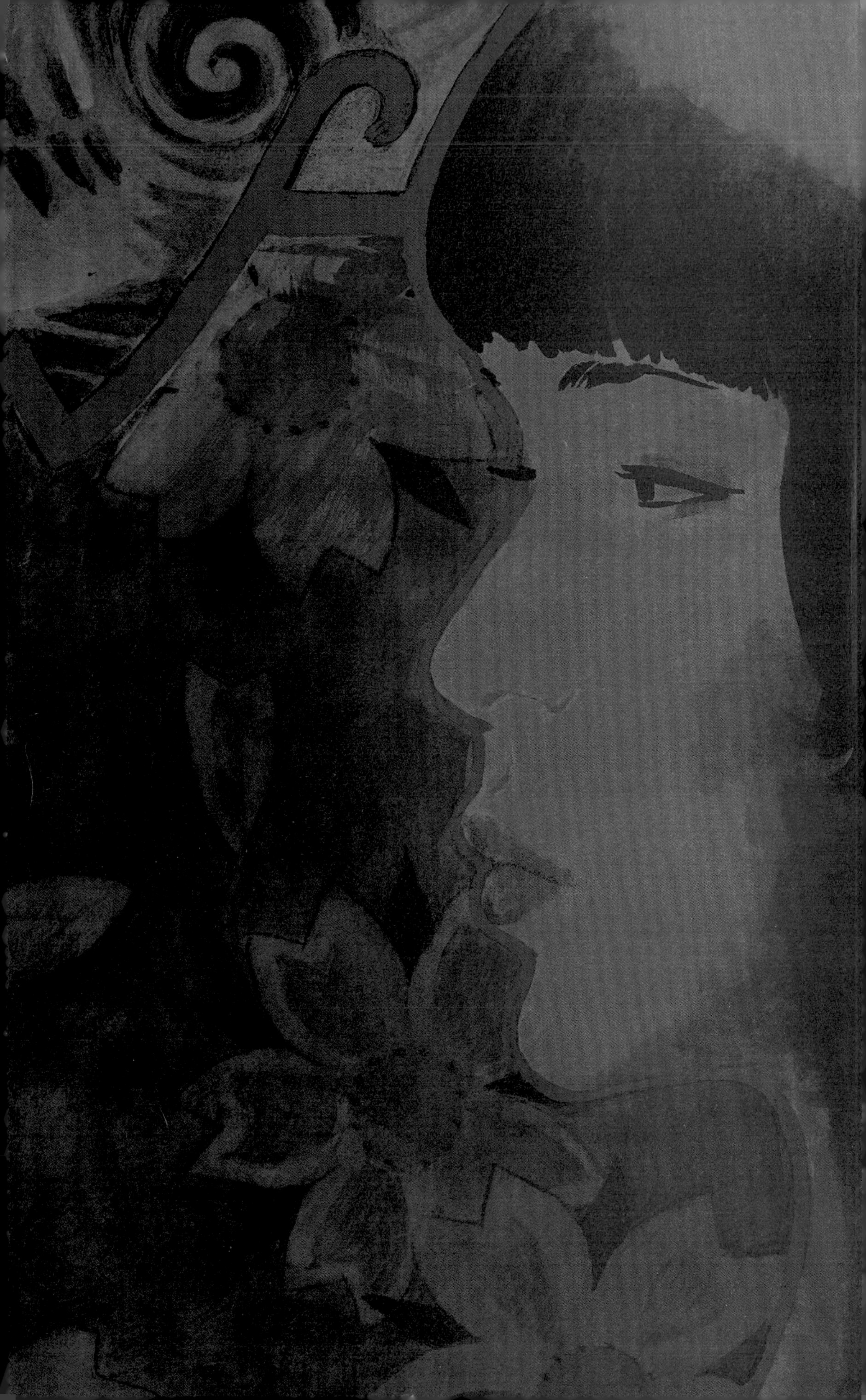

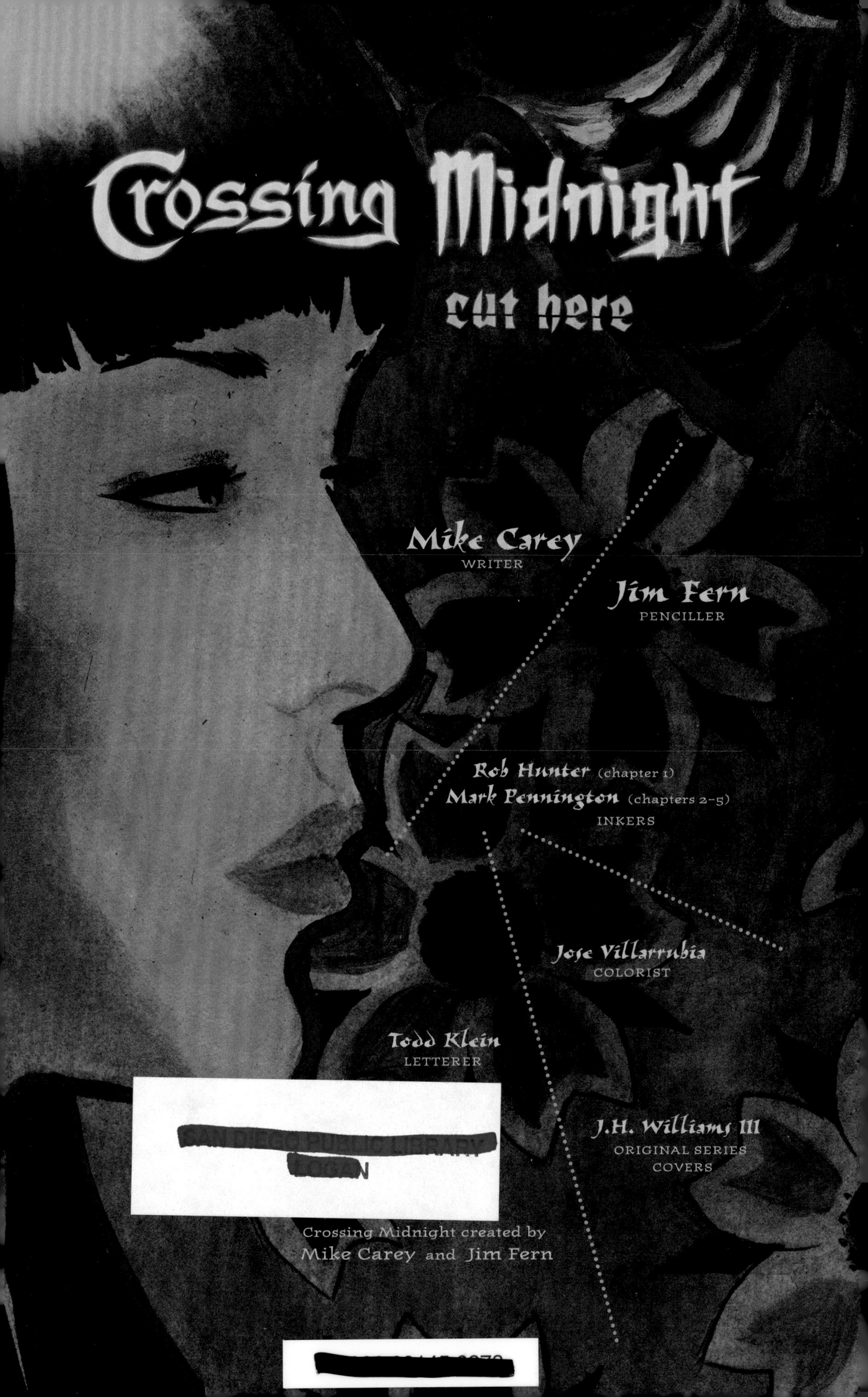

Crossing Midnight

cut here

Mike Carey
WRITER

Jim Fern
PENCILLER

Rob Hunter (chapter 1)
Mark Pennington (chapters 2-5)
INKERS

Jose Villarrubia
COLORIST

Todd Klein
LETTERER

J.H. Williams III
ORIGINAL SERIES
COVERS

Crossing Midnight created by
Mike Carey and Jim Fern

KAREN BERGER
Senior VP-Executive Editor

KAREN BERGER &
PORNSAK PICHETSHOTE
Editors-original series

BOB HARRAS
Editor-collected edition

ROBBIN BROSTERMAN
Senior Art Director

PAUL LEVITZ
President & Publisher

GEORG BREWER
VP-Design & DC Direct Creative

RICHARD BRUNING
Senior VP-Creative Director

PATRICK CALDON
Executive VP-Finance & Operations

CHRIS CARAMALIS
VP-Finance

JOHN CUNNINGHAM
VP-Marketing

TERRI CUNNINGHAM
VP-Managing Editor

ALISON GILL
VP-Manufacturing

HANK KANALZ
VP-General Manager, WildStorm

JIM LEE
Editorial Director-WildStorm

PAULA LOWITT
Senior VP-Business & Legal Affairs

MARYELLEN MCLAUGHLIN
VP-Advertising & Custom Publishing

JOHN NEE
VP-Business Development

GREGORY NOVECK
Senior VP-Creative Affairs

SUE POHJA
VP-Book Trade Sales

CHERYL RUBIN
Senior VP-Brand Management

JEFF TROJAN
VP-Business Development, DC Direct

BOB WAYNE
VP-Sales

Cover illustration by J. H. Williams III
Logo design by Terry Marks
Publication design by Amelia Grohman

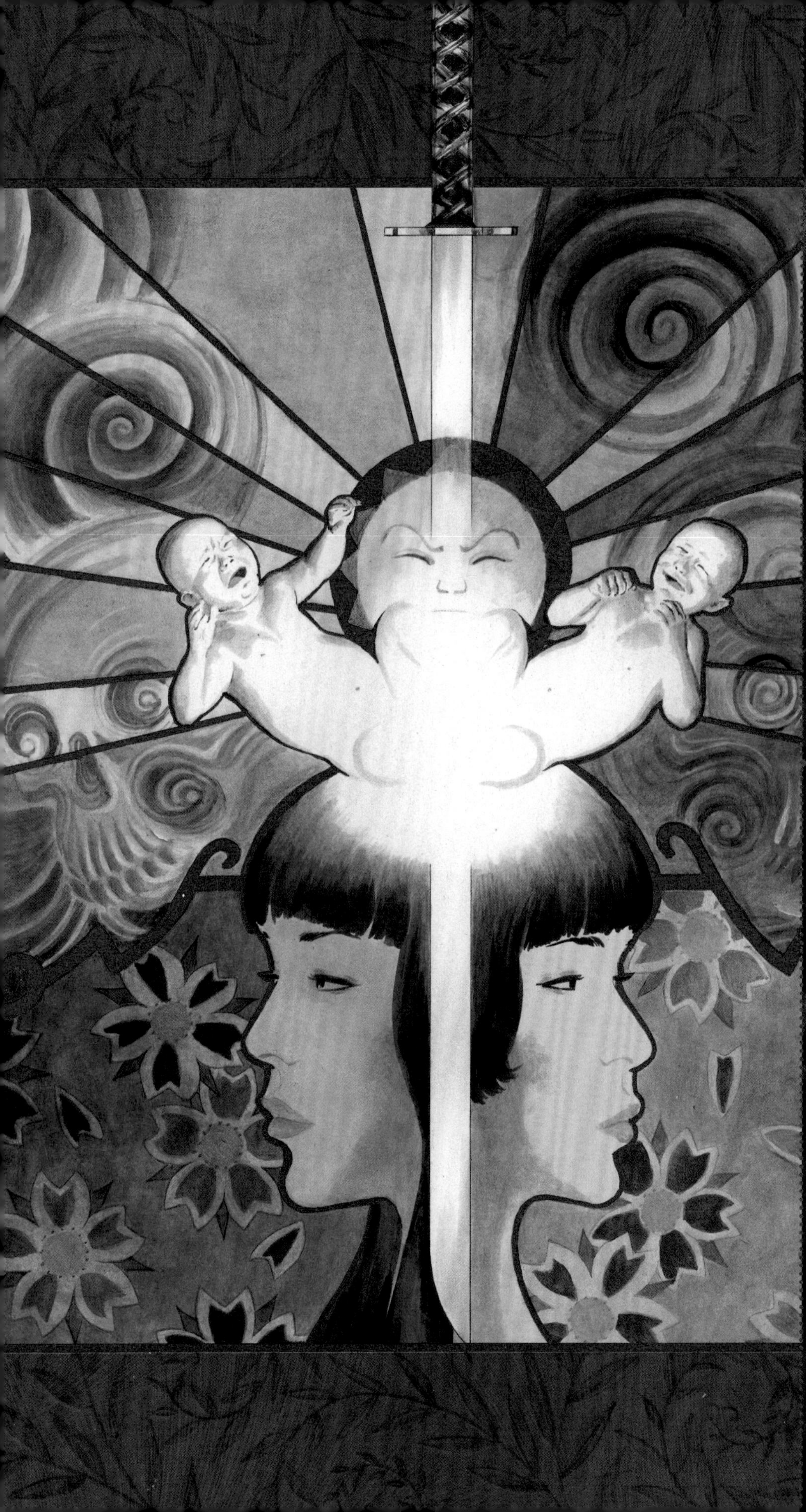

chapter one

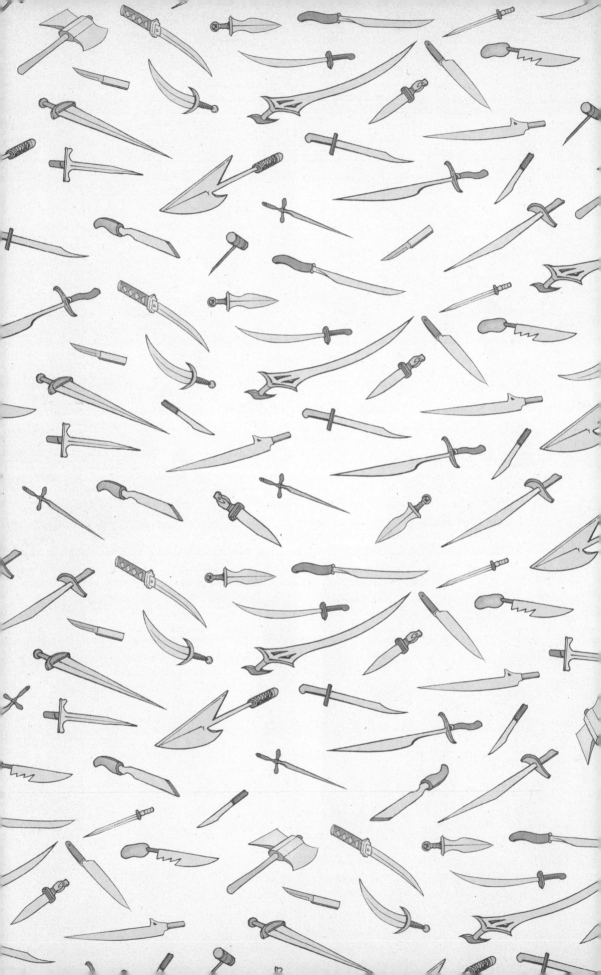

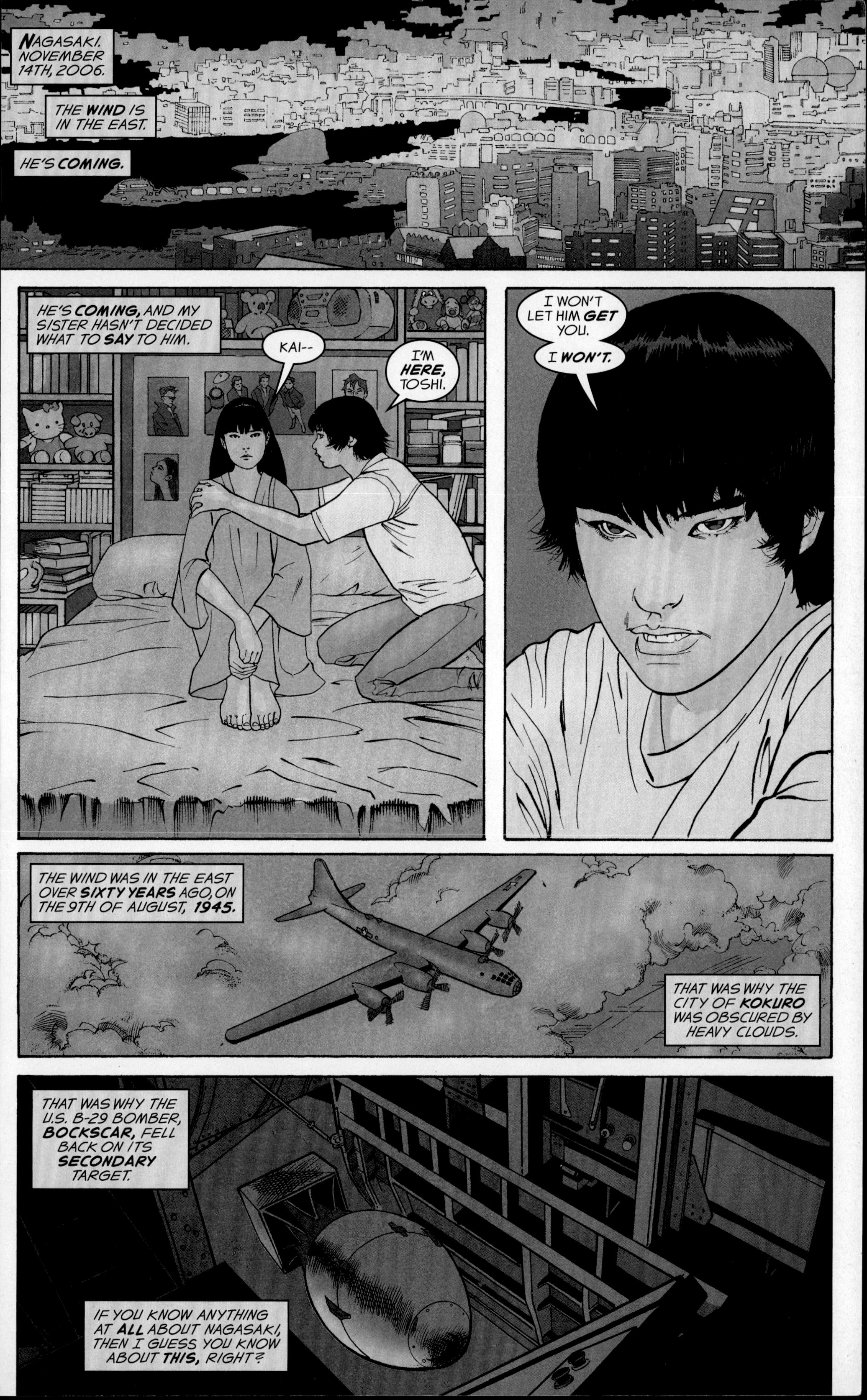
NAGASAKI. NOVEMBER 14TH, 2006.
THE WIND IS IN THE EAST.
HE'S COMING.
HE'S COMING, AND MY SISTER HASN'T DECIDED WHAT TO SAY TO HIM.
KAI--
I'M HERE, TOSHI.
I WON'T LET HIM GET YOU.
I WON'T.
THE WIND WAS IN THE EAST OVER SIXTY YEARS AGO, ON THE 9TH OF AUGUST, 1945.
THAT WAS WHY THE CITY OF KOKURO WAS OBSCURED BY HEAVY CLOUDS.
THAT WAS WHY THE U.S. B-29 BOMBER, BOCKSCAR, FELL BACK ON ITS SECONDARY TARGET.
IF YOU KNOW ANYTHING AT ALL ABOUT NAGASAKI, THEN I GUESS YOU KNOW ABOUT THIS, RIGHT?

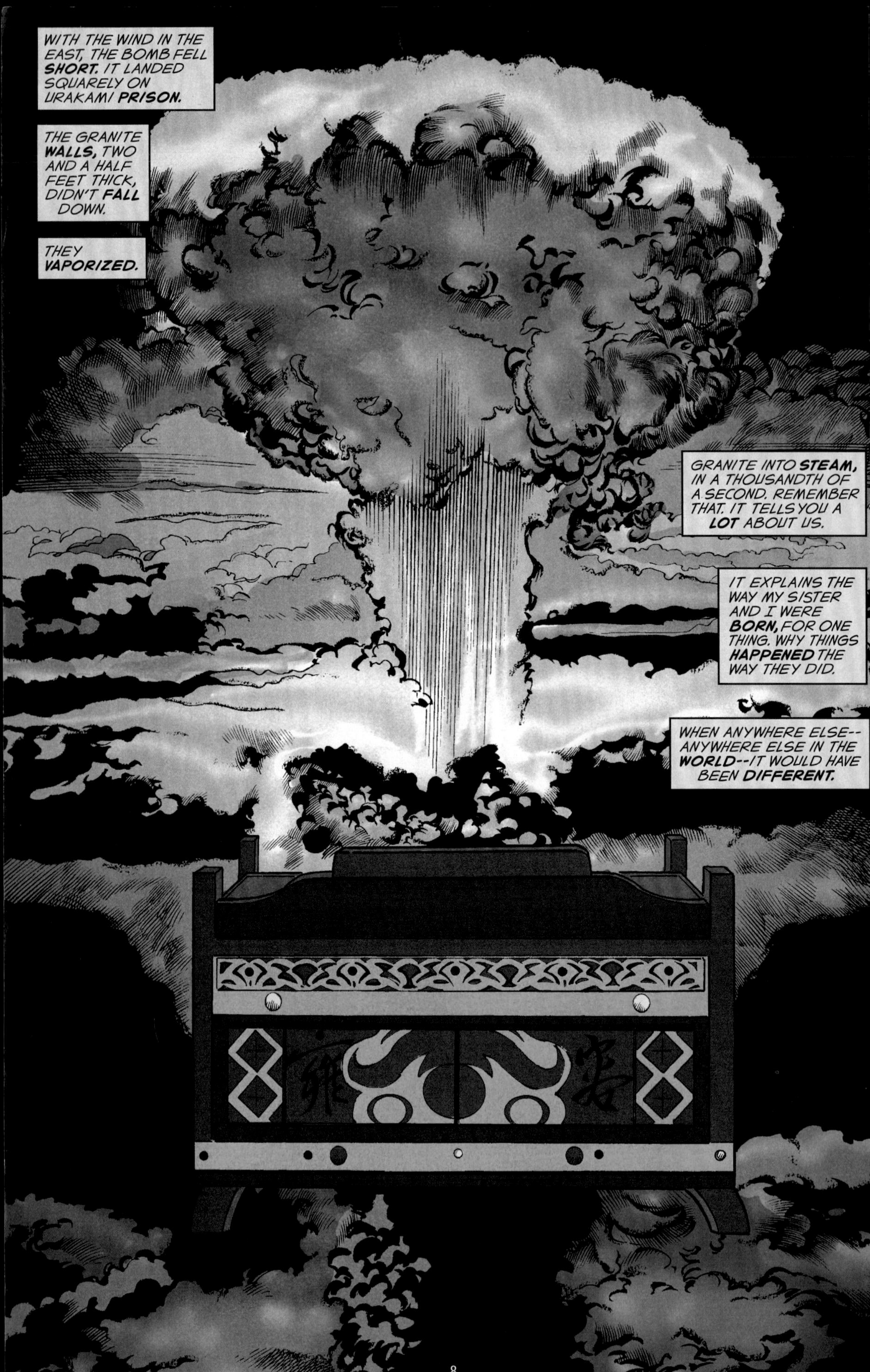
WITH THE WIND IN THE EAST, THE BOMB FELL SHORT. IT LANDED SQUARELY ON URAKAMI PRISON.
THE GRANITE WALLS, TWO AND A HALF FEET THICK, DIDN'T FALL DOWN.
THEY VAPORIZED.
GRANITE INTO STEAM, IN A THOUSANDTH OF A SECOND. REMEMBER THAT. IT TELLS YOU A LOT ABOUT US.
IT EXPLAINS THE WAY MY SISTER AND I WERE BORN, FOR ONE THING. WHY THINGS HAPPENED THE WAY THEY DID.
WHEN ANYWHERE ELSE--ANYWHERE ELSE IN THE WORLD--IT WOULD HAVE BEEN DIFFERENT.

MY **GRANDMA**, AKIKO HARA. SHE'S A **HIBAKUSHA**-- A SURVIVOR OF THE BOMB. VERY **TOUGH**.

SHE BROUGHT HER CHILDREN TO NAGASAKI AFTER GRANDDAD **HIDESHI** DIED AND KEPT THEM **ALIVE** BY WORKING AT THE PORT.

SHE WASN'T **RELIGIOUS** BACK THEN. SHE ONLY BROUGHT THE SHRINE WITH HER BECAUSE HER **OWN** MOTHER INSISTED.

BUT--GRANITE INTO **STEAM**. THAT CHANGES THE WAY YOU **THINK**.

HERE WE ARE.

WHEN MY MOM, **MIYA**, GOT PREGNANT, GRANDMA AKIKO TOLD DAD HE HAD TO **PRAY** FOR A SAFE DELIVERY.

PRAY TO THE **KAMI.** THE SPIRITS WHO **LIVED** IN THE SHRINE.

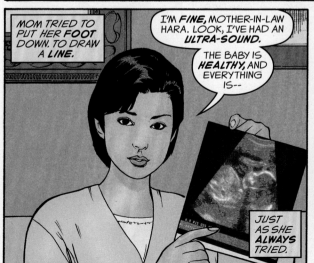

MOM TRIED TO PUT HER **FOOT** DOWN. TO DRAW A **LINE**.

I'M **FINE,** MOTHER-IN-LAW HARA. LOOK, I'VE HAD AN **ULTRA-SOUND.**

THE BABY IS **HEALTHY,** AND EVERYTHING IS--

JUST AS SHE **ALWAYS** TRIED.

BUT YOU COULDN'T **ARGUE** WITH GRANDMA AKIKO.

SHE'D JUST **STARE** AT YOU WITH HER BURNED FACE UNTIL YOU STUMBLED INTO **SILENCE.**

9

THE KAMI ARE SORT OF A **FOLKLORE** THING. NOT QUITE GODS, NOT QUITE **DEMONS**.

OH **SPIRITS** OF THIS SHRINE, LOOK UPON US WITH **FAVOR**.

AND BLESS MY WIFE'S **WOMB**.

SPIRITS OF **NATURE**. SPIRITS OF EVERYTHING.

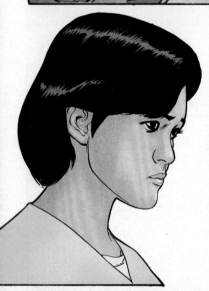

LET OUR CHILD BE BORN **HEALTHY**, WITH NO COMPLICA- TIONS.

AND--UMM-- ACCEPT OUR **OFFERING** IN RETURN.

AND WE'LL BE HUMBLE AND **THANKFUL** UNTO YOU.

AND...ER...**REPAY** YOUR KINDNESS WITH OUR **WORSHIP**.

THAT WAS REALLY **HUMILIATING**, YASUO.

WHEN ARE YOU **EVER** GOING TO STAND UP TO HER?

I'M SORRY, MIYA. I DIDN'T THINK THERE WAS ANY **HARM** IN IT.

IT DOESN'T **MEAN** ANYTHING. THAT SHRINE IS JUST A FAMILY **RELIC**.

WE DON'T EVEN KNOW WHICH KAMI IT'S MEANT TO BE **DEDI- CATED** TO.

I **LOVE** YOU, MIYA.

I **KNOW** THAT, STUPID. THAT'S THE **POINT**.

WHY DO I NEED **DIVINE** PROTECTION WHEN I'VE GOT **YOU**?

ON THE 14TH OF NOVEMBER AT 6 A.M., MY MOM'S **WATER** BROKE.

DAD WAS TERRIFIED THE CAR WOULDN'T START, BUT THAT MORNING IT WENT LIKE A DREAM.

HE TOOK HER TO THE UNIVERSITY HOSPITAL, WHERE HE SPENT THE DAY PACING AND FRETTING.

IT WAS AN **EIGHTEEN-HOUR** LABOR.

ALMOST. **ALMOST** EIGHTEEN HOURS.

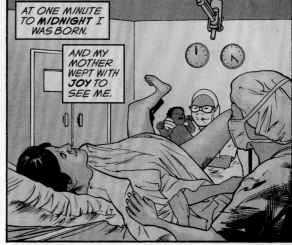

AT ONE MINUTE TO **MIDNIGHT** I WAS BORN.

AND MY MOTHER WEPT WITH **JOY** TO SEE ME.

BUT WHEN THEY PUT ME ON HER BREAST, SHE **CONTINUED** TO WEEP.

BECAUSE THE PAIN HADN'T **STOPPED.**

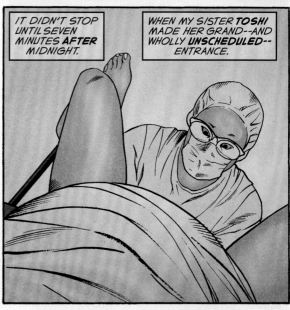

IT DIDN'T STOP UNTIL SEVEN MINUTES **AFTER** MIDNIGHT.

WHEN MY SISTER **TOSHI** MADE HER GRAND--AND WHOLLY **UNSCHEDULED**--ENTRANCE.

SOMETIMES ONE BABY LIES **BEHIND** THE OTHER, THE HOSPITAL SAID.

AND WHEN THE DOCTOR HEARS **ONE** HEALTHY HEARTBEAT, HE MAY STOP AT **THAT.**

EVEN WITH AN ULTRA-SOUND--IF THE **ANGLE** ISN'T SET UP RIGHT...

OUR PARENTS DIDN'T MIND; NEVER EVEN **THOUGHT** ABOUT SUING. THEY WERE **BURSTING** WITH HAPPINESS.

AND THEY GAVE US THEIR **LOVE** ABSOLUTELY AND UNCON-DITIONALLY.

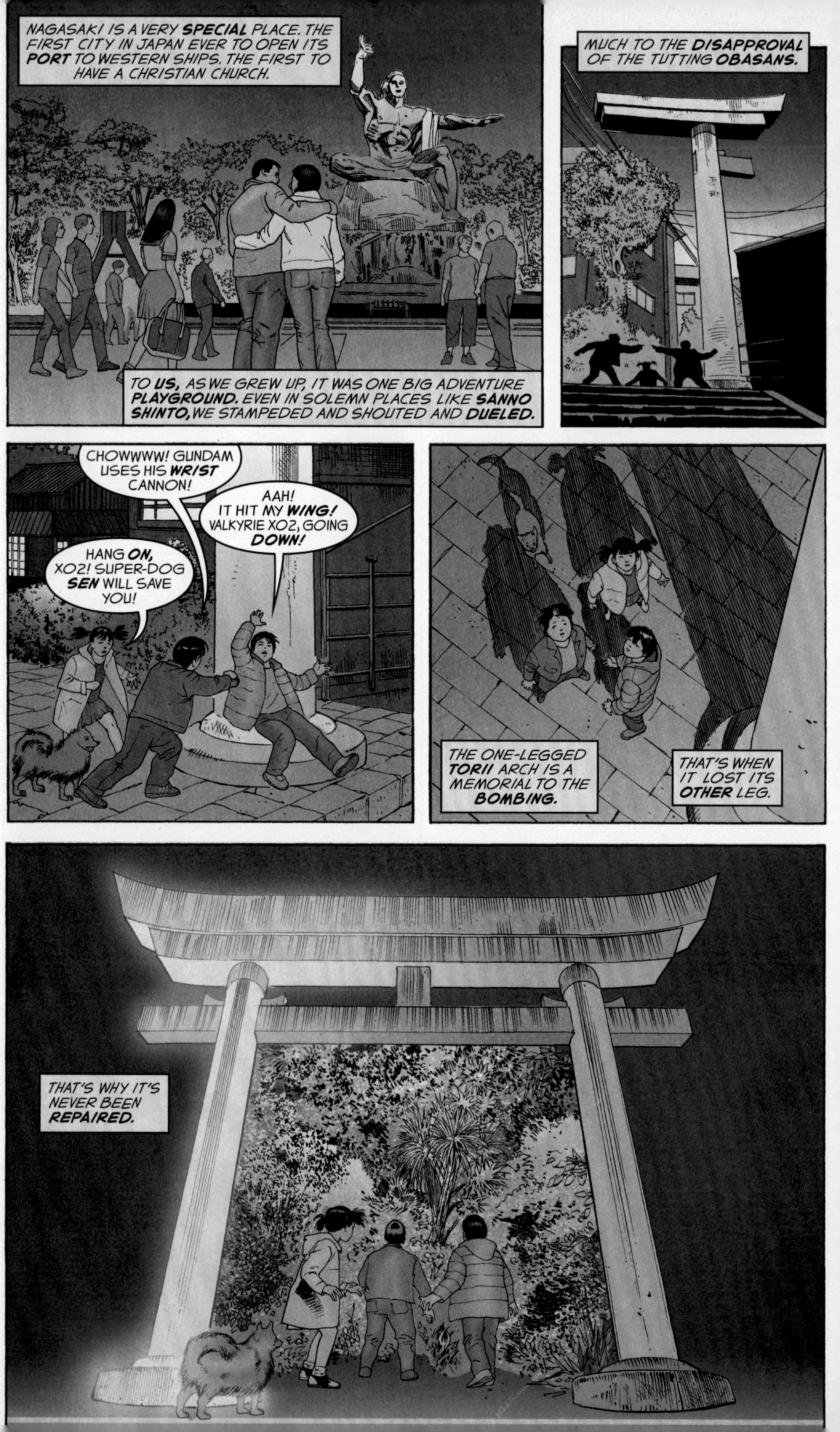
NAGASAKI IS A VERY SPECIAL PLACE. THE FIRST CITY IN JAPAN EVER TO OPEN ITS PORT TO WESTERN SHIPS. THE FIRST TO HAVE A CHRISTIAN CHURCH.
TO US, AS WE GREW UP, IT WAS ONE BIG ADVENTURE PLAYGROUND. EVEN IN SOLEMN PLACES LIKE SANNO SHINTO, WE STAMPEDED AND SHOUTED AND DUELED.
MUCH TO THE DISAPPROVAL OF THE TUTTING OBASANS.
CHOWWWW! GUNDAM USES HIS WRIST CANNON!
AAH! IT HIT MY WING! VALKYRIE XO2, GOING DOWN!
HANG ON, XO2! SUPER-DOG SEN WILL SAVE YOU!
THE ONE-LEGGED TORII ARCH IS A MEMORIAL TO THE BOMBING.
THAT'S WHEN IT LOST ITS OTHER LEG.
THAT'S WHY IT'S NEVER BEEN REPAIRED.

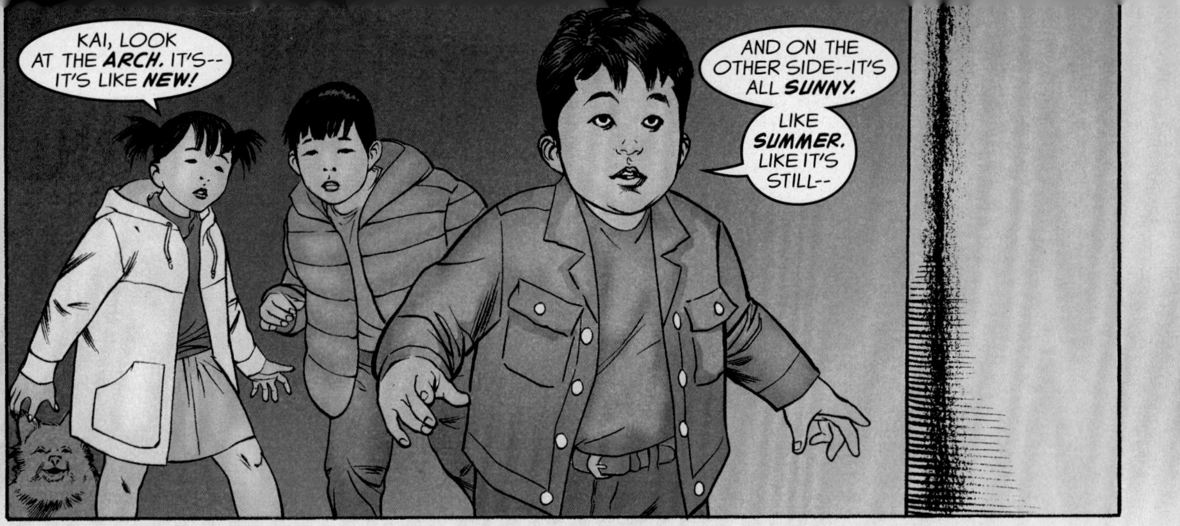
KAI, LOOK AT THE **ARCH.** IT'S-- IT'S LIKE **NEW!**
AND ON THE OTHER SIDE--IT'S ALL **SUNNY.**
LIKE **SUMMER.** LIKE IT'S STILL--

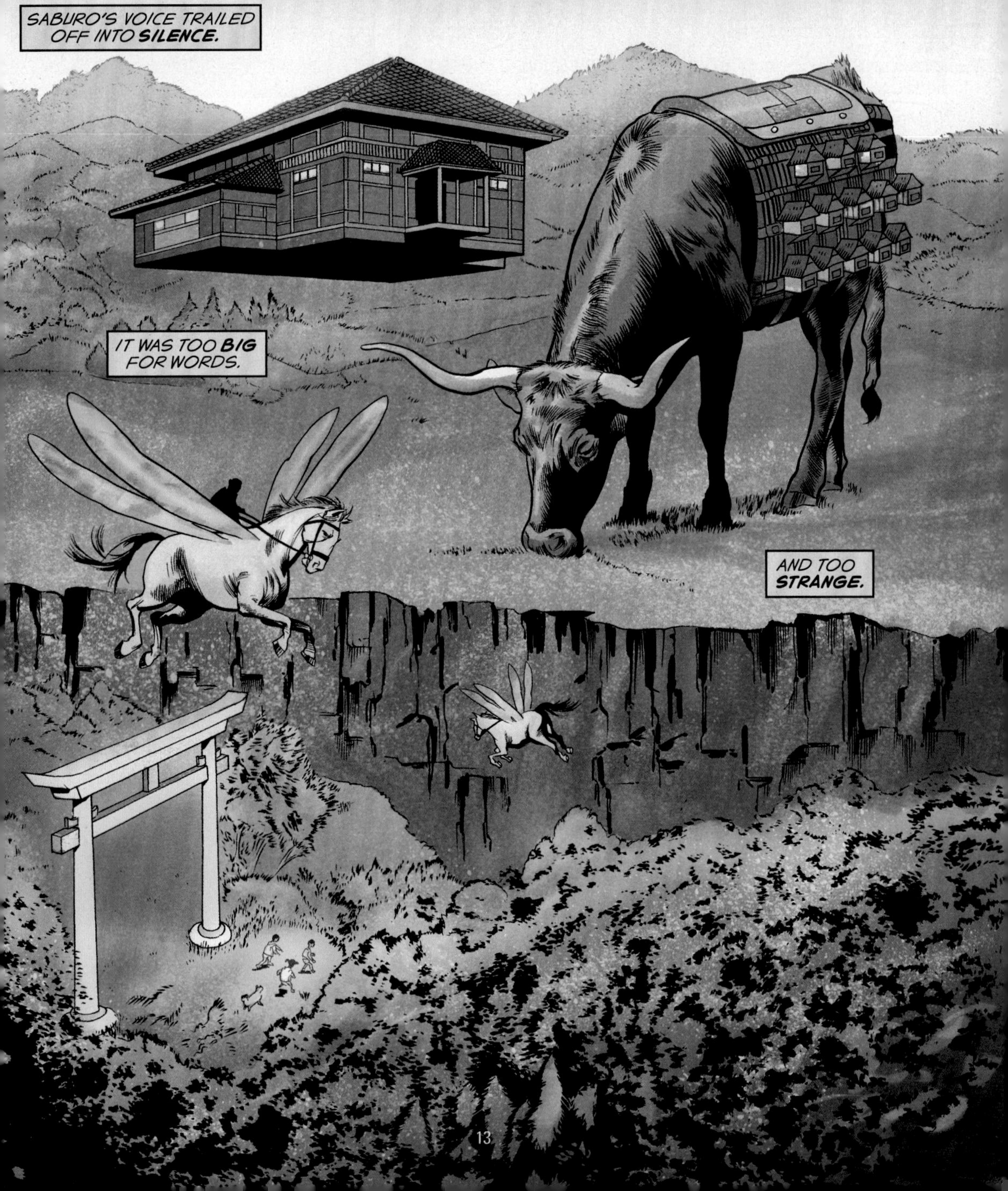
SABURO'S VOICE TRAILED OFF INTO **SILENCE.**
IT WAS TOO **BIG** FOR WORDS.
AND TOO **STRANGE.**

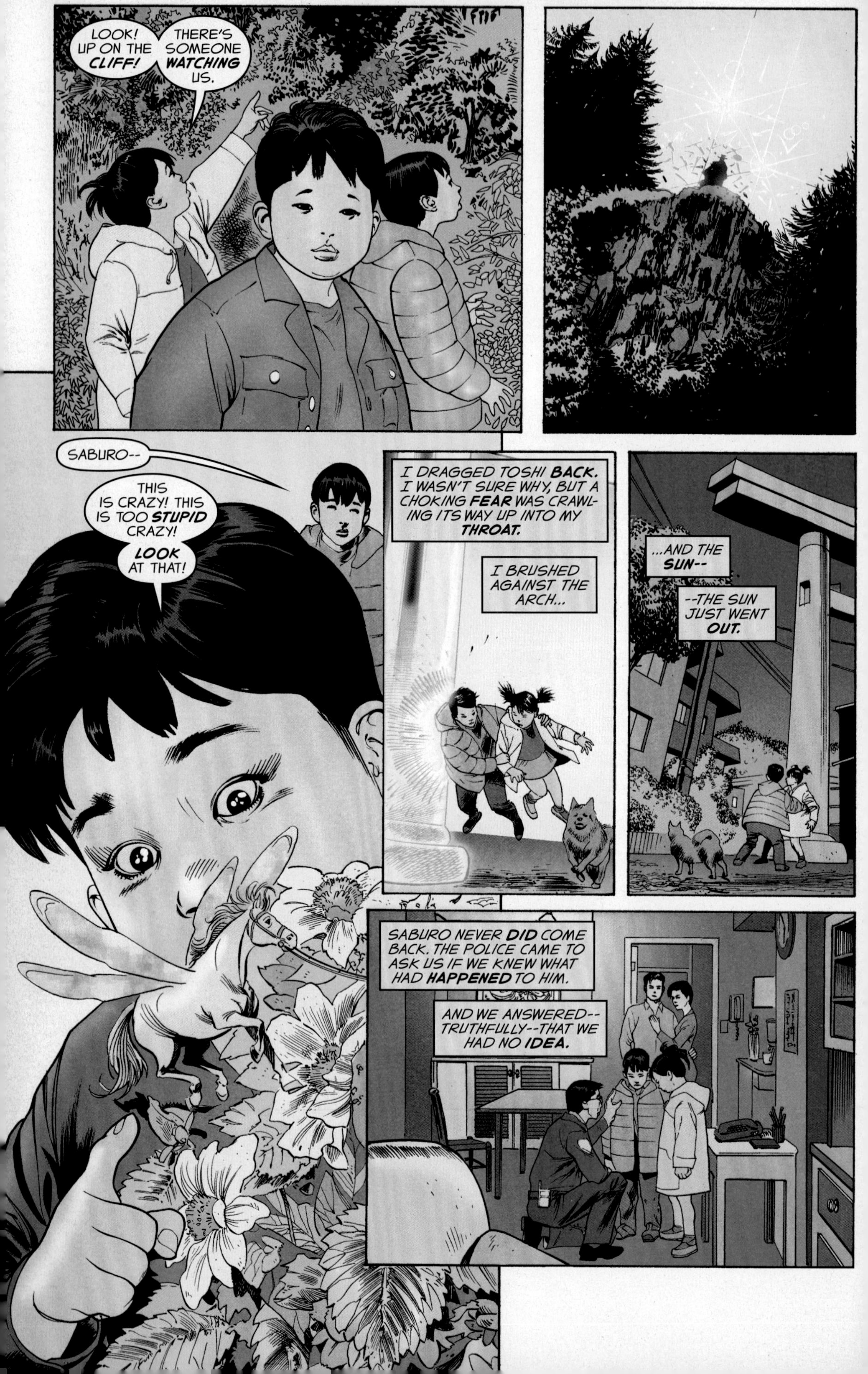
LOOK! UP ON THE CLIFF!
THERE'S SOMEONE WATCHING US.
SABURO--
THIS IS CRAZY! THIS IS TOO STUPID CRAZY!
LOOK AT THAT!
I DRAGGED TOSHI BACK. I WASN'T SURE WHY, BUT A CHOKING FEAR WAS CRAWLING ITS WAY UP INTO MY THROAT.
I BRUSHED AGAINST THE ARCH...
...AND THE SUN--
--THE SUN JUST WENT OUT.
SABURO NEVER DID COME BACK. THE POLICE CAME TO ASK US IF WE KNEW WHAT HAD HAPPENED TO HIM.
AND WE ANSWERED--TRUTHFULLY--THAT WE HAD NO IDEA.

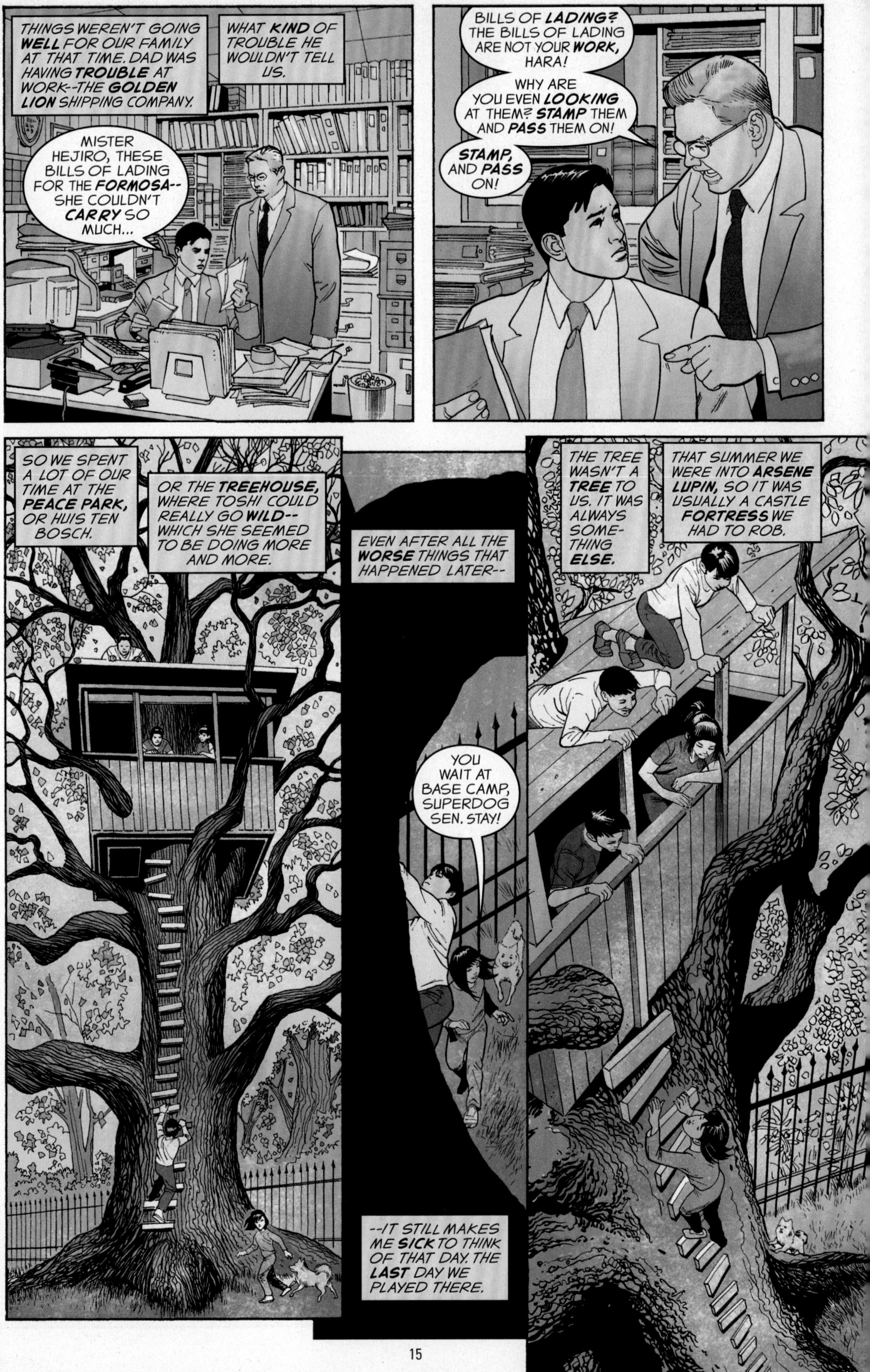

THINGS WEREN'T GOING WELL FOR OUR FAMILY AT THAT TIME. DAD WAS HAVING TROUBLE AT WORK--THE GOLDEN LION SHIPPING COMPANY.
WHAT KIND OF TROUBLE HE WOULDN'T TELL US.
MISTER HEJIRO, THESE BILLS OF LADING FOR THE FORMOSA-- SHE COULDN'T CARRY SO MUCH...
BILLS OF LADING? THE BILLS OF LADING ARE NOT YOUR WORK, HARA!
WHY ARE YOU EVEN LOOKING AT THEM? STAMP THEM AND PASS THEM ON!
STAMP, AND PASS ON!
SO WE SPENT A LOT OF OUR TIME AT THE PEACE PARK, OR HUIS TEN BOSCH.
OR THE TREEHOUSE, WHERE TOSHI COULD REALLY GO WILD-- WHICH SHE SEEMED TO BE DOING MORE AND MORE.
EVEN AFTER ALL THE WORSE THINGS THAT HAPPENED LATER--
YOU WAIT AT BASE CAMP, SUPERDOG SEN. STAY!
--IT STILL MAKES ME SICK TO THINK OF THAT DAY. THE LAST DAY WE PLAYED THERE.
THE TREE WASN'T A TREE TO US. IT WAS ALWAYS SOME-THING ELSE.
THAT SUMMER WE WERE INTO ARSENE LUPIN, SO IT WAS USUALLY A CASTLE FORTRESS WE HAD TO ROB.

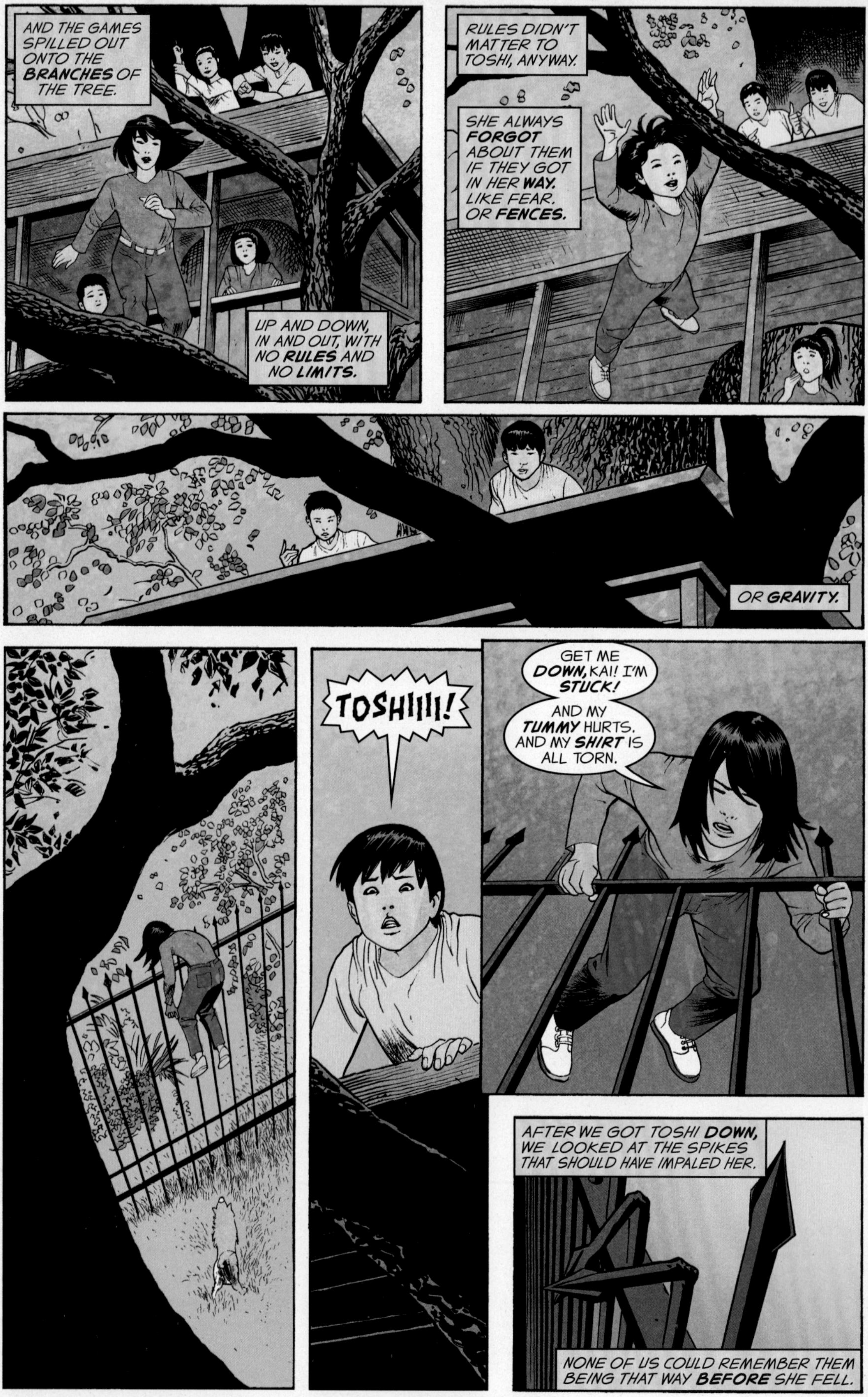

AND THE GAMES SPILLED OUT ONTO THE BRANCHES OF THE TREE.
UP AND DOWN, IN AND OUT, WITH NO RULES AND NO LIMITS.
RULES DIDN'T MATTER TO TOSHI, ANYWAY.
SHE ALWAYS FORGOT ABOUT THEM IF THEY GOT IN HER WAY. LIKE FEAR. OR FENCES.
OR GRAVITY.
TOSHIIII!
GET ME DOWN, KAI! I'M STUCK!
AND MY TUMMY HURTS. AND MY SHIRT IS ALL TORN.
AFTER WE GOT TOSHI DOWN, WE LOOKED AT THE SPIKES THAT SHOULD HAVE IMPALED HER.
NONE OF US COULD REMEMBER THEM BEING THAT WAY BEFORE SHE FELL.

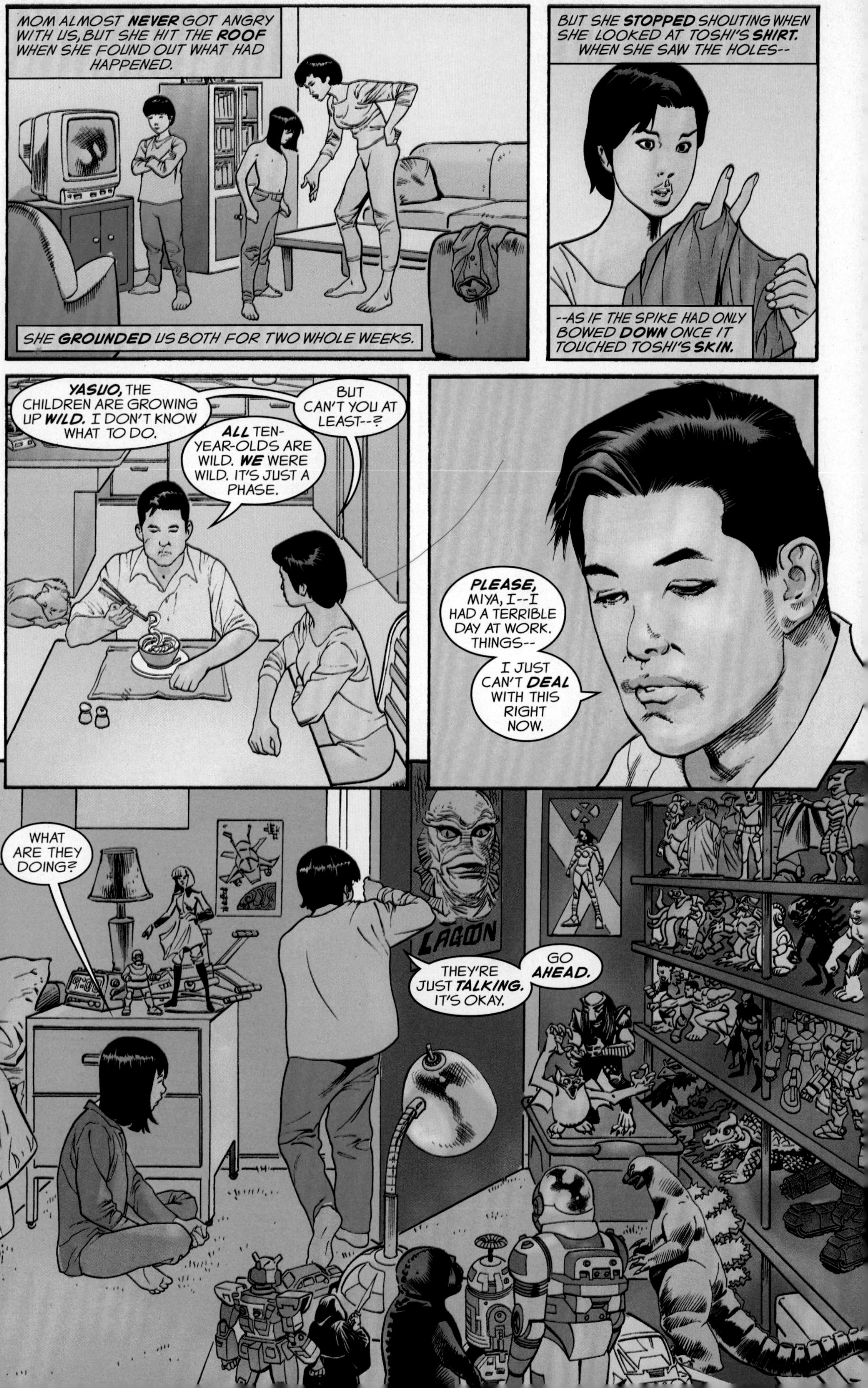
MOM ALMOST NEVER GOT ANGRY WITH US, BUT SHE HIT THE ROOF WHEN SHE FOUND OUT WHAT HAD HAPPENED.
SHE GROUNDED US BOTH FOR TWO WHOLE WEEKS.
BUT SHE STOPPED SHOUTING WHEN SHE LOOKED AT TOSHI'S SHIRT. WHEN SHE SAW THE HOLES--
--AS IF THE SPIKE HAD ONLY BOWED DOWN ONCE IT TOUCHED TOSHI'S SKIN.
YASUO, THE CHILDREN ARE GROWING UP WILD. I DON'T KNOW WHAT TO DO.
ALL TEN-YEAR-OLDS ARE WILD. WE WERE WILD. IT'S JUST A PHASE.
BUT CAN'T YOU AT LEAST--?
PLEASE, MIYA, I--I HAD A TERRIBLE DAY AT WORK. THINGS--
I JUST CAN'T DEAL WITH THIS RIGHT NOW.
WHAT ARE THEY DOING?
LAGOON
THEY'RE JUST TALKING. IT'S OKAY.
GO AHEAD.

THE PENKNIFE WAS **MINE**: A GIFT FROM GRANDMA. BUT I NEVER **USED** IT.

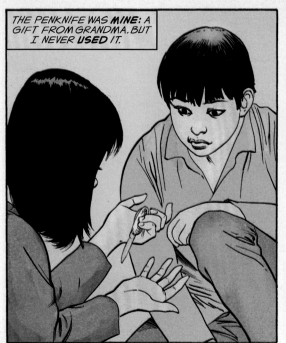

WE DECIDED IT WAS **EXPENDABLE.**

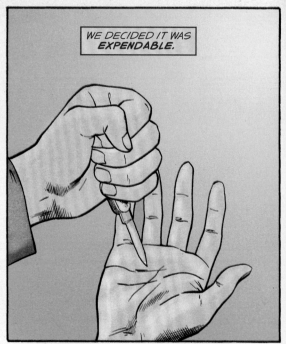

IT--

--IT WON'T GO **IN.**

SNAP

COOOOOOOL!

18

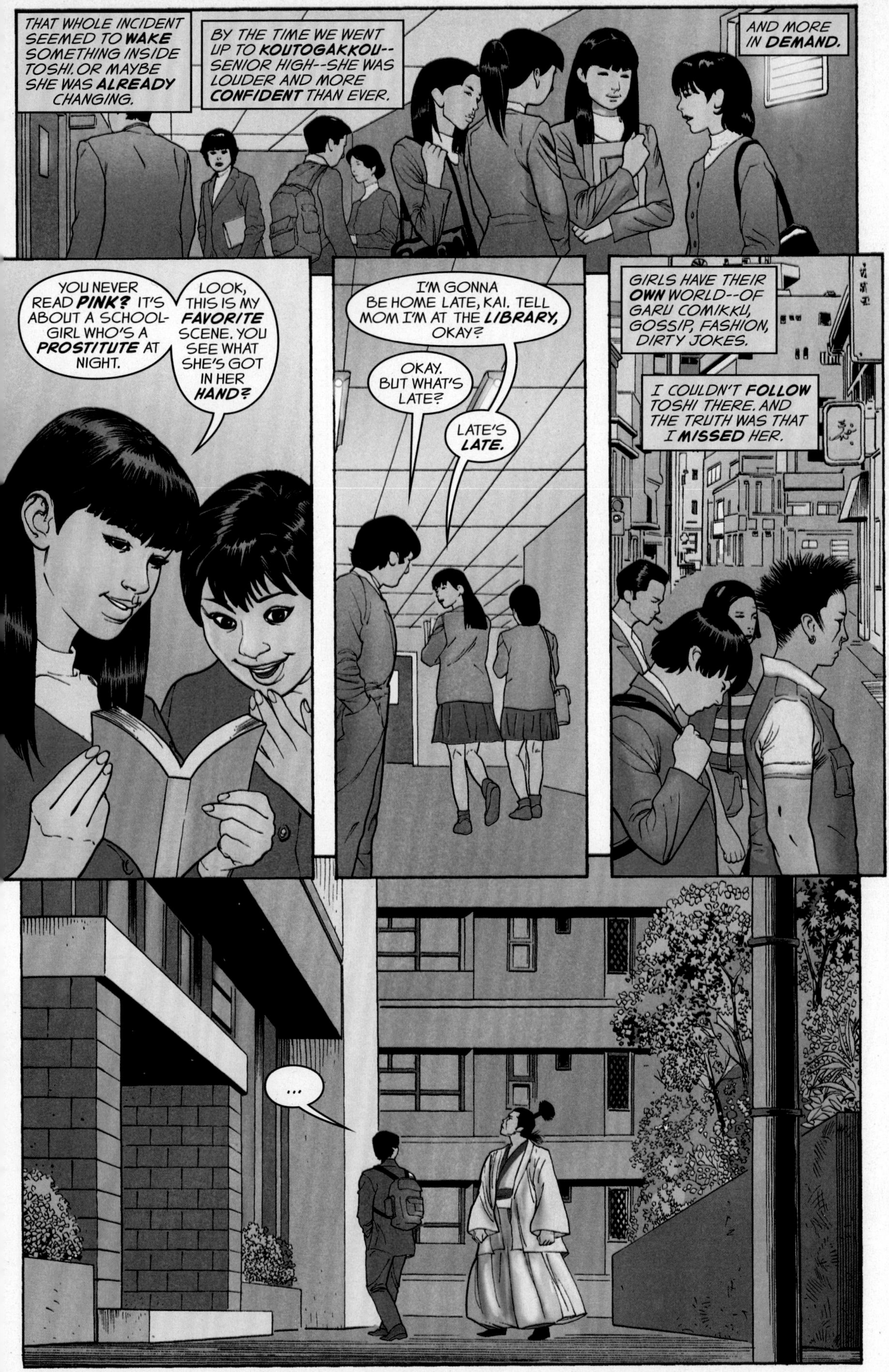
THAT WHOLE INCIDENT SEEMED TO WAKE SOMETHING INSIDE TOSHI. OR MAYBE SHE WAS ALREADY CHANGING.
BY THE TIME WE WENT UP TO KOUTOGAKKOU--SENIOR HIGH--SHE WAS LOUDER AND MORE CONFIDENT THAN EVER.
AND MORE IN DEMAND.
YOU NEVER READ PINK? IT'S ABOUT A SCHOOL-GIRL WHO'S A PROSTITUTE AT NIGHT.
LOOK, THIS IS MY FAVORITE SCENE. YOU SEE WHAT SHE'S GOT IN HER HAND?
I'M GONNA BE HOME LATE, KAI. TELL MOM I'M AT THE LIBRARY, OKAY?
OKAY. BUT WHAT'S LATE?
LATE'S LATE.
GIRLS HAVE THEIR OWN WORLD--OF GARU COMIKKU, GOSSIP, FASHION, DIRTY JOKES.
I COULDN'T FOLLOW TOSHI THERE. AND THE TRUTH WAS THAT I MISSED HER.
...

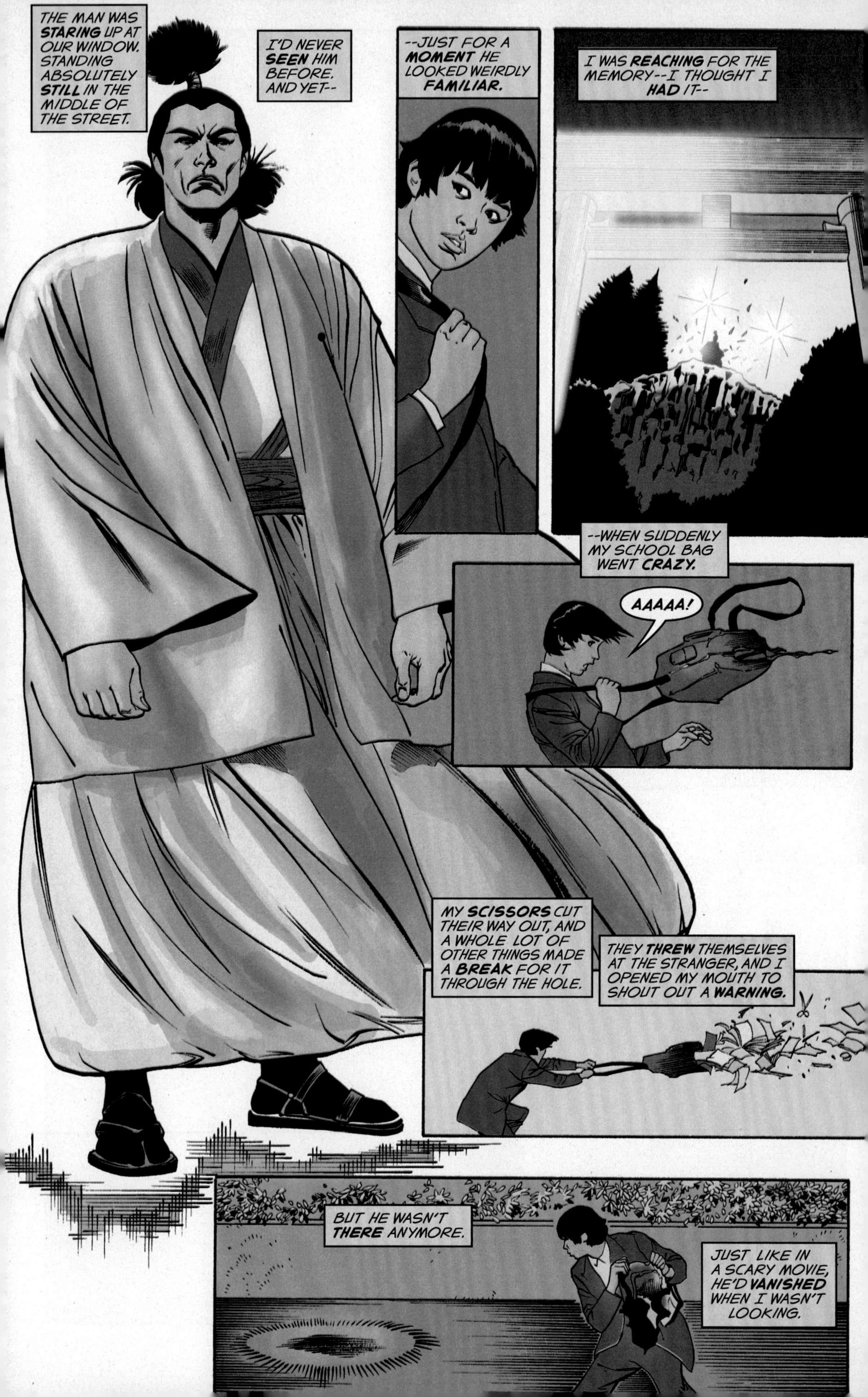
THE MAN WAS STARING UP AT OUR WINDOW. STANDING ABSOLUTELY STILL IN THE MIDDLE OF THE STREET.
I'D NEVER SEEN HIM BEFORE. AND YET--
--JUST FOR A MOMENT HE LOOKED WEIRDLY FAMILIAR.
I WAS REACHING FOR THE MEMORY--I THOUGHT I HAD IT--
--WHEN SUDDENLY MY SCHOOL BAG WENT CRAZY.
AAAAA!
MY SCISSORS CUT THEIR WAY OUT, AND A WHOLE LOT OF OTHER THINGS MADE A BREAK FOR IT THROUGH THE HOLE.
THEY THREW THEMSELVES AT THE STRANGER, AND I OPENED MY MOUTH TO SHOUT OUT A WARNING.
BUT HE WASN'T THERE ANYMORE.
JUST LIKE IN A SCARY MOVIE, HE'D VANISHED WHEN I WASN'T LOOKING.

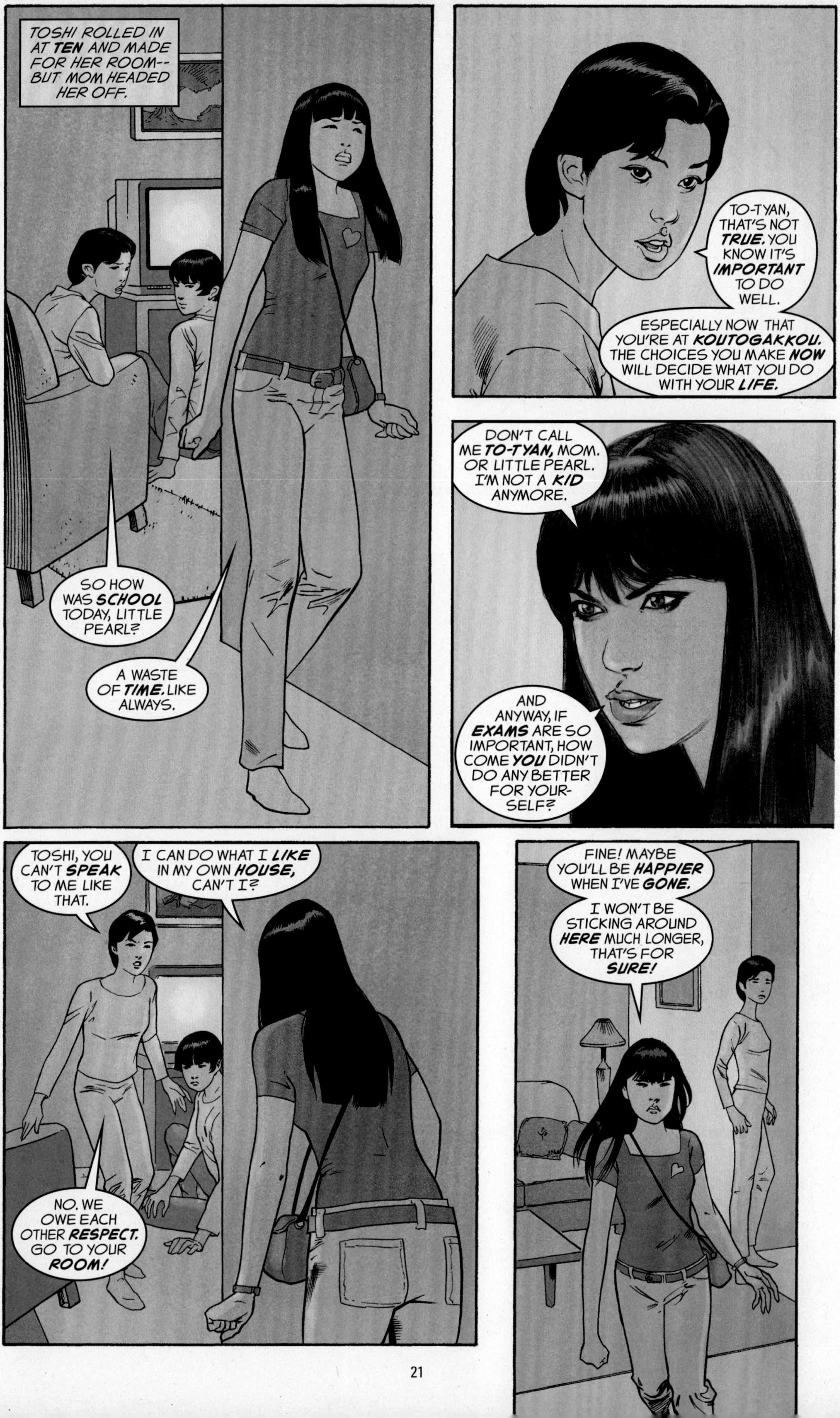
TOSHI ROLLED IN AT TEN AND MADE FOR HER ROOM-- BUT MOM HEADED HER OFF.
SO HOW WAS SCHOOL TODAY, LITTLE PEARL?
A WASTE OF TIME. LIKE ALWAYS.
TO-TYAN, THAT'S NOT TRUE. YOU KNOW IT'S IMPORTANT TO DO WELL.
ESPECIALLY NOW THAT YOU'RE AT KOUTOGAKKOU. THE CHOICES YOU MAKE NOW WILL DECIDE WHAT YOU DO WITH YOUR LIFE.
DON'T CALL ME TO-TYAN, MOM. OR LITTLE PEARL. I'M NOT A KID ANYMORE.
AND ANYWAY, IF EXAMS ARE SO IMPORTANT, HOW COME YOU DIDN'T DO ANY BETTER FOR YOUR-SELF?
TOSHI, YOU CAN'T SPEAK TO ME LIKE THAT.
I CAN DO WHAT I LIKE IN MY OWN HOUSE, CAN'T I?
NO. WE OWE EACH OTHER RESPECT. GO TO YOUR ROOM!
FINE! MAYBE YOU'LL BE HAPPIER WHEN I'VE GONE.
I WON'T BE STICKING AROUND HERE MUCH LONGER, THAT'S FOR SURE!

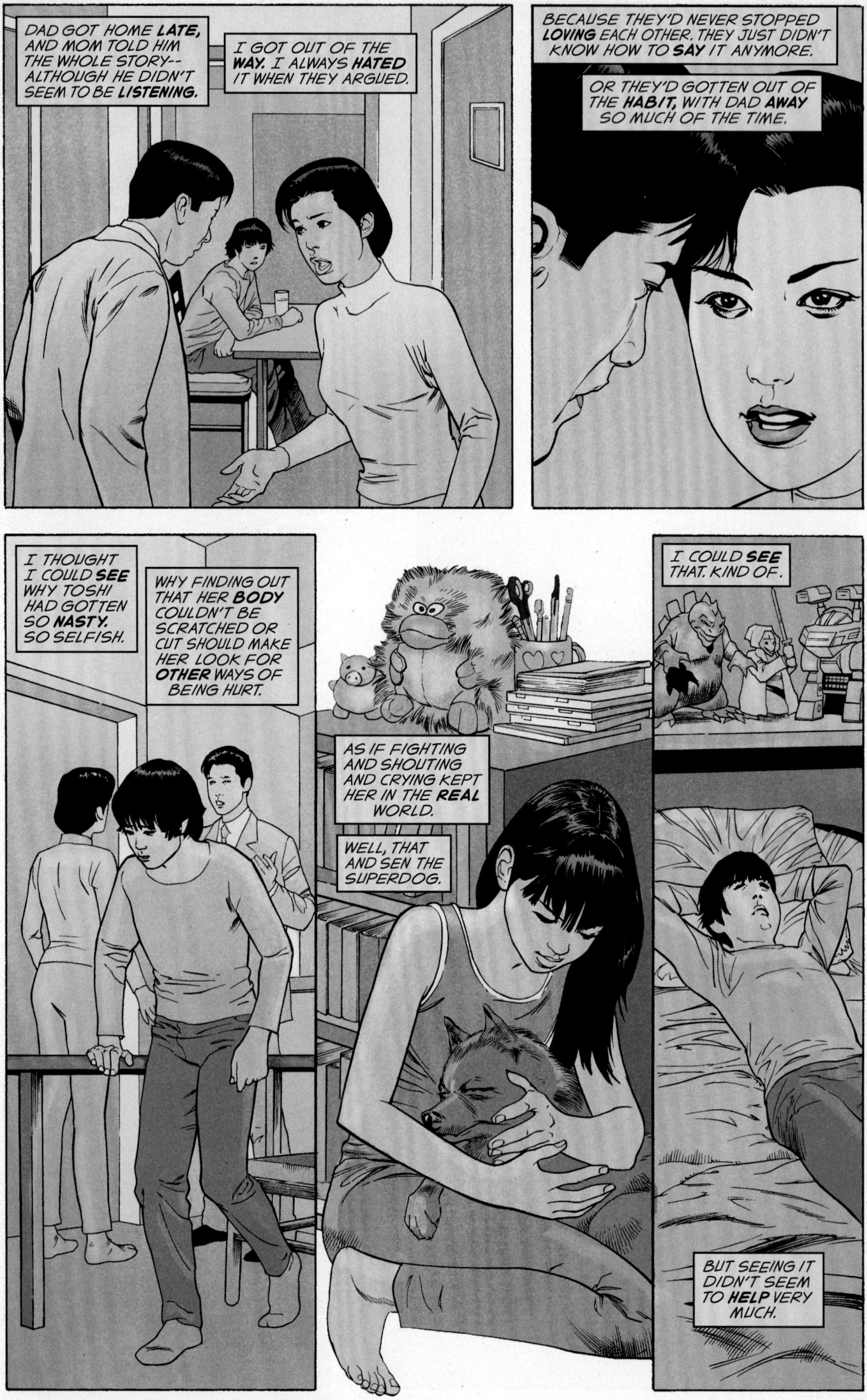

DAD GOT HOME **LATE,** AND MOM TOLD HIM THE WHOLE STORY-- ALTHOUGH HE DIDN'T SEEM TO BE **LISTENING.**
I GOT OUT OF THE **WAY.** I ALWAYS **HATED** IT WHEN THEY ARGUED.
BECAUSE THEY'D NEVER STOPPED **LOVING** EACH OTHER. THEY JUST DIDN'T KNOW HOW TO **SAY** IT ANYMORE.
OR THEY'D GOTTEN OUT OF THE **HABIT,** WITH DAD **AWAY** SO MUCH OF THE TIME.
I THOUGHT I COULD **SEE** WHY TOSHI HAD GOTTEN SO **NASTY.** SO SELFISH.
WHY FINDING OUT THAT HER **BODY** COULDN'T BE SCRATCHED OR CUT SHOULD MAKE HER LOOK FOR **OTHER** WAYS OF BEING HURT.
AS IF FIGHTING AND SHOUTING AND CRYING KEPT HER IN THE **REAL** WORLD.
WELL, THAT AND SEN THE SUPERDOG.
I COULD **SEE** THAT. KIND OF.
BUT SEEING IT DIDN'T SEEM TO **HELP** VERY MUCH.

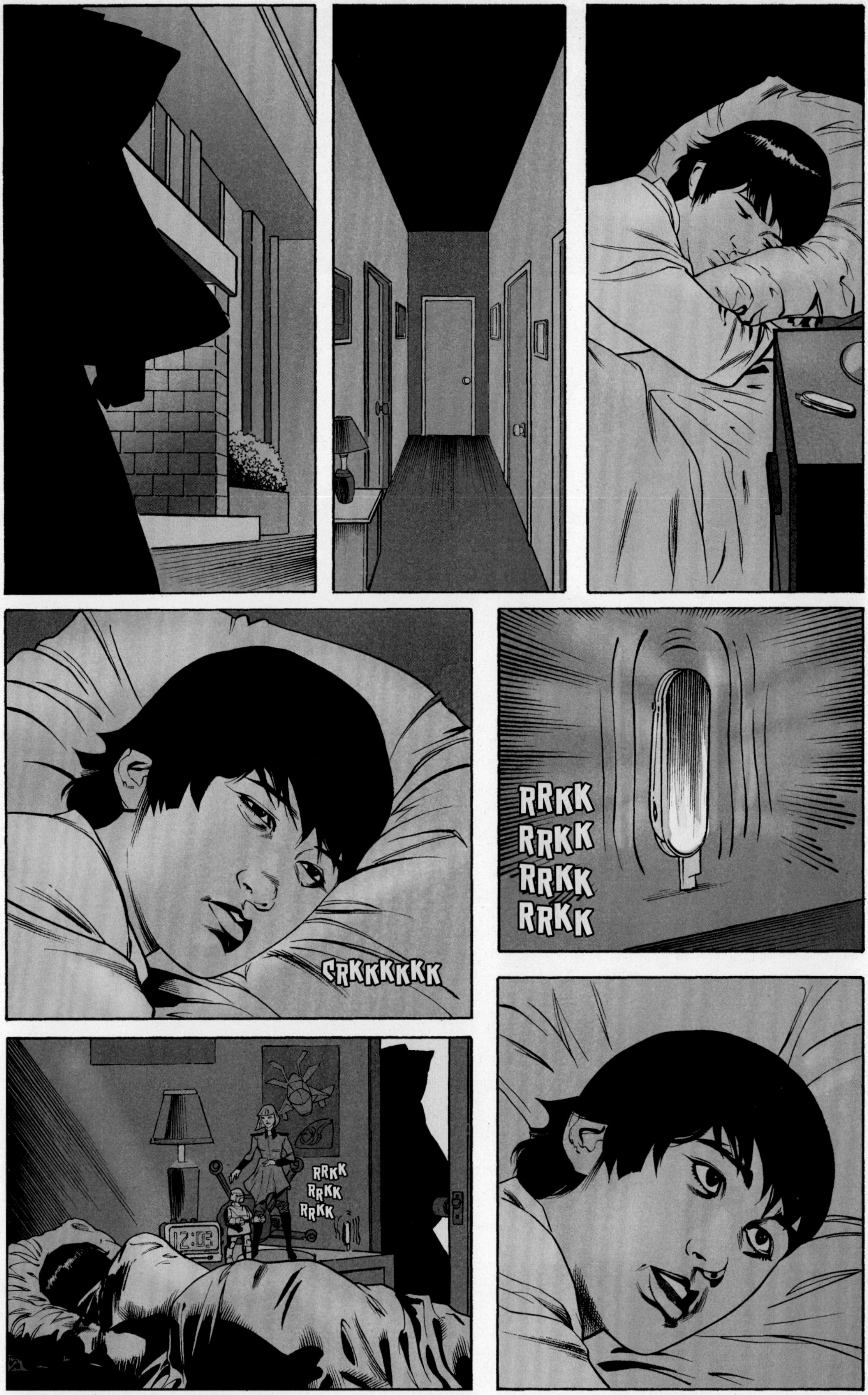
CRKKKKKK
RRKK
RRKK
RRKK
RRKK
RRKK
RRKK
RRKK
12:03

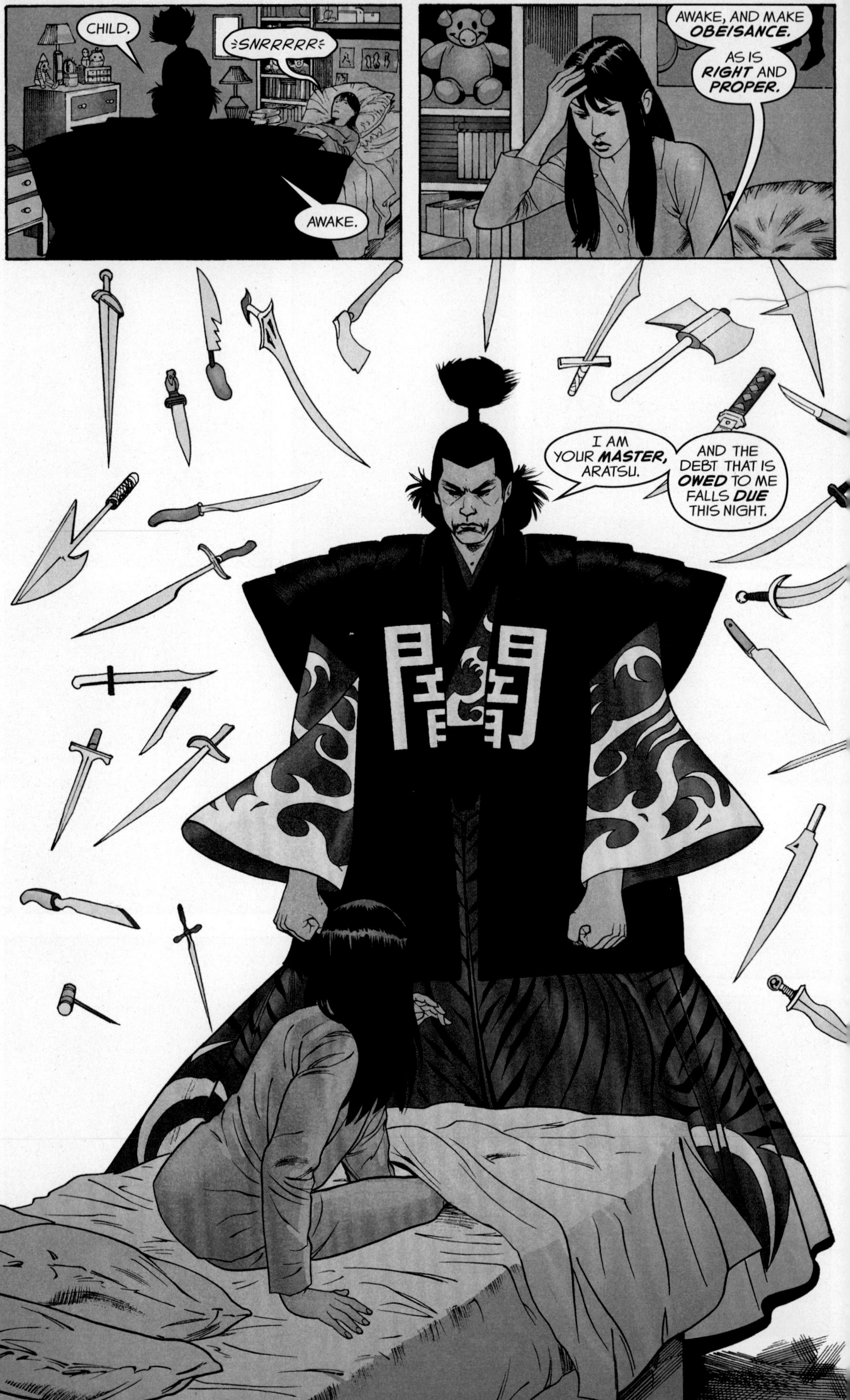
CHILD.
SNRRRRR
AWAKE.
AWAKE, AND MAKE OBEISANCE.
AS IS RIGHT AND PROPER.
I AM YOUR MASTER, ARATSU.
AND THE DEBT THAT IS OWED TO ME FALLS DUE THIS NIGHT.

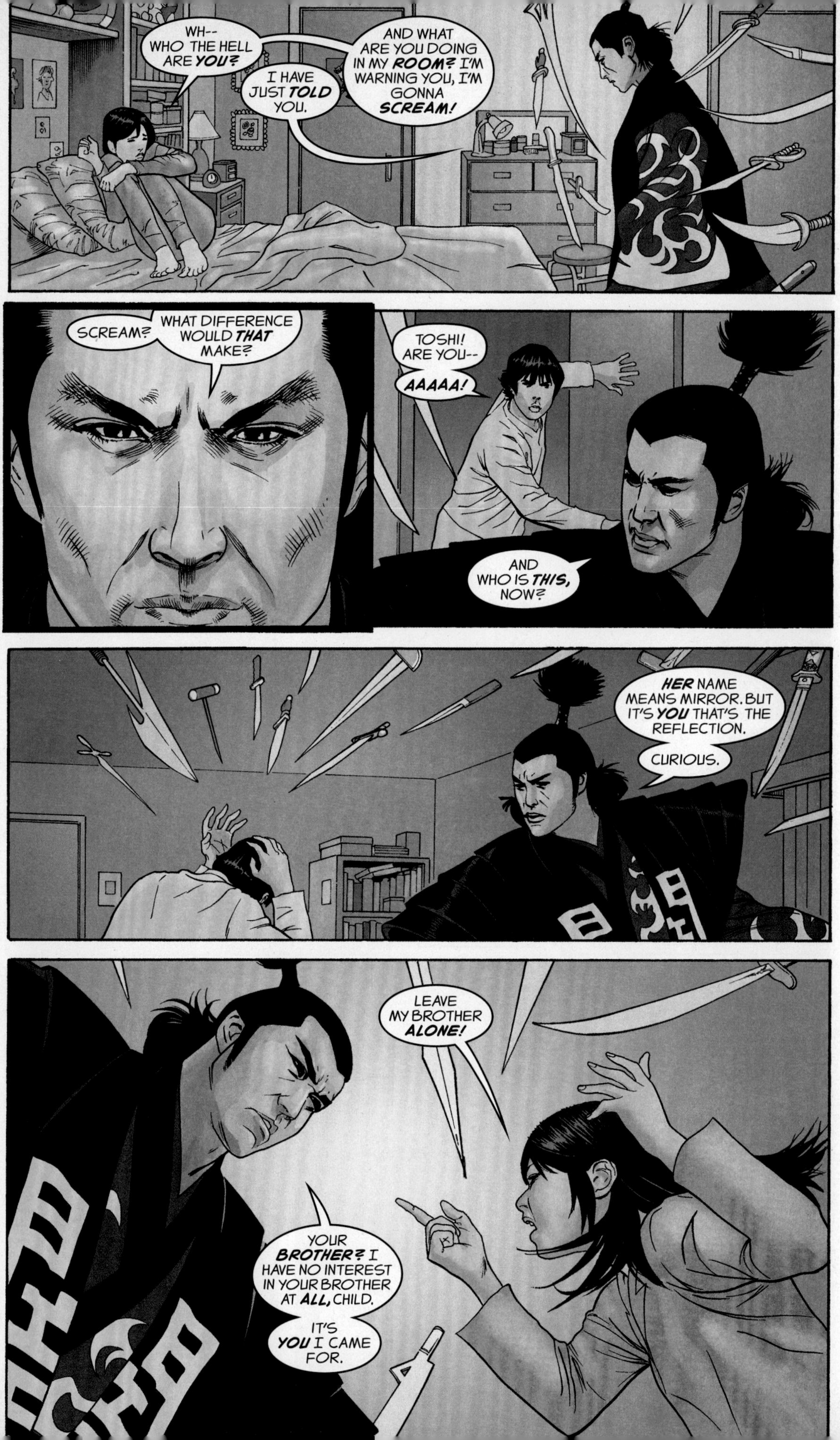
WH-- WHO THE HELL ARE YOU?
AND WHAT ARE YOU DOING IN MY ROOM? I'M WARNING YOU, I'M GONNA SCREAM!
I HAVE JUST TOLD YOU.
SCREAM?
WHAT DIFFERENCE WOULD THAT MAKE?
TOSHI! ARE YOU--
AAAAA!
AND WHO IS THIS, NOW?
HER NAME MEANS MIRROR. BUT IT'S YOU THAT'S THE REFLECTION.
CURIOUS.
LEAVE MY BROTHER ALONE!
YOUR BROTHER? I HAVE NO INTEREST IN YOUR BROTHER AT ALL, CHILD.
IT'S YOU I CAME FOR.

A **PROMISE** WAS MADE. A FAVOR FOR A **FAVOR**.

WHAT? WHAT ARE YOU **TALKING** ABOUT?

"ACCEPT OUR **OFFERING** IN RETURN." YOUR **FATHER'S** WORDS.

BUT HE DID NOT **SPECIFY** WHAT OFFERING HE **MEANT**.

I **CHOOSE** YOU.

I **OPENED** MY MOUTH TO **SPEAK**. THE KNIVES MOVED **IN** JUST A LITTLE CLOSER.

AND MY **HAND** CAME UP, BY SOME KIND OF **REFLEX**.

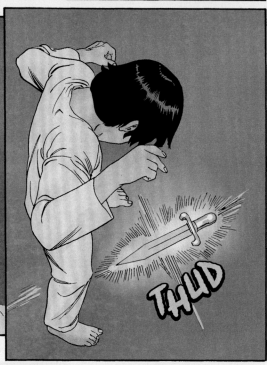

THUD

I NEVER MADE ANY PROMISE TO YOU.

YOU'RE **BOUND** BY YASUO HARA'S WORDS.

SO **ANSWER**. WILL YOU COME WITH ME?

NO.

I **WON'T**.

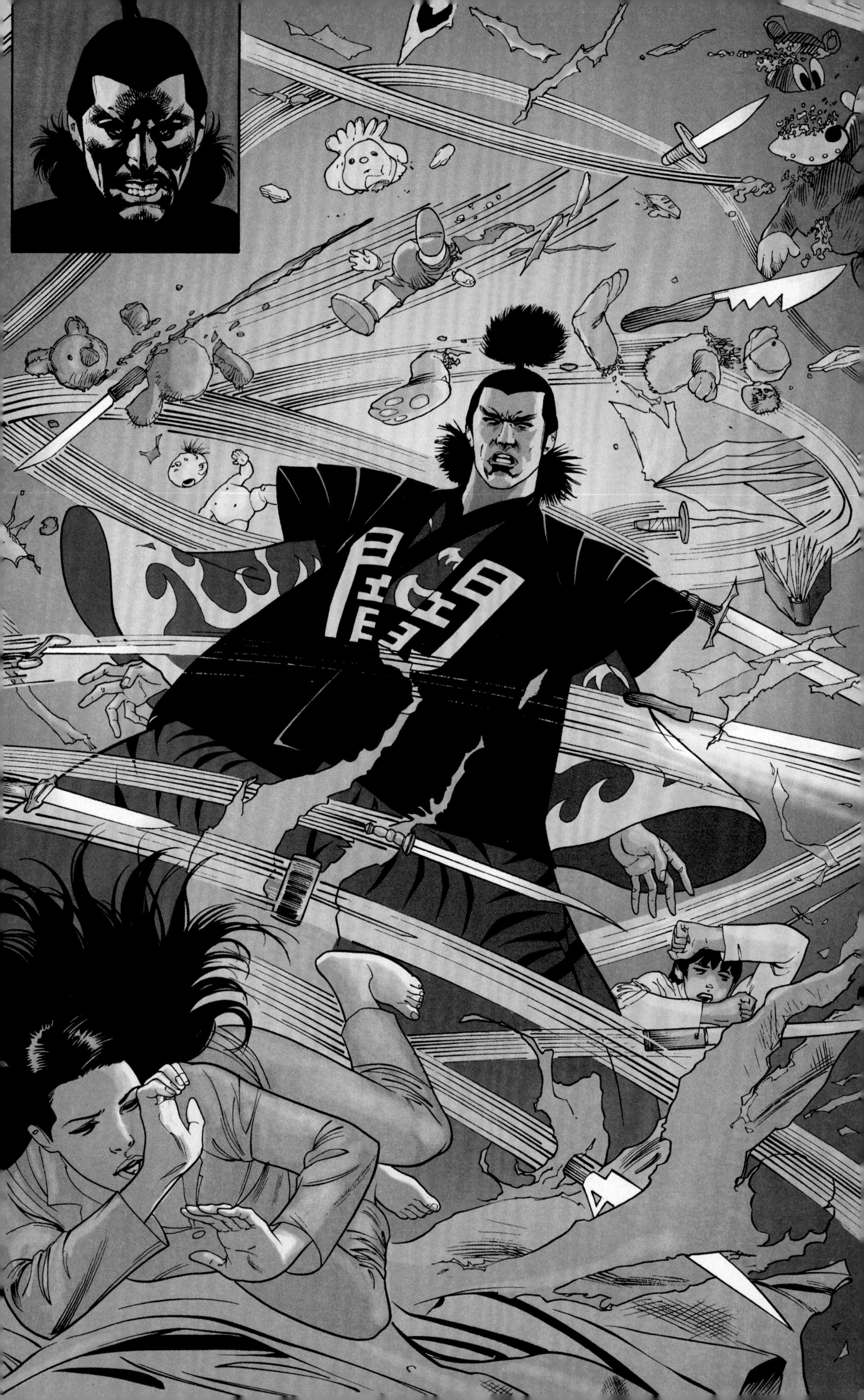

SAYING **NO** TO ME DRAWS DOWN **CONSEQUENCES.**

CONSIDER THIS A **WARNING.** I WILL **RETURN** WHEN YOU HAVE HAD TIME TO **CONSIDER.**

THERE WAS A **SOUND** AS HE WALKED PAST ME LIKE A **WHIP,** SLICING THROUGH THE AIR.

HIS **FOOTSTEPS** FADED INTO NOTHING. INTO **NOWHERE.**

TOSHI, ARE YOU **ALL RIGHT?**

I--I DON'T **KNOW.** LOOK WHAT HE DID.

LOOK WHAT HE **DID!**

I'LL GET MOM AND **DAD,** OKAY? JUST-- JUST **WAIT.**

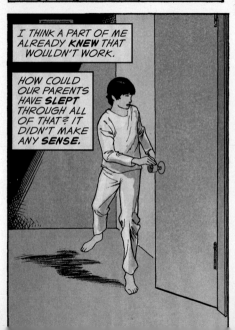

I THINK A PART OF ME ALREADY **KNEW** THAT WOULDN'T WORK.

HOW COULD OUR PARENTS HAVE **SLEPT** THROUGH ALL OF THAT? IT DIDN'T MAKE ANY **SENSE.**

BUT THEY **HAD.**

EVEN THOUGH EVERY DOG IN THE **NEIGHBORHOOD** WAS BARKING.

EVERY DOG--?

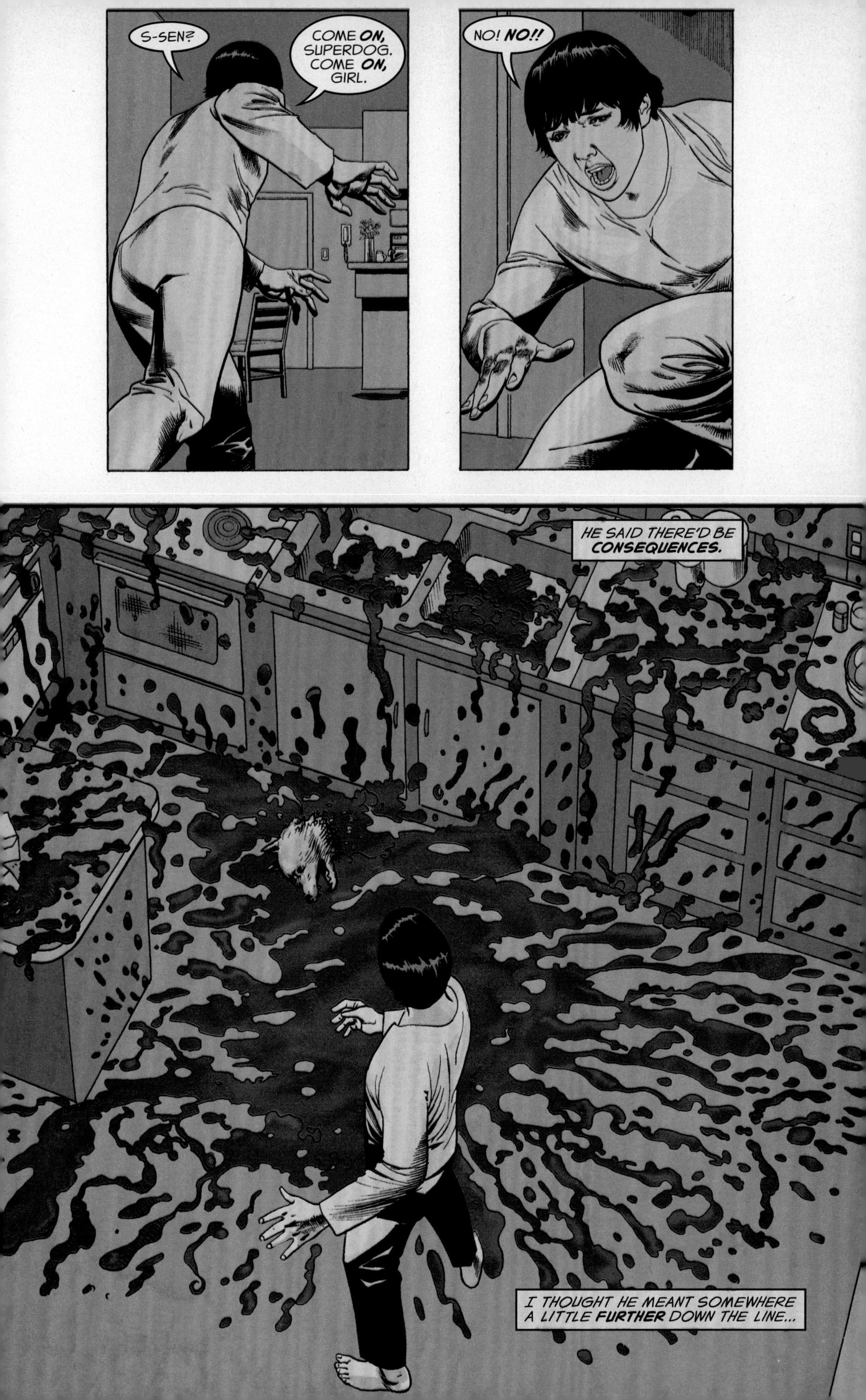
S-SEN?
COME ON, SUPERDOG. COME ON, GIRL.
NO! NO!!
HE SAID THERE'D BE CONSEQUENCES.
I THOUGHT HE MEANT SOMEWHERE A LITTLE FURTHER DOWN THE LINE...

chapter two

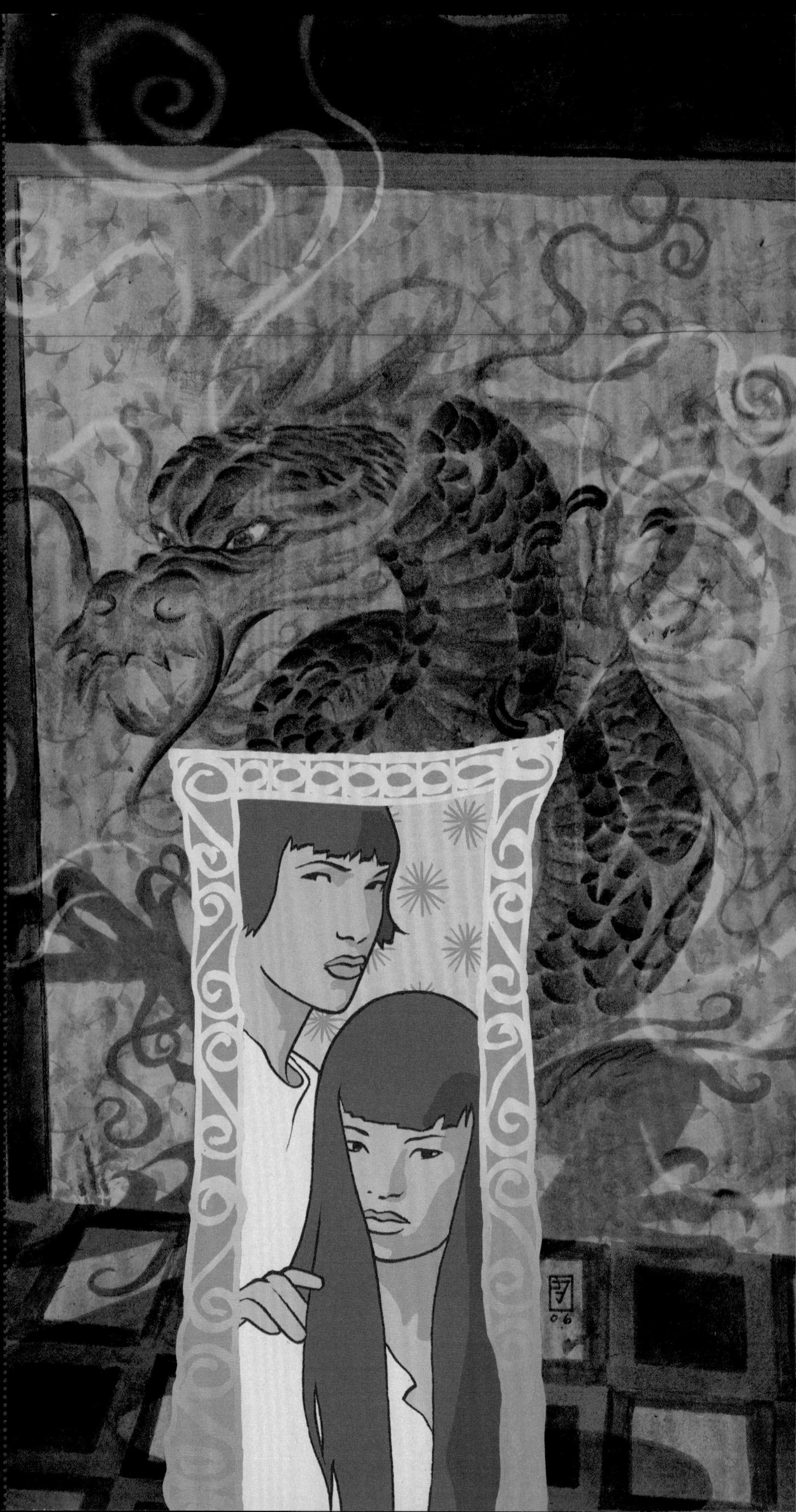

TELL US WHAT *HAPPENED.* IN YOUR OWN WORDS.

IT SOUNDED LIKE A *REASONABLE* ENOUGH REQUEST.

I WAS ACTUALLY ABOUT TO *TRY*--

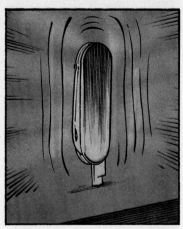

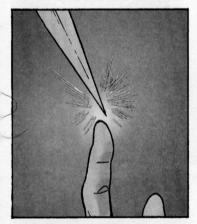

--BUT THE WORDS DIDN'T *COME.*

I DON'T REALLY--

I JUST--

--WOKE UP AND *FOUND* HER.

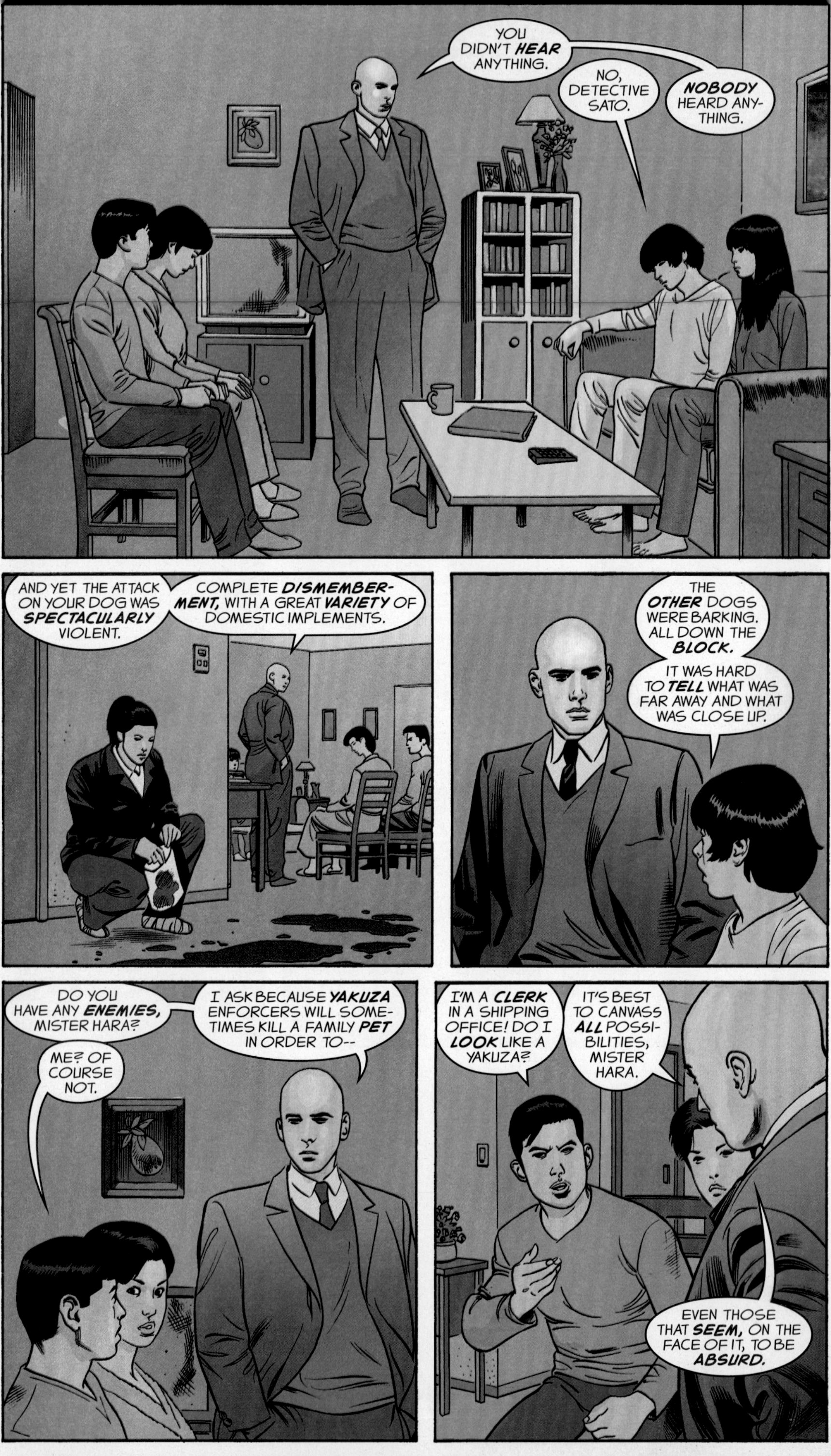
YOU DIDN'T HEAR ANYTHING.
NO, DETECTIVE SATO.
NOBODY HEARD ANY-THING.
AND YET THE ATTACK ON YOUR DOG WAS SPECTACULARLY VIOLENT.
COMPLETE DISMEMBER-MENT, WITH A GREAT VARIETY OF DOMESTIC IMPLEMENTS.
THE OTHER DOGS WERE BARKING. ALL DOWN THE BLOCK.
IT WAS HARD TO TELL WHAT WAS FAR AWAY AND WHAT WAS CLOSE UP.
DO YOU HAVE ANY ENEMIES, MISTER HARA?
ME? OF COURSE NOT.
I ASK BECAUSE YAKUZA ENFORCERS WILL SOME-TIMES KILL A FAMILY PET IN ORDER TO--
I'M A CLERK IN A SHIPPING OFFICE! DO I LOOK LIKE A YAKUZA?
IT'S BEST TO CANVASS ALL POSSI-BILITIES, MISTER HARA.
EVEN THOSE THAT SEEM, ON THE FACE OF IT, TO BE ABSURD.

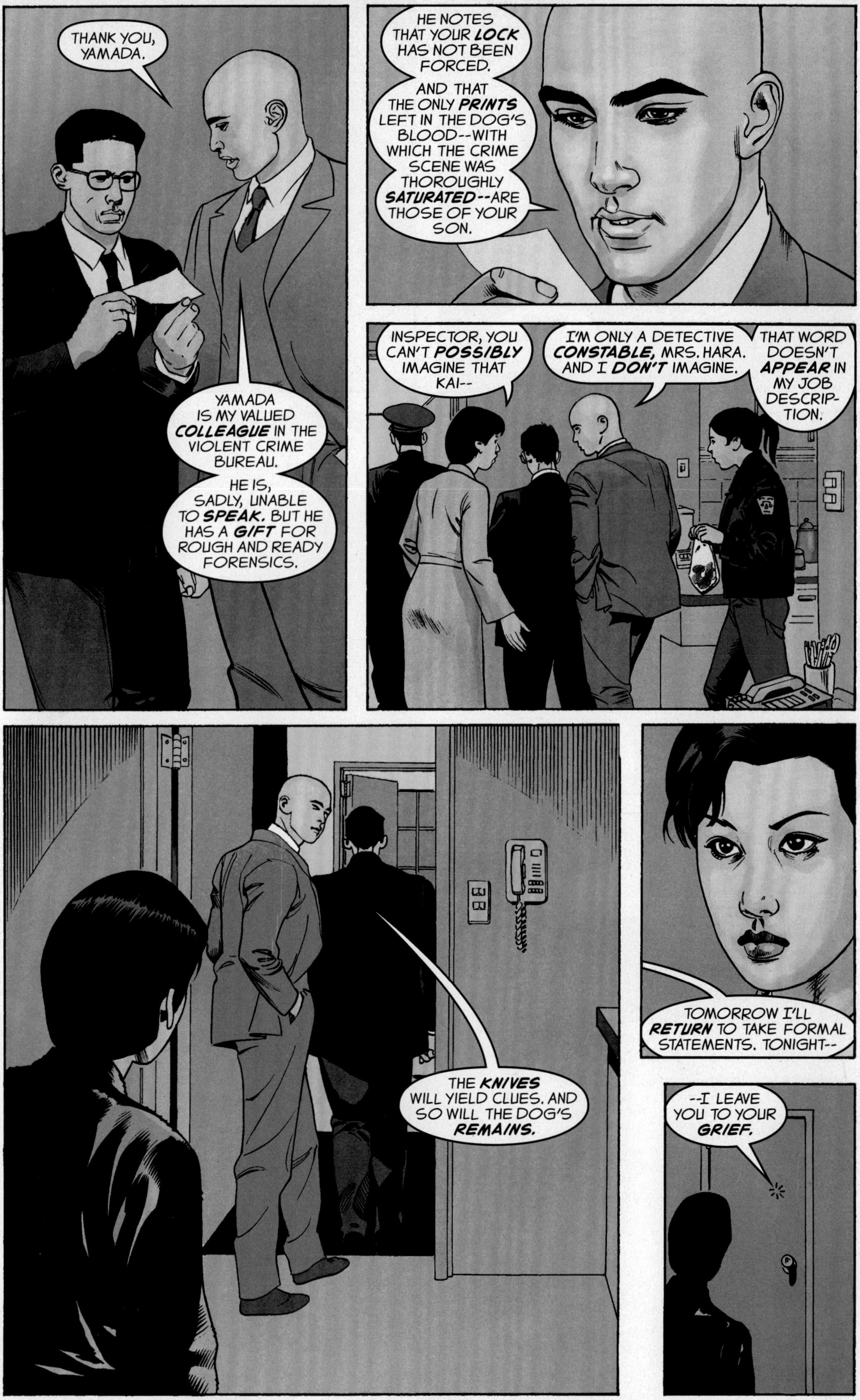
THANK YOU, YAMADA.
YAMADA IS MY VALUED COLLEAGUE IN THE VIOLENT CRIME BUREAU.
HE IS, SADLY, UNABLE TO SPEAK. BUT HE HAS A GIFT FOR ROUGH AND READY FORENSICS.
HE NOTES THAT YOUR LOCK HAS NOT BEEN FORCED.
AND THAT THE ONLY PRINTS LEFT IN THE DOG'S BLOOD--WITH WHICH THE CRIME SCENE WAS THOROUGHLY SATURATED--ARE THOSE OF YOUR SON.
INSPECTOR, YOU CAN'T POSSIBLY IMAGINE THAT KAI--
I'M ONLY A DETECTIVE CONSTABLE, MRS. HARA. AND I DON'T IMAGINE.
THAT WORD DOESN'T APPEAR IN MY JOB DESCRIPTION.
THE KNIVES WILL YIELD CLUES. AND SO WILL THE DOG'S REMAINS.
TOMORROW I'LL RETURN TO TAKE FORMAL STATEMENTS. TONIGHT--
--I LEAVE YOU TO YOUR GRIEF.

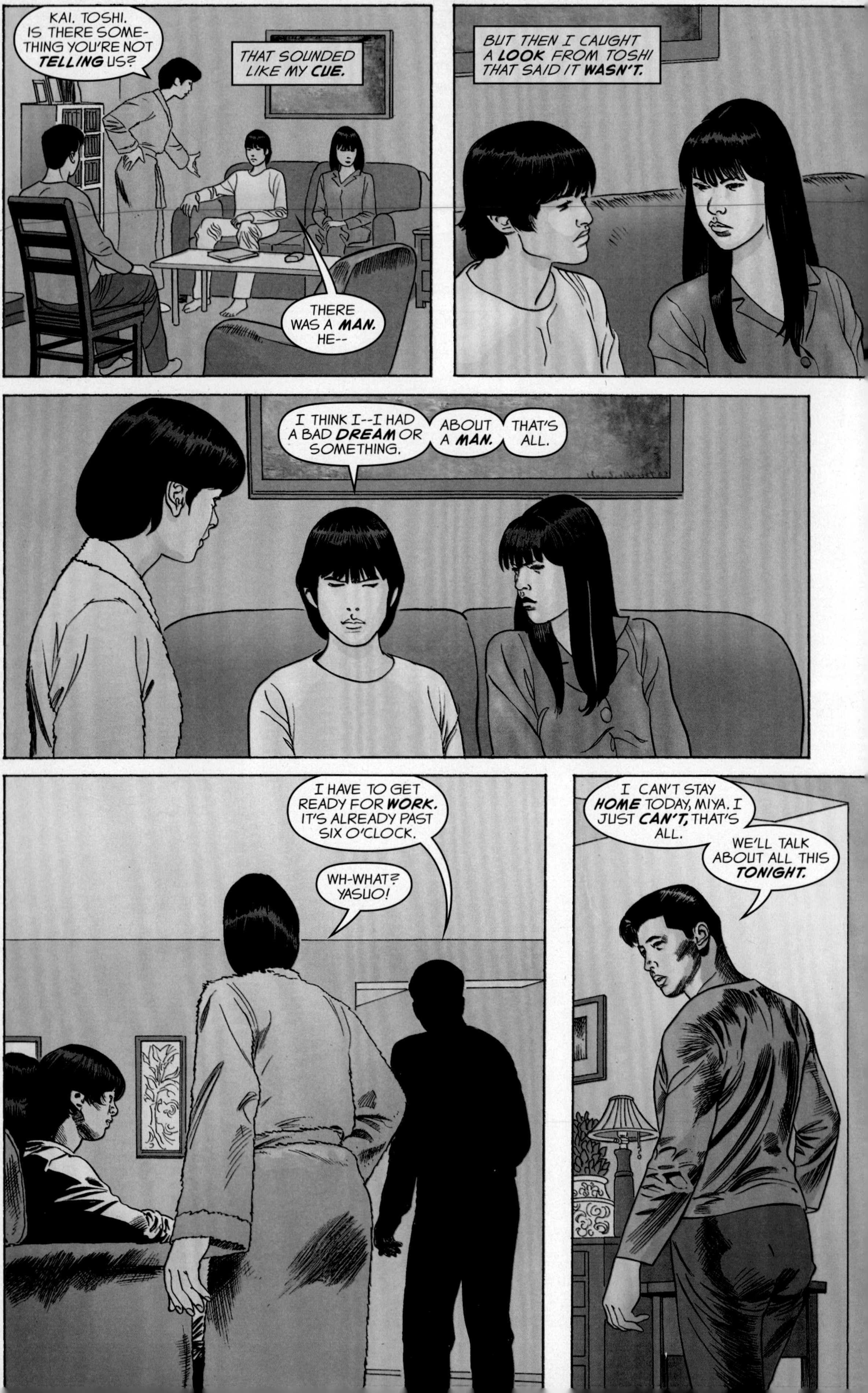
KAI. TOSHI. IS THERE SOMETHING YOU'RE NOT TELLING US?
THAT SOUNDED LIKE MY CUE.
THERE WAS A MAN. HE--
BUT THEN I CAUGHT A LOOK FROM TOSHI THAT SAID IT WASN'T.
I THINK I--I HAD A BAD DREAM OR SOMETHING.
ABOUT A MAN.
THAT'S ALL.
I HAVE TO GET READY FOR WORK. IT'S ALREADY PAST SIX O'CLOCK.
WH-WHAT? YASUO!
I CAN'T STAY HOME TODAY, MIYA. I JUST CAN'T, THAT'S ALL.
WE'LL TALK ABOUT ALL THIS TONIGHT.

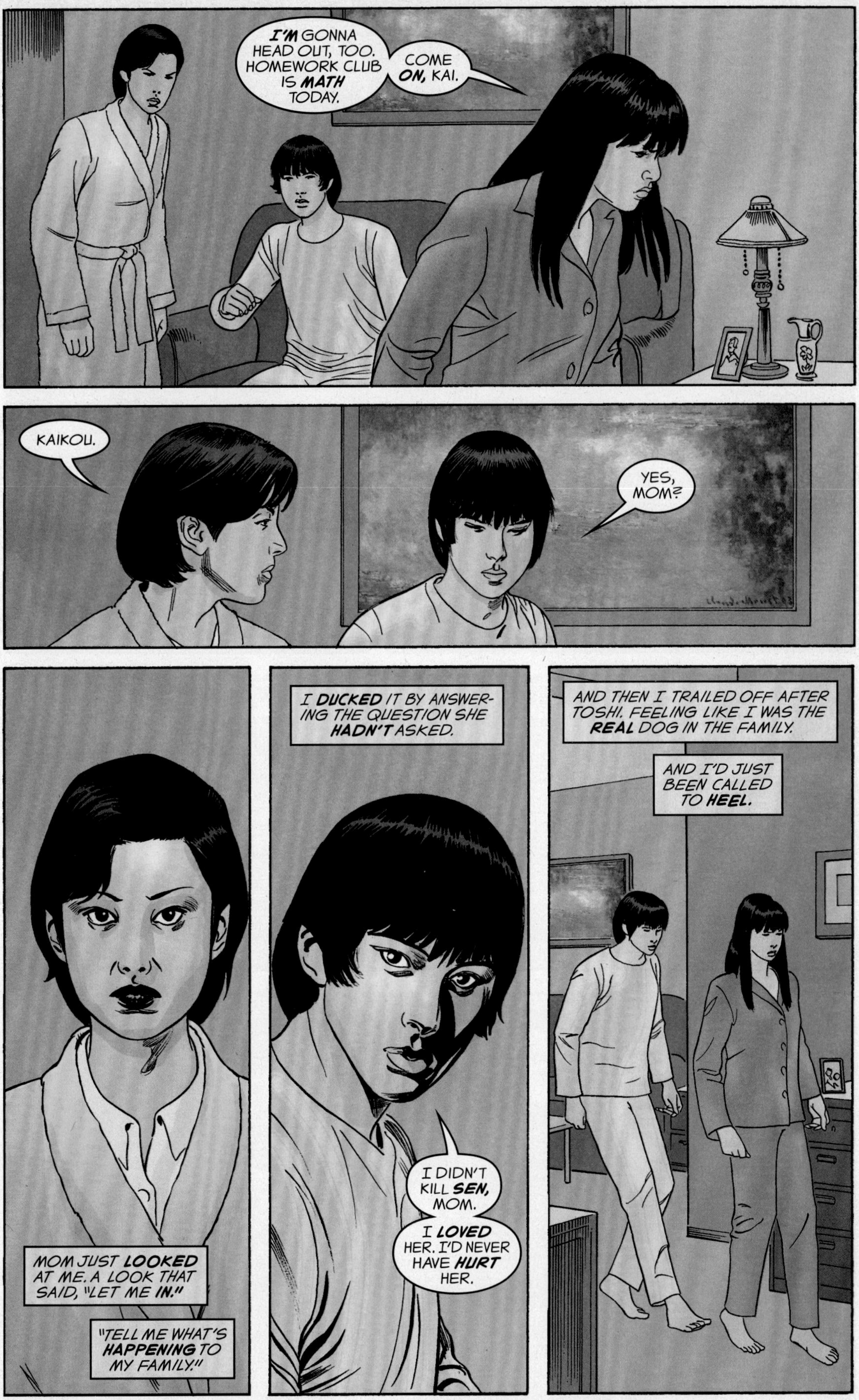
I'M GONNA HEAD OUT, TOO. HOMEWORK CLUB IS MATH TODAY.
COME ON, KAI.
KAIKOU.
YES, MOM?
MOM JUST LOOKED AT ME. A LOOK THAT SAID, "LET ME IN."
"TELL ME WHAT'S HAPPENING TO MY FAMILY."
I DUCKED IT BY ANSWERING THE QUESTION SHE HADN'T ASKED.
I DIDN'T KILL SEN, MOM.
I LOVED HER. I'D NEVER HAVE HURT HER.
AND THEN I TRAILED OFF AFTER TOSHI. FEELING LIKE I WAS THE REAL DOG IN THE FAMILY.
AND I'D JUST BEEN CALLED TO HEEL.

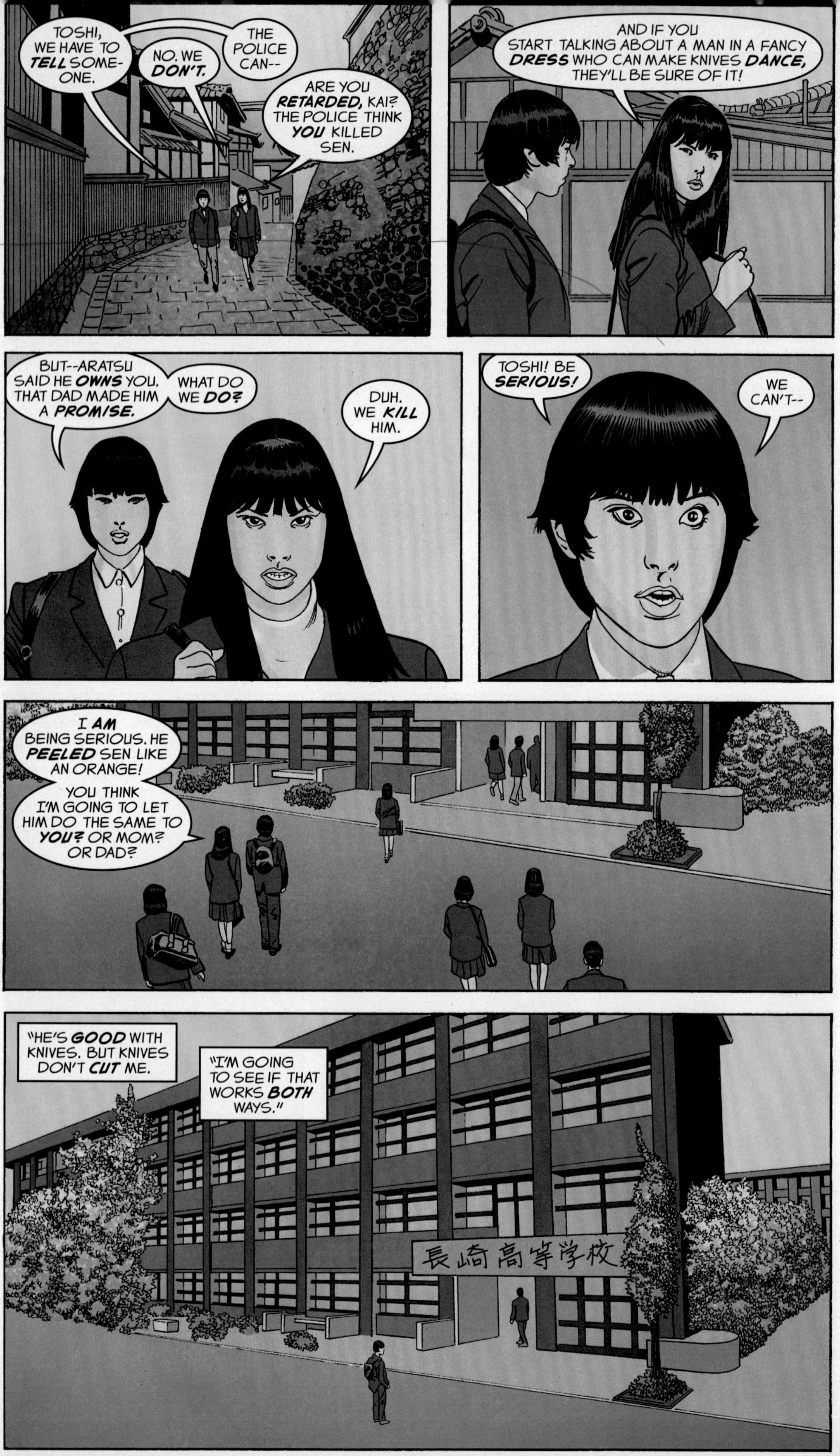
TOSHI, WE HAVE TO TELL SOME-ONE.
THE POLICE CAN--
NO. WE DON'T.
ARE YOU RETARDED, KAI? THE POLICE THINK YOU KILLED SEN.
AND IF YOU START TALKING ABOUT A MAN IN A FANCY DRESS WHO CAN MAKE KNIVES DANCE, THEY'LL BE SURE OF IT!
BUT--ARATSU SAID HE OWNS YOU. THAT DAD MADE HIM A PROMISE.
WHAT DO WE DO?
DUH. WE KILL HIM.
TOSHI! BE SERIOUS!
WE CAN'T--
I AM BEING SERIOUS. HE PEELED SEN LIKE AN ORANGE!
YOU THINK I'M GOING TO LET HIM DO THE SAME TO YOU? OR MOM? OR DAD?
"HE'S GOOD WITH KNIVES. BUT KNIVES DON'T CUT ME.
"I'M GOING TO SEE IF THAT WORKS BOTH WAYS."
長崎高等学校

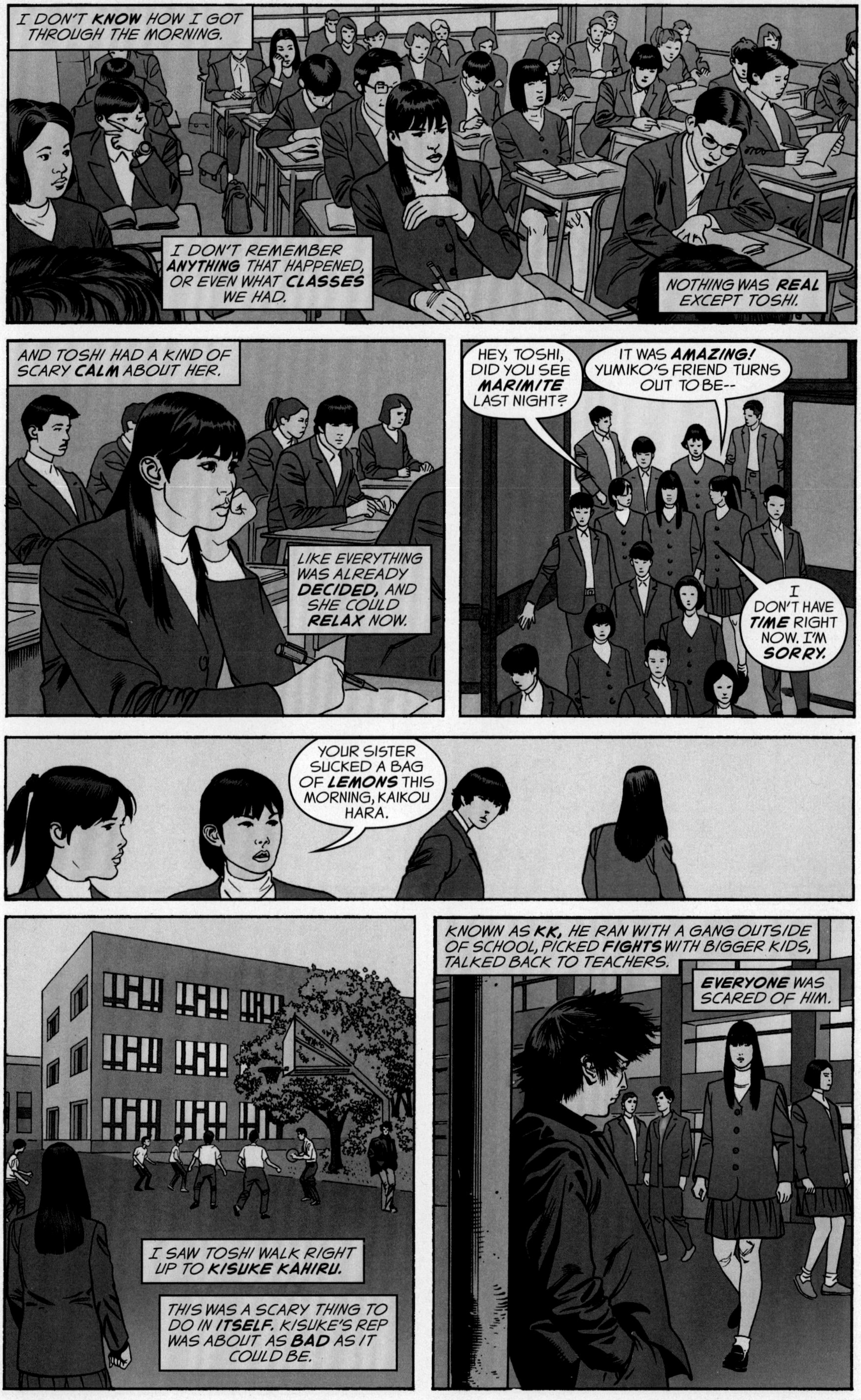
I DON'T **KNOW** HOW I GOT THROUGH THE MORNING.
I DON'T REMEMBER **ANYTHING** THAT HAPPENED, OR EVEN WHAT **CLASSES** WE HAD.
NOTHING WAS **REAL** EXCEPT TOSHI.
AND TOSHI HAD A KIND OF SCARY **CALM** ABOUT HER.
LIKE EVERYTHING WAS ALREADY **DECIDED,** AND SHE COULD **RELAX** NOW.
HEY, TOSHI, DID YOU SEE **MARIMITE** LAST NIGHT?
IT WAS **AMAZING!** YUMIKO'S FRIEND TURNS OUT TO BE--
I DON'T HAVE **TIME** RIGHT NOW. I'M **SORRY.**
YOUR SISTER SUCKED A BAG OF **LEMONS** THIS MORNING, KAIKOU HARA.
I SAW TOSHI WALK RIGHT UP TO **KISUKE KAHIRU.**
THIS WAS A SCARY THING TO DO IN **ITSELF.** KISUKE'S REP WAS ABOUT AS **BAD** AS IT COULD BE.
KNOWN AS **KK,** HE RAN WITH A GANG OUTSIDE OF SCHOOL, PICKED **FIGHTS** WITH BIGGER KIDS, TALKED BACK TO TEACHERS.
EVERYONE WAS SCARED OF HIM.

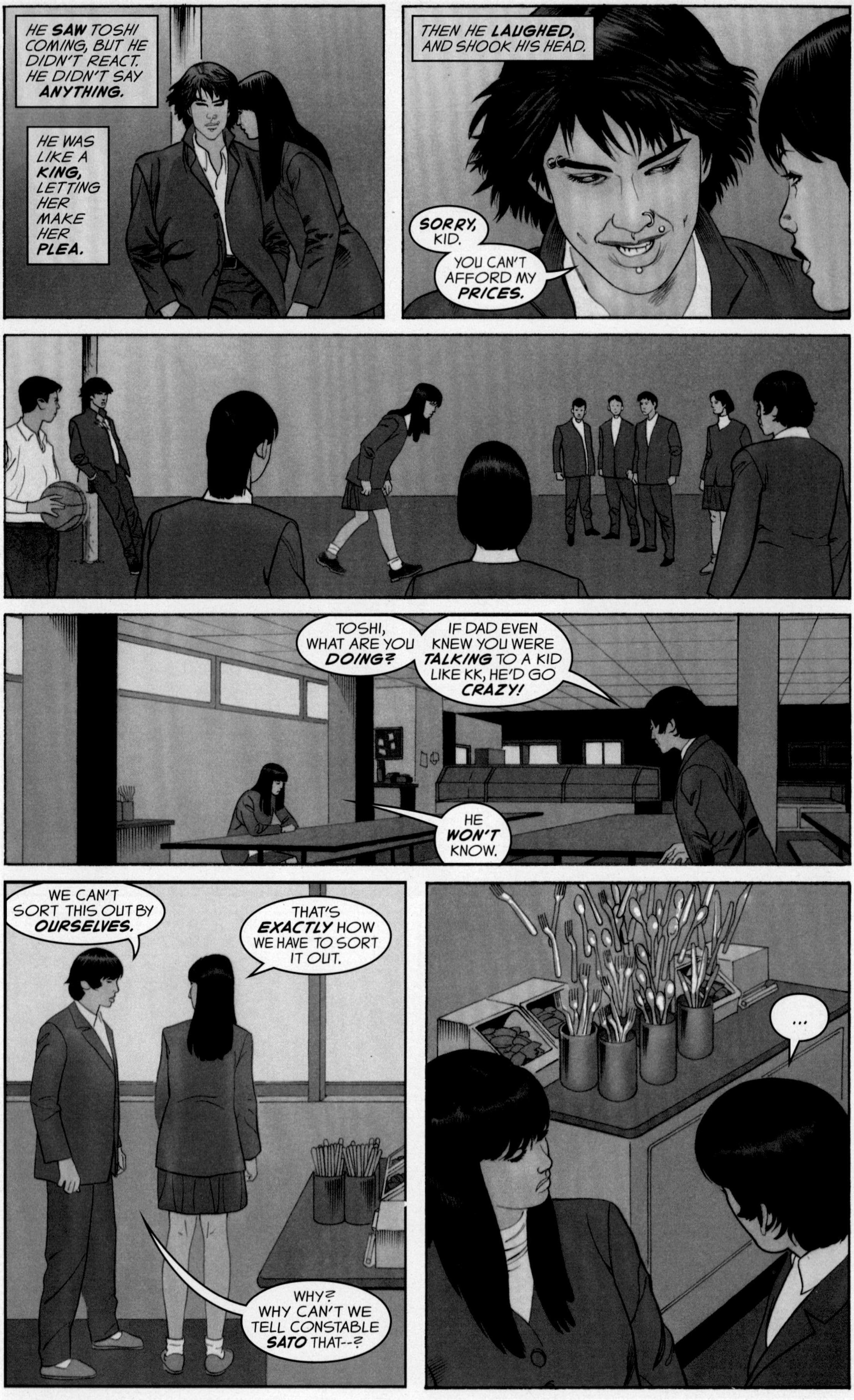
HE SAW TOSHI COMING, BUT HE DIDN'T REACT. HE DIDN'T SAY ANYTHING.
HE WAS LIKE A KING, LETTING HER MAKE HER PLEA.
THEN HE LAUGHED, AND SHOOK HIS HEAD.
SORRY, KID.
YOU CAN'T AFFORD MY PRICES.
TOSHI, WHAT ARE YOU DOING?
IF DAD EVEN KNEW YOU WERE TALKING TO A KID LIKE KK, HE'D GO CRAZY!
HE WON'T KNOW.
WE CAN'T SORT THIS OUT BY OURSELVES.
THAT'S EXACTLY HOW WE HAVE TO SORT IT OUT.
WHY? WHY CAN'T WE TELL CONSTABLE SATO THAT--?
...

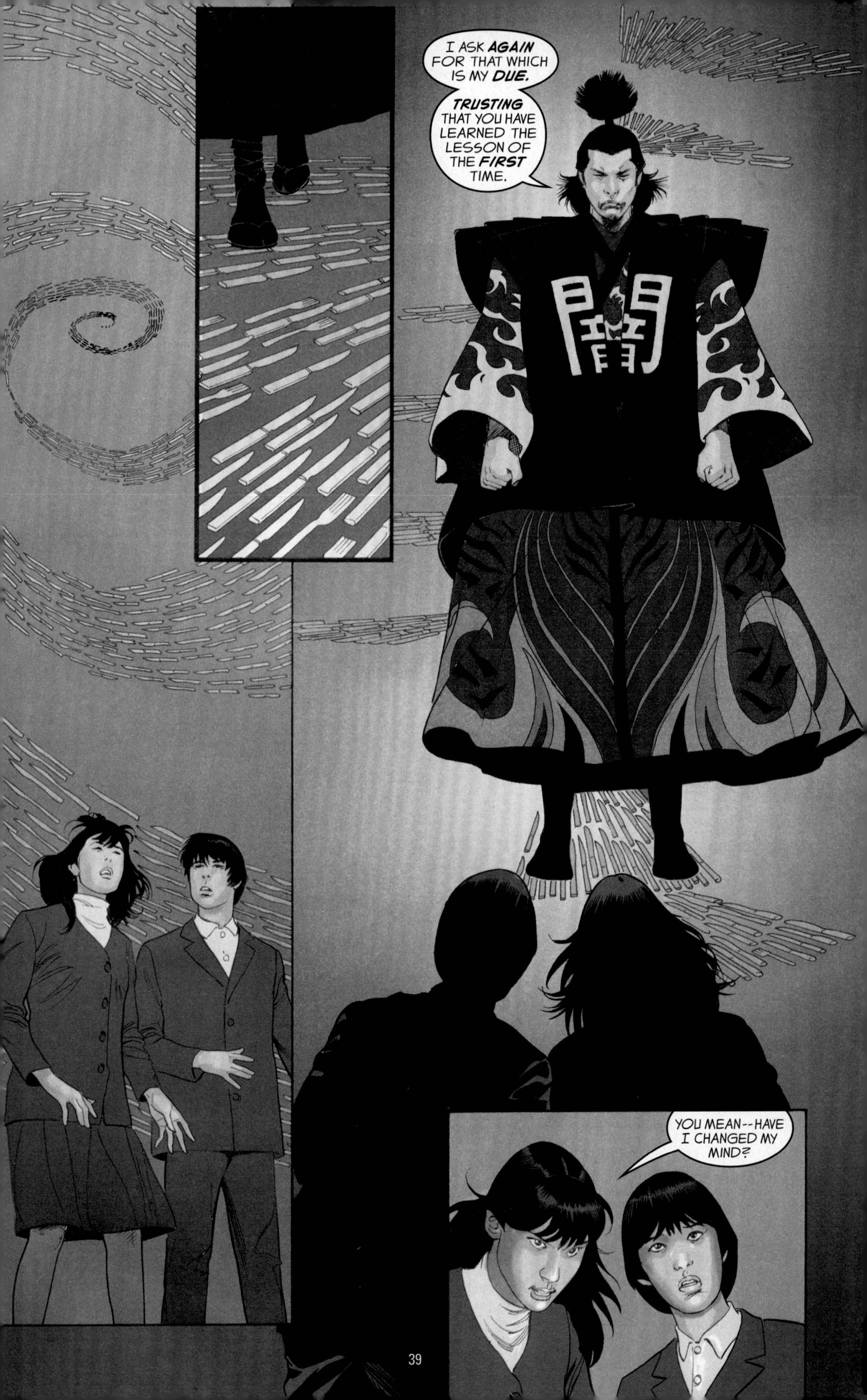
I ASK AGAIN FOR THAT WHICH IS MY DUE.
TRUSTING THAT YOU HAVE LEARNED THE LESSON OF THE FIRST TIME.
YOU MEAN--HAVE I CHANGED MY MIND?

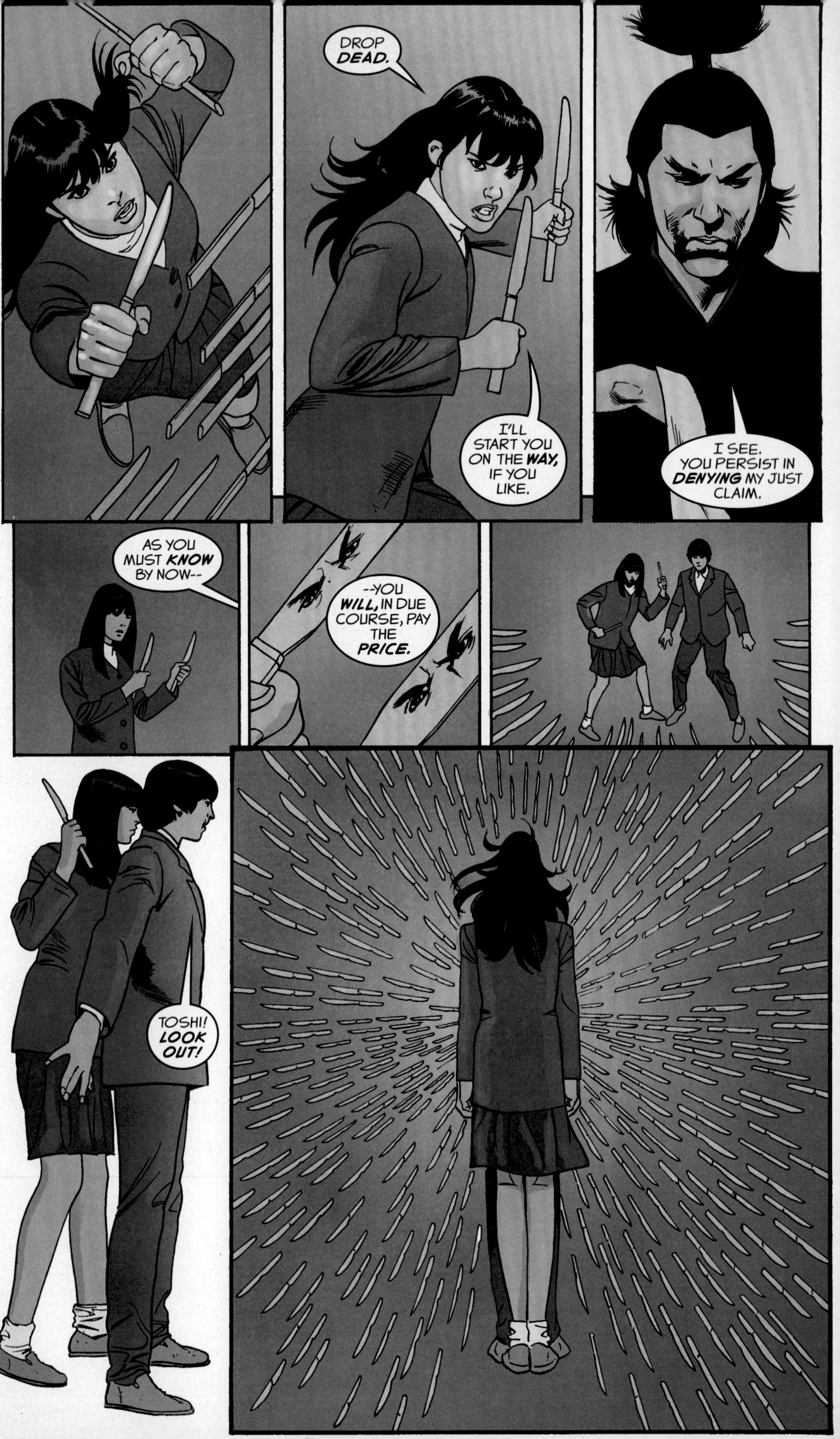
DROP DEAD.
I'LL START YOU ON THE WAY, IF YOU LIKE.
I SEE. YOU PERSIST IN DENYING MY JUST CLAIM.
AS YOU MUST KNOW BY NOW--
--YOU WILL, IN DUE COURSE, PAY THE PRICE.
TOSHI! LOOK OUT!

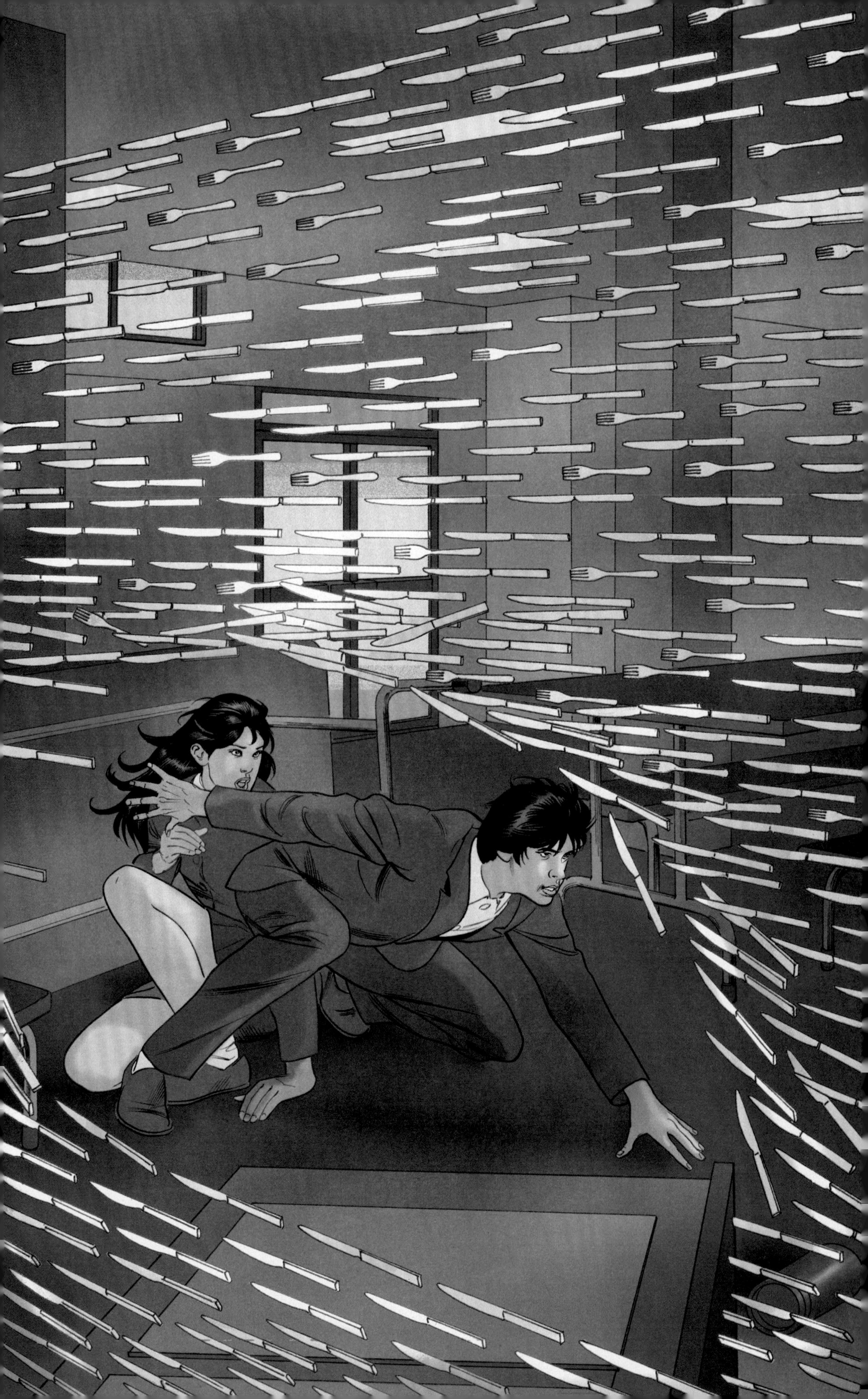

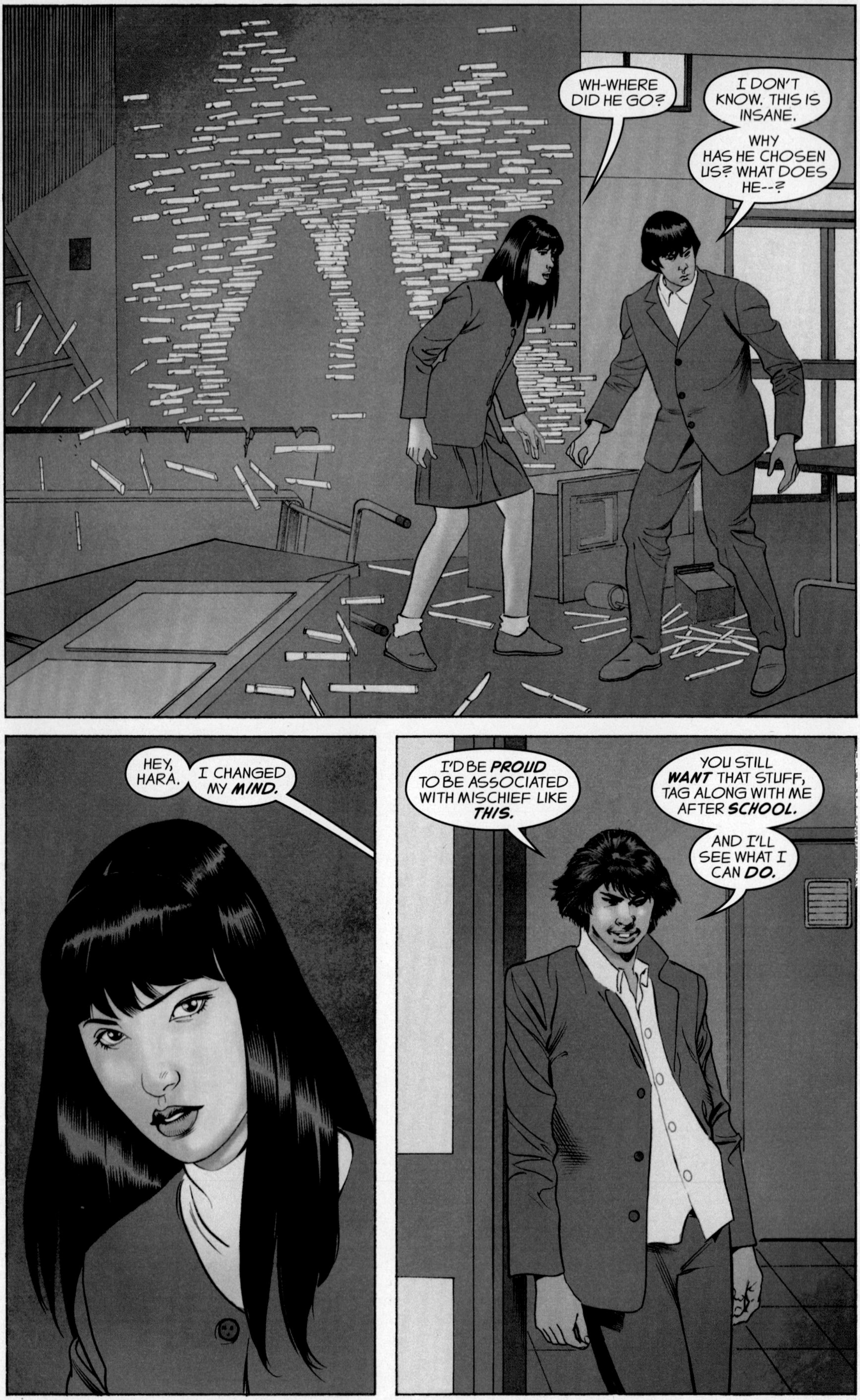
WH-WHERE DID HE GO?
I DON'T KNOW. THIS IS INSANE.
WHY HAS HE CHOSEN US? WHAT DOES HE--?
HEY, HARA.
I CHANGED MY MIND.
I'D BE PROUD TO BE ASSOCIATED WITH MISCHIEF LIKE THIS.
YOU STILL WANT THAT STUFF, TAG ALONG WITH ME AFTER SCHOOL.
AND I'LL SEE WHAT I CAN DO.

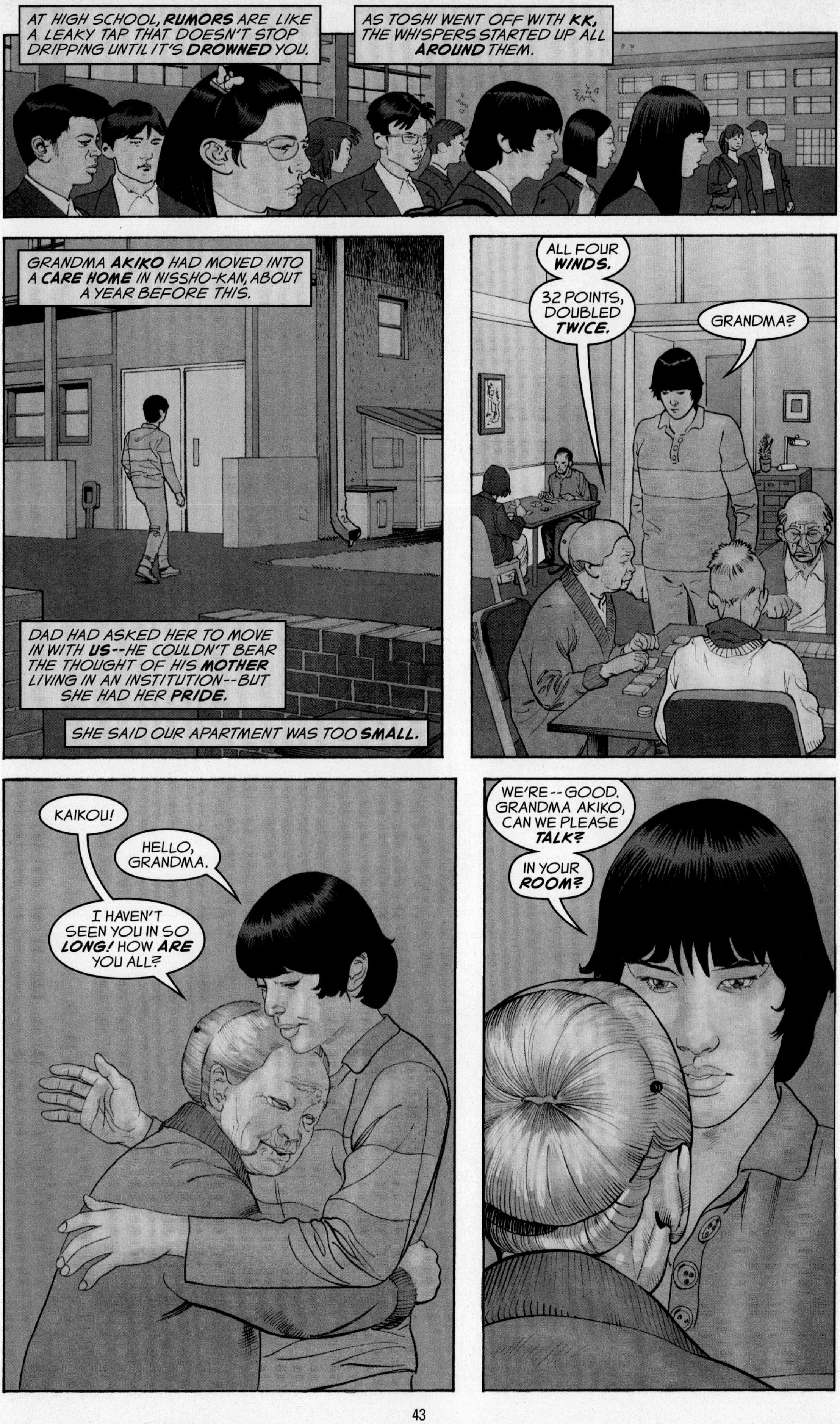
AT HIGH SCHOOL, RUMORS ARE LIKE A LEAKY TAP THAT DOESN'T STOP DRIPPING UNTIL IT'S DROWNED YOU.
AS TOSHI WENT OFF WITH KK, THE WHISPERS STARTED UP ALL AROUND THEM.
GRANDMA AKIKO HAD MOVED INTO A CARE HOME IN NISSHO-KAN, ABOUT A YEAR BEFORE THIS.
DAD HAD ASKED HER TO MOVE IN WITH US--HE COULDN'T BEAR THE THOUGHT OF HIS MOTHER LIVING IN AN INSTITUTION--BUT SHE HAD HER PRIDE.
SHE SAID OUR APARTMENT WAS TOO SMALL.
ALL FOUR WINDS.
32 POINTS, DOUBLED TWICE.
GRANDMA?
KAIKOU!
HELLO, GRANDMA.
I HAVEN'T SEEN YOU IN SO LONG! HOW ARE YOU ALL?
WE'RE--GOOD. GRANDMA AKIKO, CAN WE PLEASE TALK?
IN YOUR ROOM?

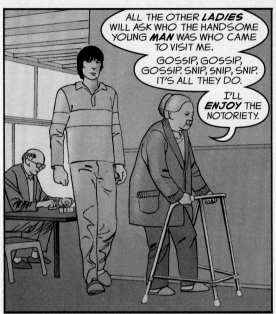

ALL THE OTHER *LADIES* WILL ASK WHO THE HANDSOME YOUNG *MAN* WAS WHO CAME TO VISIT ME.

GOSSIP, GOSSIP, GOSSIP. SNIP, SNIP, SNIP. IT'S ALL THEY DO.

I'LL *ENJOY* THE NOTORIETY.

NOW, WHAT DID YOU WANT TO *TALK* ABOUT, KAIKOU?

THE TIME JUST BEFORE WE WERE *BORN.* DID DAD GET INTO *DEBT* BACK THEN?

OR MAKE A-- A *BARGAIN?* A *PROMISE* TO SOMEONE?

ONLY TO THE *KAMI.*

WHEN HE GAVE HIS *OFFERING* AT THE SHRINE.

THE *SHRINE?*

MY LITTLE *WOODEN* SHRINE. THE ONE I BROUGHT WITH ME FROM *KUMATOMO.*

AND DAD *PRAYED* AT IT?

JUST THAT ONCE--TO PLEASE *ME.* HE ASKED THAT YOU SHOULD BE BORN *SAFE* AND HEALTHY.

AND HE MADE AN *OFFERING* OF RICE CAKES.

GRANDMA, WHERE DID THE SHRINE *COME* FROM?

IT'S BEEN IN OUR FAMILY FOR *CENTURIES,* KAIKOU. AS TO WHERE IT *CAME* FROM--

--I CAN ONLY TELL YOU WHAT MY *MOTHER* TOLD ME.

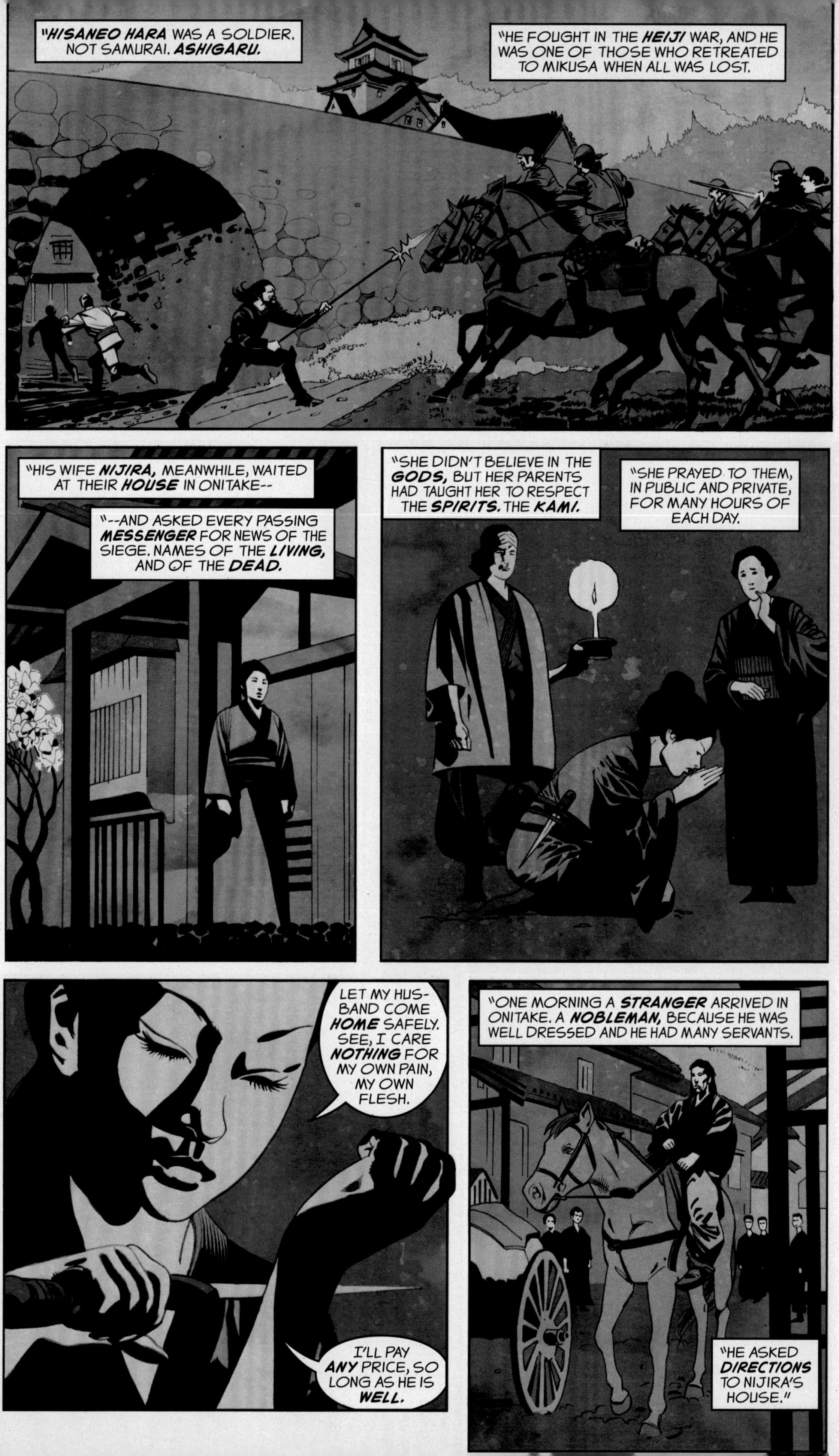

"HISANEO HARA WAS A SOLDIER. NOT SAMURAI. ASHIGARU.
"HE FOUGHT IN THE HEIJI WAR, AND HE WAS ONE OF THOSE WHO RETREATED TO MIKUSA WHEN ALL WAS LOST.
"HIS WIFE NIJIRA, MEANWHILE, WAITED AT THEIR HOUSE IN ONITAKE--
"--AND ASKED EVERY PASSING MESSENGER FOR NEWS OF THE SIEGE. NAMES OF THE LIVING, AND OF THE DEAD.
"SHE DIDN'T BELIEVE IN THE GODS, BUT HER PARENTS HAD TAUGHT HER TO RESPECT THE SPIRITS. THE KAMI.
"SHE PRAYED TO THEM, IN PUBLIC AND PRIVATE, FOR MANY HOURS OF EACH DAY.
LET MY HUSBAND COME HOME SAFELY. SEE, I CARE NOTHING FOR MY OWN PAIN, MY OWN FLESH.
I'LL PAY ANY PRICE, SO LONG AS HE IS WELL.
"ONE MORNING A STRANGER ARRIVED IN ONITAKE. A NOBLEMAN, BECAUSE HE WAS WELL DRESSED AND HE HAD MANY SERVANTS.
"HE ASKED DIRECTIONS TO NIJIRA'S HOUSE."

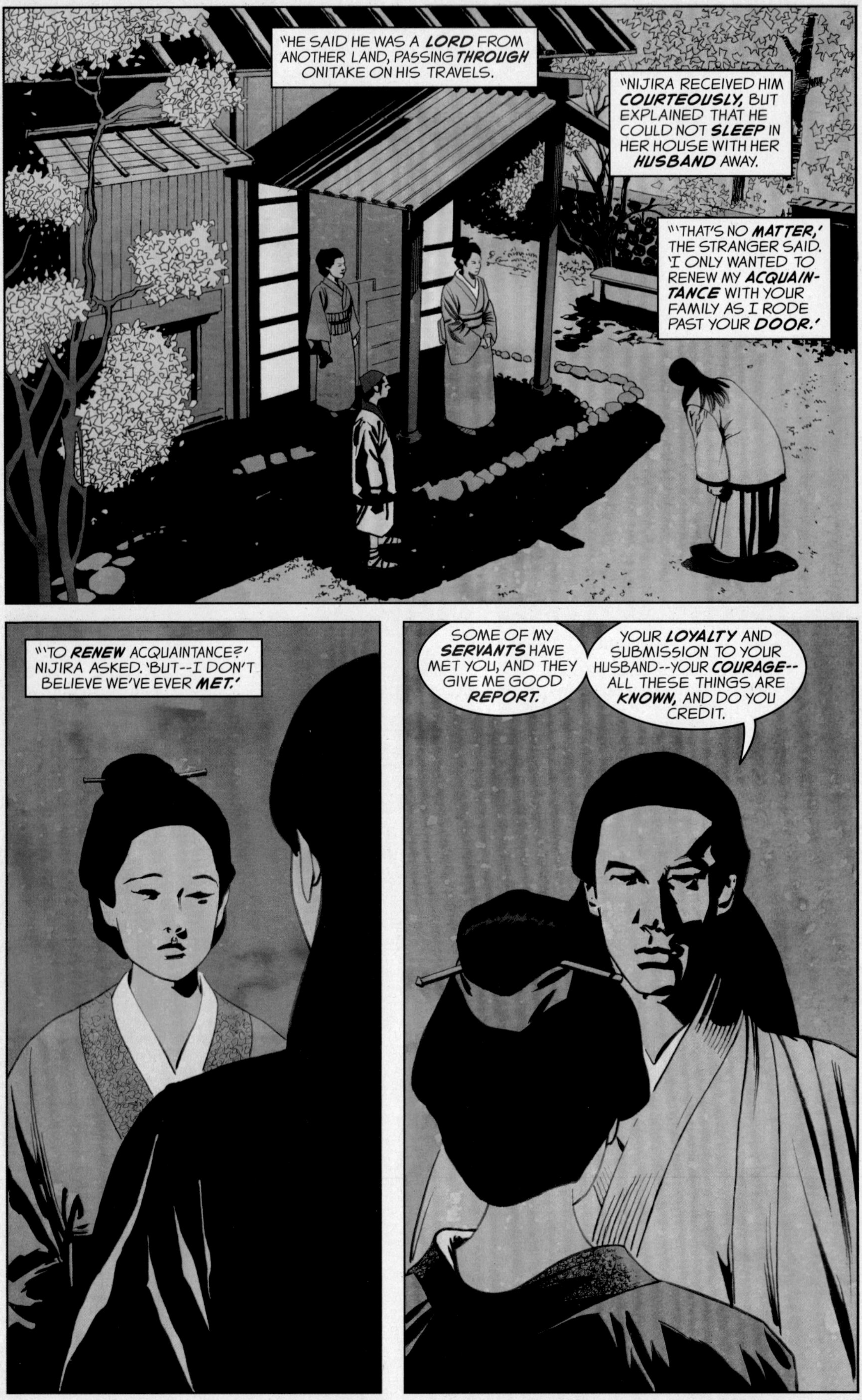
"HE SAID HE WAS A LORD FROM ANOTHER LAND, PASSING THROUGH ONITAKE ON HIS TRAVELS.
"NIJIRA RECEIVED HIM COURTEOUSLY, BUT EXPLAINED THAT HE COULD NOT SLEEP IN HER HOUSE WITH HER HUSBAND AWAY.
"'THAT'S NO MATTER,' THE STRANGER SAID. 'I ONLY WANTED TO RENEW MY ACQUAINTANCE WITH YOUR FAMILY AS I RODE PAST YOUR DOOR.'
"'TO RENEW ACQUAINTANCE?' NIJIRA ASKED. 'BUT--I DON'T BELIEVE WE'VE EVER MET.'
SOME OF MY SERVANTS HAVE MET YOU, AND THEY GIVE ME GOOD REPORT.
YOUR LOYALTY AND SUBMISSION TO YOUR HUSBAND--YOUR COURAGE--ALL THESE THINGS ARE KNOWN, AND DO YOU CREDIT.

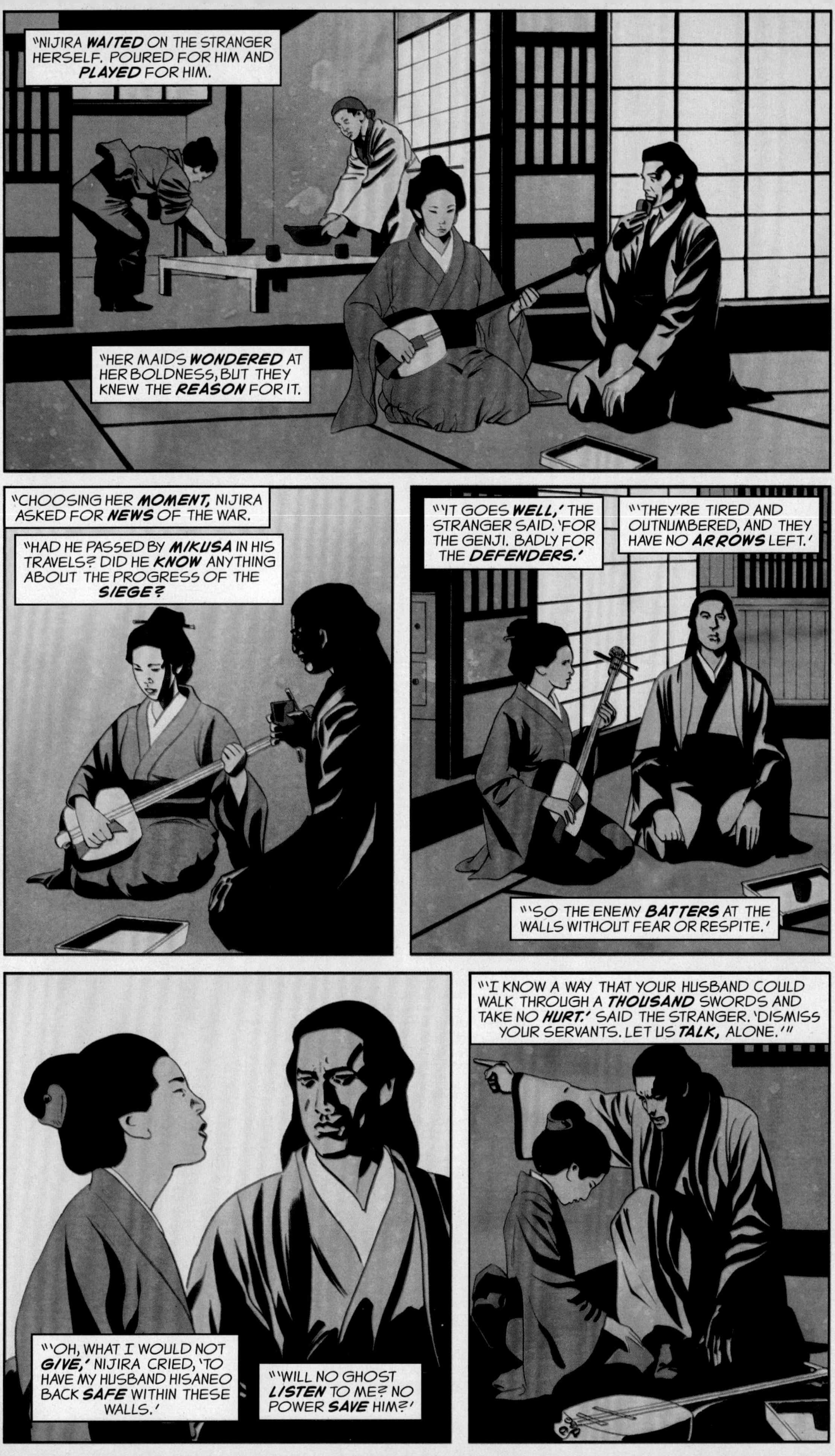
"NIJIRA WAITED ON THE STRANGER HERSELF. POURED FOR HIM AND PLAYED FOR HIM.
"HER MAIDS WONDERED AT HER BOLDNESS, BUT THEY KNEW THE REASON FOR IT.
"CHOOSING HER MOMENT, NIJIRA ASKED FOR NEWS OF THE WAR.
"HAD HE PASSED BY MIKUSA IN HIS TRAVELS? DID HE KNOW ANYTHING ABOUT THE PROGRESS OF THE SIEGE?
"'IT GOES WELL,' THE STRANGER SAID. 'FOR THE GENJI. BADLY FOR THE DEFENDERS.'
"'THEY'RE TIRED AND OUTNUMBERED, AND THEY HAVE NO ARROWS LEFT.'
"'SO THE ENEMY BATTERS AT THE WALLS WITHOUT FEAR OR RESPITE.'
"'OH, WHAT I WOULD NOT GIVE,' NIJIRA CRIED, 'TO HAVE MY HUSBAND HISANEO BACK SAFE WITHIN THESE WALLS.'
"'WILL NO GHOST LISTEN TO ME? NO POWER SAVE HIM?'
"'I KNOW A WAY THAT YOUR HUSBAND COULD WALK THROUGH A THOUSAND SWORDS AND TAKE NO HURT,' SAID THE STRANGER. 'DISMISS YOUR SERVANTS. LET US TALK, ALONE.'"

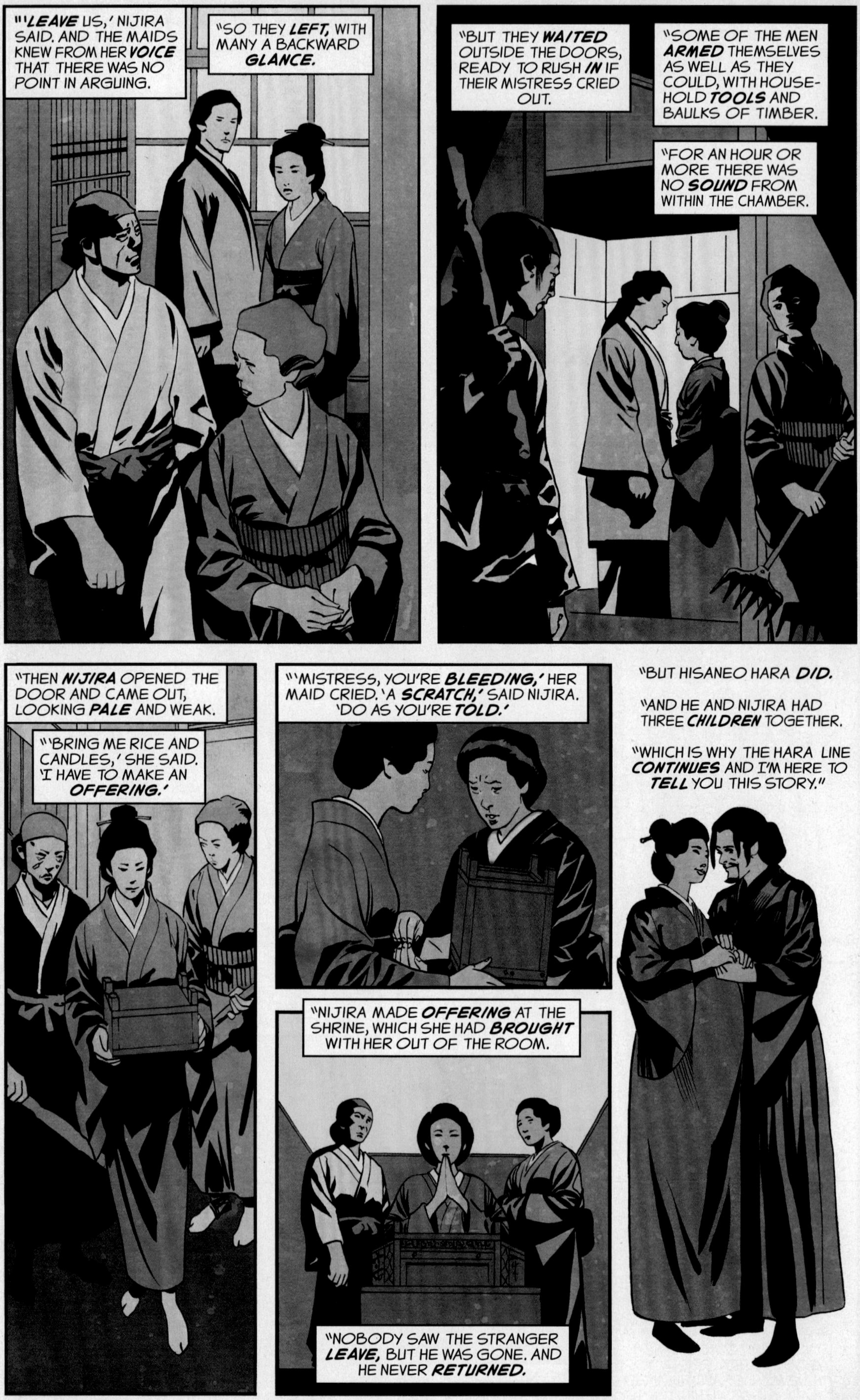
"'LEAVE US,' NIJIRA SAID. AND THE MAIDS KNEW FROM HER VOICE THAT THERE WAS NO POINT IN ARGUING.
"SO THEY LEFT, WITH MANY A BACKWARD GLANCE.
"BUT THEY WAITED OUTSIDE THE DOORS, READY TO RUSH IN IF THEIR MISTRESS CRIED OUT.
"SOME OF THE MEN ARMED THEMSELVES AS WELL AS THEY COULD, WITH HOUSEHOLD TOOLS AND BAULKS OF TIMBER.
"FOR AN HOUR OR MORE THERE WAS NO SOUND FROM WITHIN THE CHAMBER.
"THEN NIJIRA OPENED THE DOOR AND CAME OUT, LOOKING PALE AND WEAK.
"'BRING ME RICE AND CANDLES,' SHE SAID. 'I HAVE TO MAKE AN OFFERING.'
"'MISTRESS, YOU'RE BLEEDING,' HER MAID CRIED. 'A SCRATCH,' SAID NIJIRA. 'DO AS YOU'RE TOLD.'
"NIJIRA MADE OFFERING AT THE SHRINE, WHICH SHE HAD BROUGHT WITH HER OUT OF THE ROOM.
"NOBODY SAW THE STRANGER LEAVE, BUT HE WAS GONE. AND HE NEVER RETURNED.
"BUT HISANEO HARA DID.
"AND HE AND NIJIRA HAD THREE CHILDREN TOGETHER.
"WHICH IS WHY THE HARA LINE CONTINUES AND I'M HERE TO TELL YOU THIS STORY."

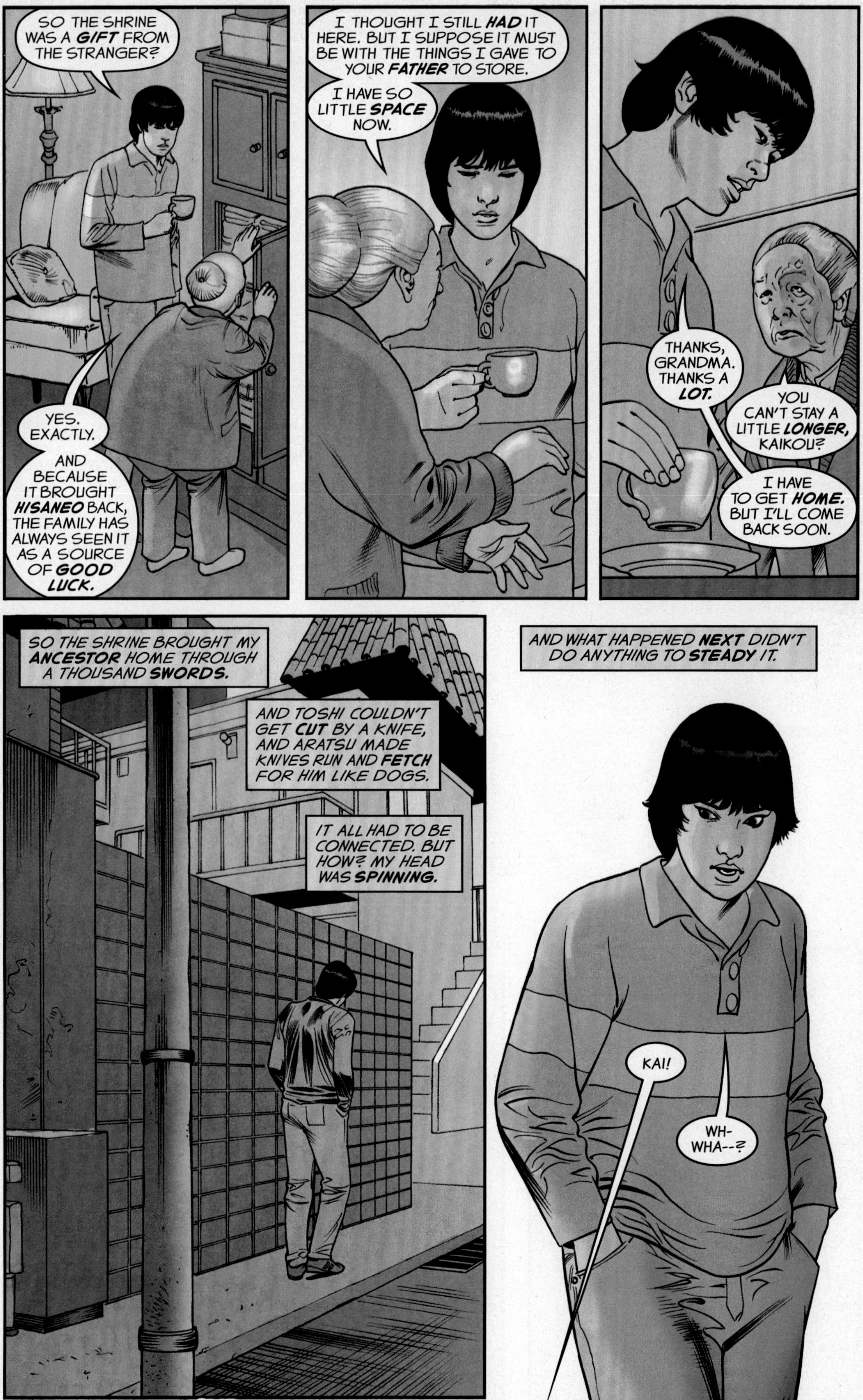
SO THE SHRINE WAS A GIFT FROM THE STRANGER?
YES. EXACTLY.
AND BECAUSE IT BROUGHT HISANEO BACK, THE FAMILY HAS ALWAYS SEEN IT AS A SOURCE OF GOOD LUCK.
I THOUGHT I STILL HAD IT HERE. BUT I SUPPOSE IT MUST BE WITH THE THINGS I GAVE TO YOUR FATHER TO STORE.
I HAVE SO LITTLE SPACE NOW.
THANKS, GRANDMA. THANKS A LOT.
YOU CAN'T STAY A LITTLE LONGER, KAIKOU?
I HAVE TO GET HOME. BUT I'LL COME BACK SOON.
SO THE SHRINE BROUGHT MY ANCESTOR HOME THROUGH A THOUSAND SWORDS.
AND TOSHI COULDN'T GET CUT BY A KNIFE, AND ARATSU MADE KNIVES RUN AND FETCH FOR HIM LIKE DOGS.
IT ALL HAD TO BE CONNECTED. BUT HOW? MY HEAD WAS SPINNING.
AND WHAT HAPPENED NEXT DIDN'T DO ANYTHING TO STEADY IT.
KAI!
WH-WHA--?

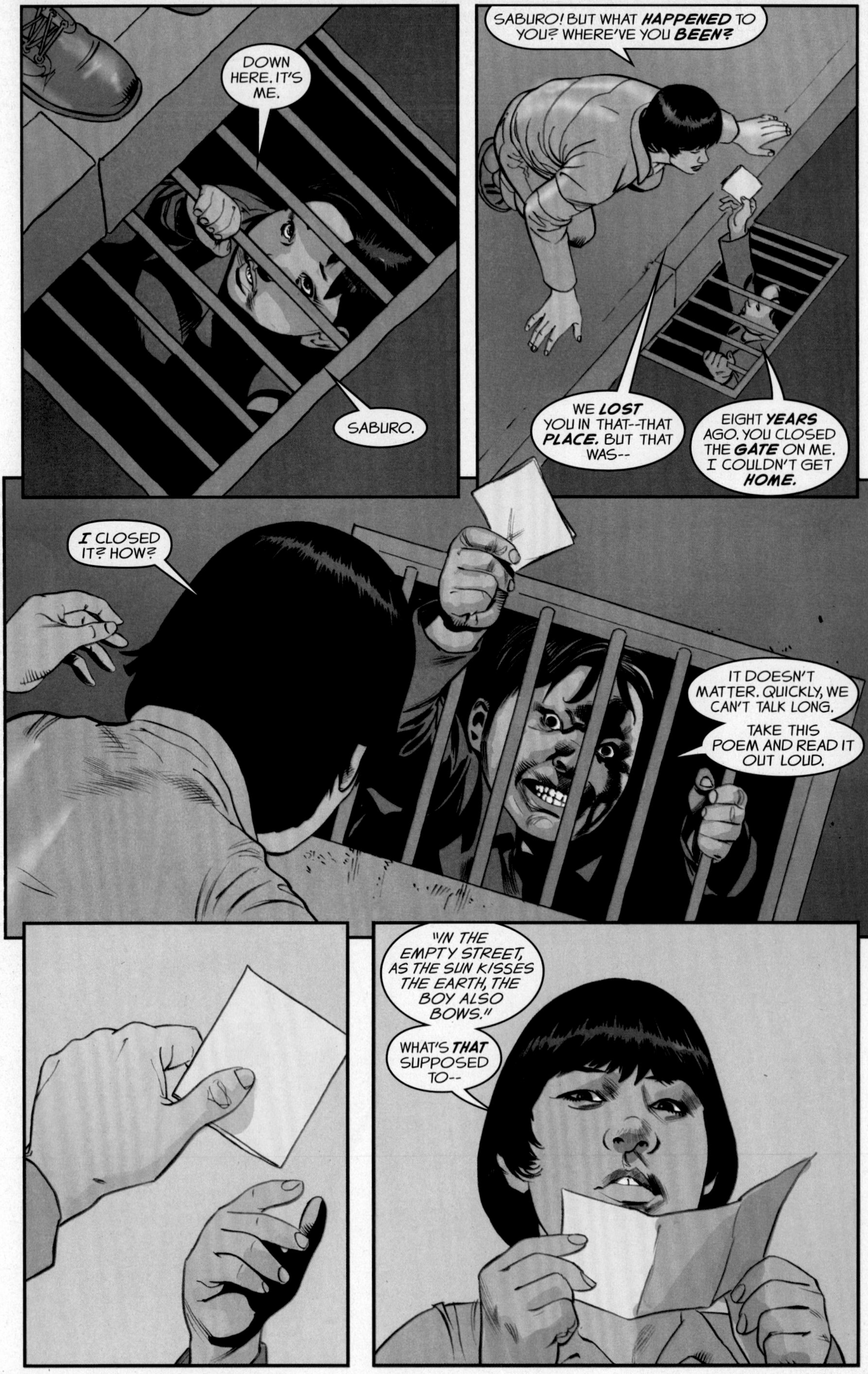
DOWN HERE. IT'S ME.
SABURO.
SABURO! BUT WHAT HAPPENED TO YOU? WHERE'VE YOU BEEN?
WE LOST YOU IN THAT--THAT PLACE. BUT THAT WAS--
EIGHT YEARS AGO. YOU CLOSED THE GATE ON ME. I COULDN'T GET HOME.
I CLOSED IT? HOW?
IT DOESN'T MATTER. QUICKLY, WE CAN'T TALK LONG.
TAKE THIS POEM AND READ IT OUT LOUD.
"IN THE EMPTY STREET, AS THE SUN KISSES THE EARTH, THE BOY ALSO BOWS."
WHAT'S THAT SUPPOSED TO--

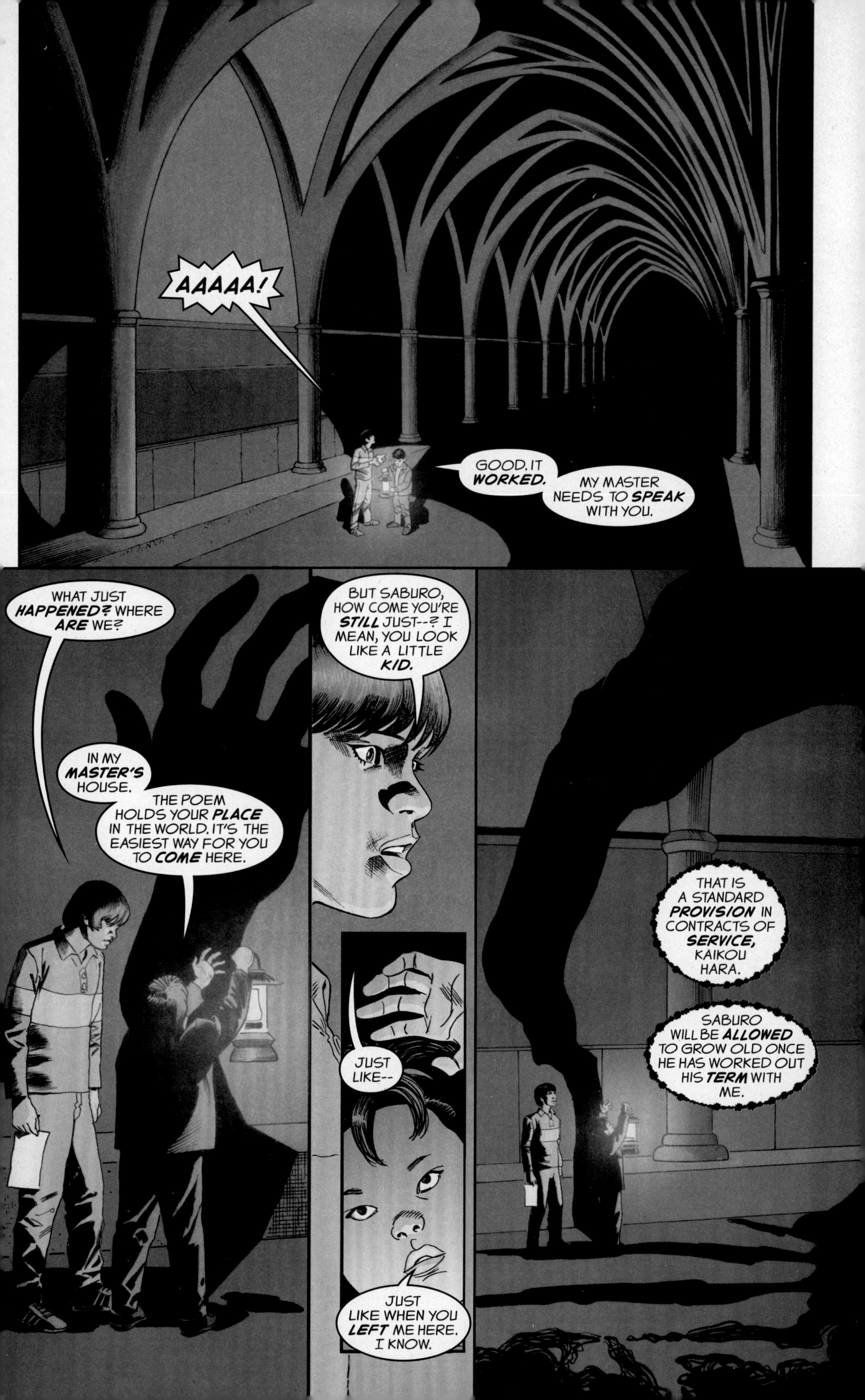
AAAAA!
GOOD. IT WORKED.
MY MASTER NEEDS TO SPEAK WITH YOU.
WHAT JUST HAPPENED? WHERE ARE WE?
IN MY MASTER'S HOUSE.
THE POEM HOLDS YOUR PLACE IN THE WORLD. IT'S THE EASIEST WAY FOR YOU TO COME HERE.
BUT SABURO, HOW COME YOU'RE STILL JUST--? I MEAN, YOU LOOK LIKE A LITTLE KID.
JUST LIKE--
JUST LIKE WHEN YOU LEFT ME HERE. I KNOW.
THAT IS A STANDARD PROVISION IN CONTRACTS OF SERVICE, KAIKOU HARA.
SABURO WILL BE ALLOWED TO GROW OLD ONCE HE HAS WORKED OUT HIS TERM WITH ME.

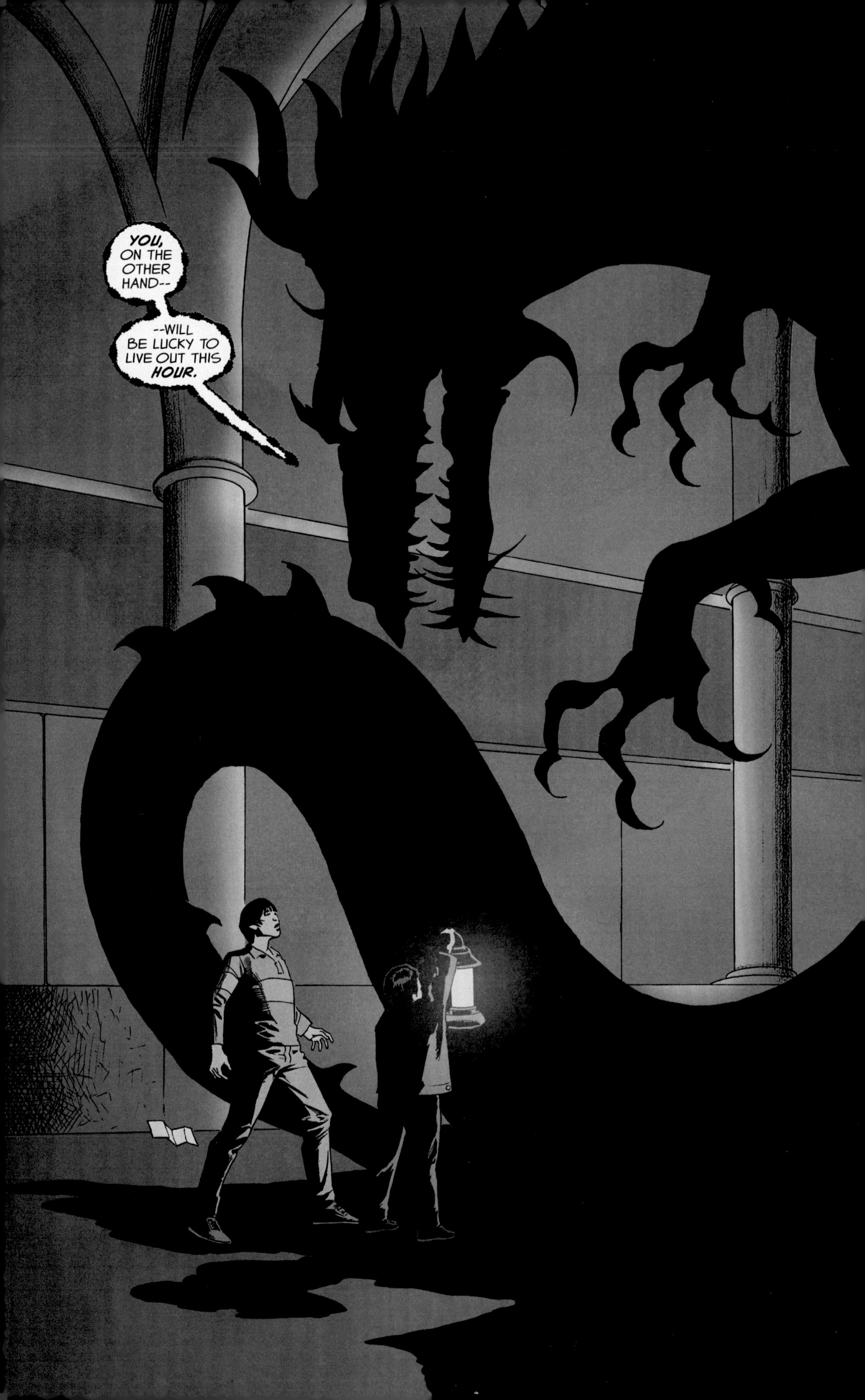
YOU, ON THE OTHER HAND--
--WILL BE LUCKY TO LIVE OUT THIS HOUR.

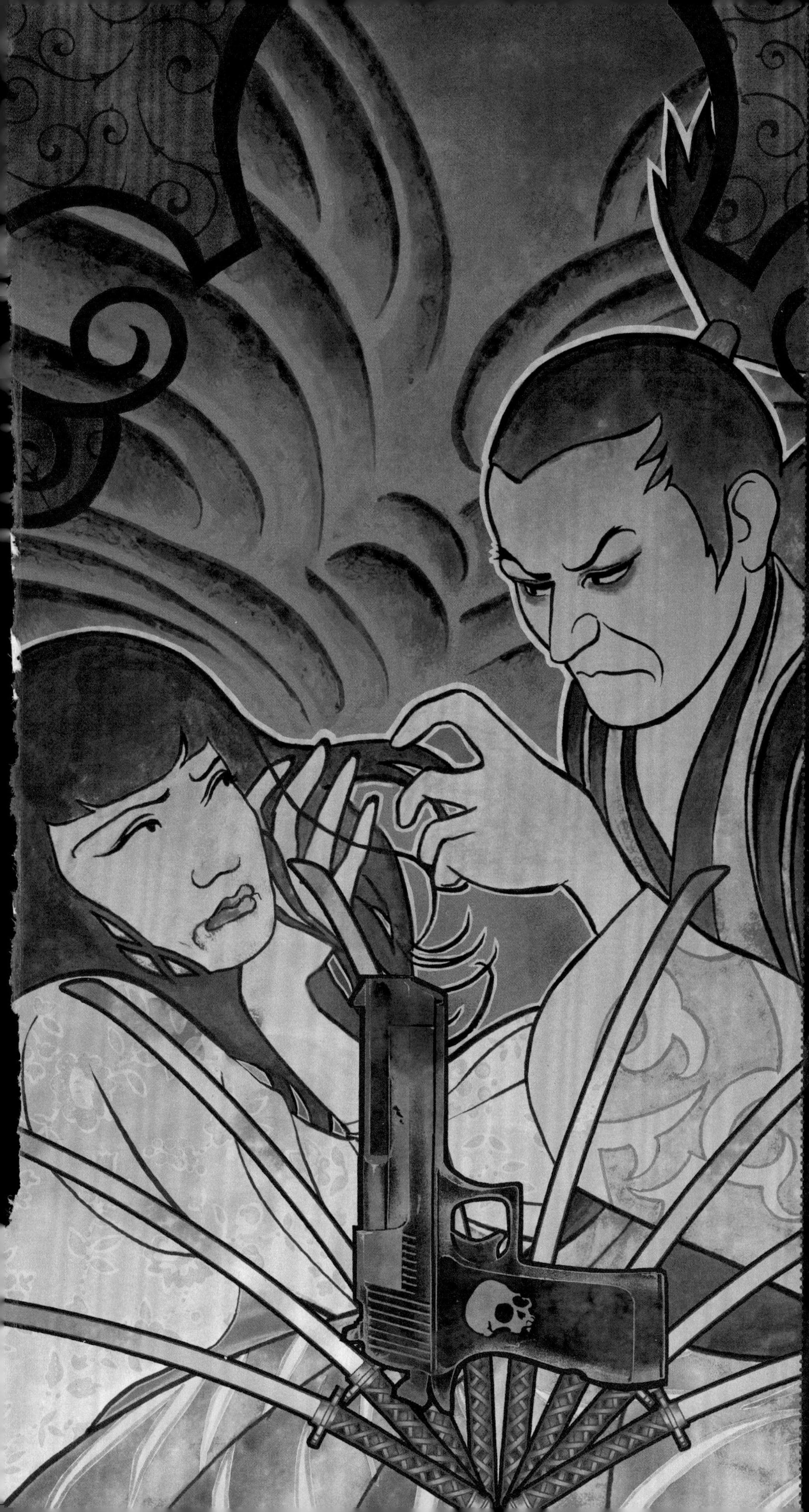

chapter three

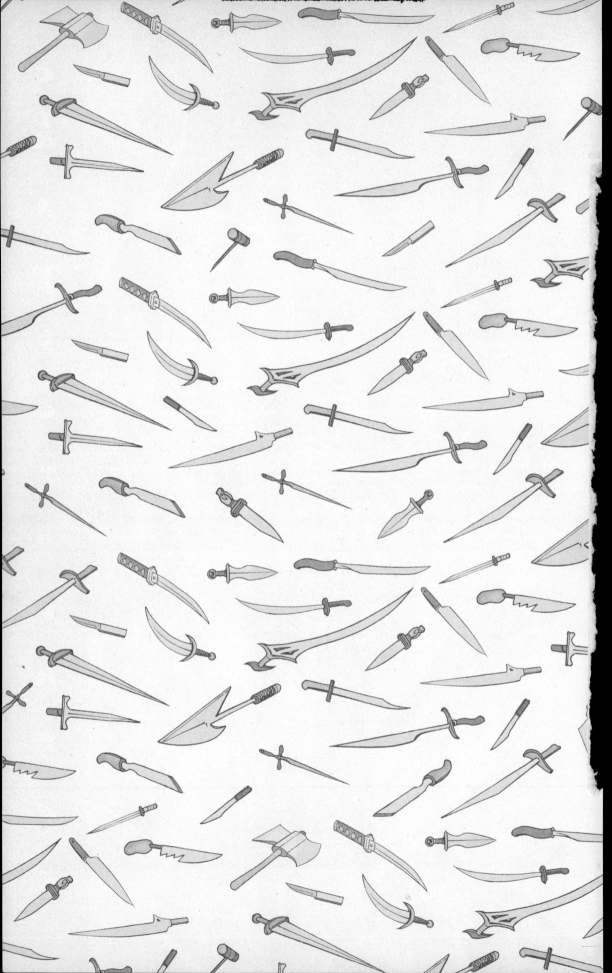

DOWN BY THE RIVER, THE HOMELESS LIVE IN CARDBOARD **BOXES** COVERED WITH TARPAULIN.

WHEN THE POLICE COME TO **EVICT** THEM, THEY RUN WITH THEIR HOUSES ON THEIR **BACKS**, LIKE SNAILS.

THAT WAS WHERE **KISUKE KAHIRU**--KK--TOOK MY **SISTER**.

IF MY DAD SAYS ANYTHING, JUST **IGNORE** HIM. AND IF HE TRIES TO **GROPE** YOU, KICK HIM IN THE **PILLS**.

PERHAPS SHE THOUGHT ABOUT THE TIME WHEN WE STEPPED THROUGH THE **SANNO SHINTO** ARCH INTO ANOTHER **WORLD**.

YOU CAN FIND OTHER WORLDS **CLOSER** THAN THAT.

KISU, THIS IS...EMPTY. GET ME ANOTHER BOTTLE OF--

SHUT YOUR **MOUTH**. WE'LL BE IN THE BATHROOM. **DON'T** COME IN.

NOW THAT IT CAME **DOWN** TO THIS, SHE FOUND THAT SHE WAS **SHAKING**.

WHAT'S IN **HERE**?

EVERYTHING.

MORE AFRAID OF THIS **BOY** THAN OF THE RABID MAGICIAN WHO MADE **KNIVES** DANCE.

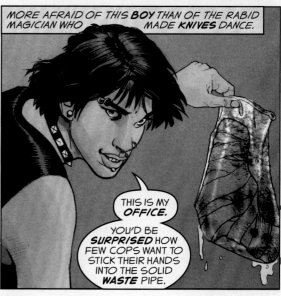

THIS IS MY **OFFICE**.

YOU'D BE **SURPRISED** HOW FEW COPS WANT TO STICK THEIR HANDS INTO THE SOLID **WASTE** PIPE.

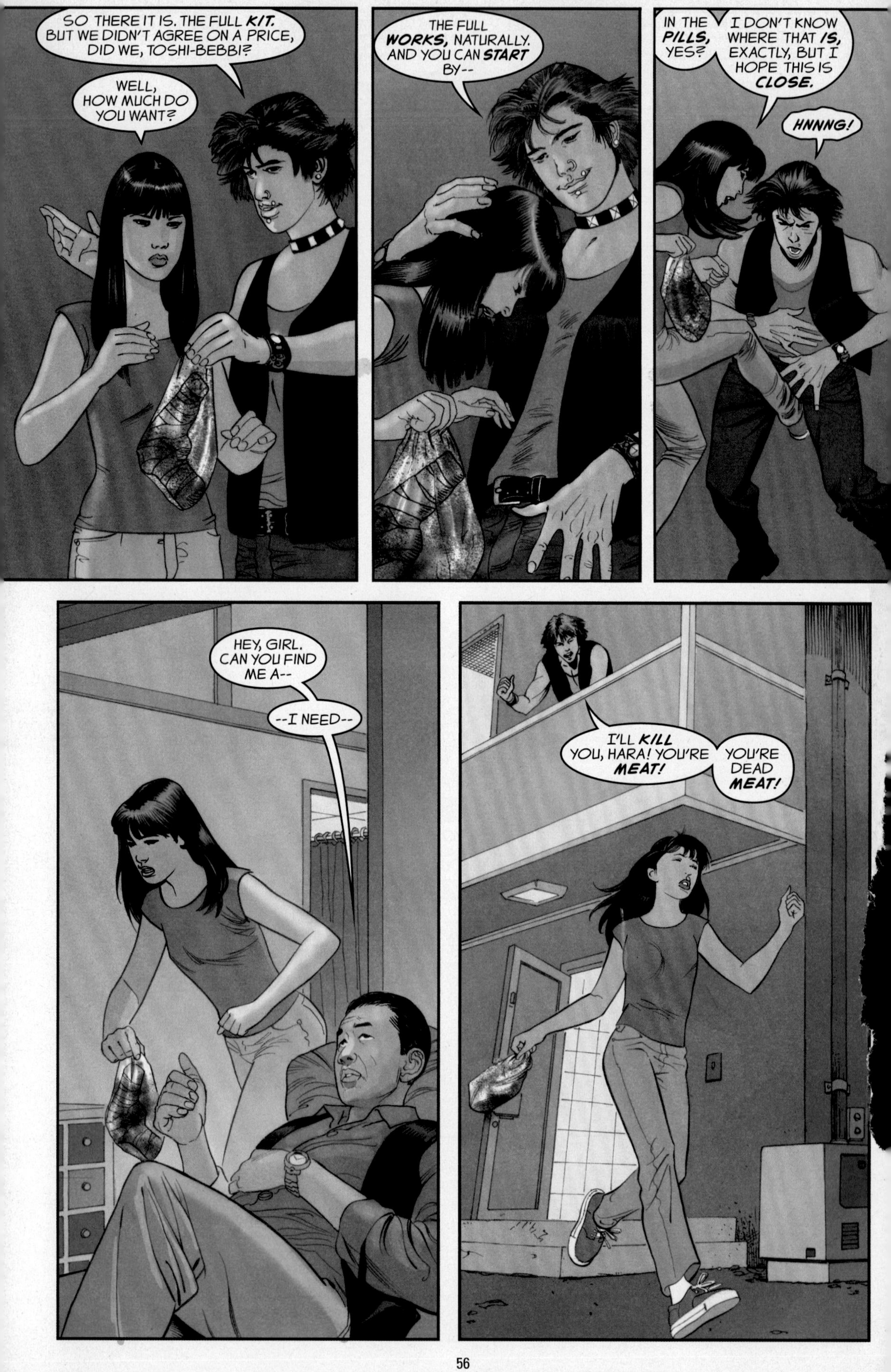
SO THERE IT IS. THE FULL KIT. BUT WE DIDN'T AGREE ON A PRICE, DID WE, TOSHI-BEBBI?
WELL, HOW MUCH DO YOU WANT?
THE FULL WORKS, NATURALLY. AND YOU CAN START BY--
IN THE PILLS, YES?
I DON'T KNOW WHERE THAT IS, EXACTLY, BUT I HOPE THIS IS CLOSE.
HNNNG!
HEY, GIRL. CAN YOU FIND ME A--
--I NEED--
I'LL KILL YOU, HARA! YOU'RE MEAT!
YOU'RE DEAD MEAT!

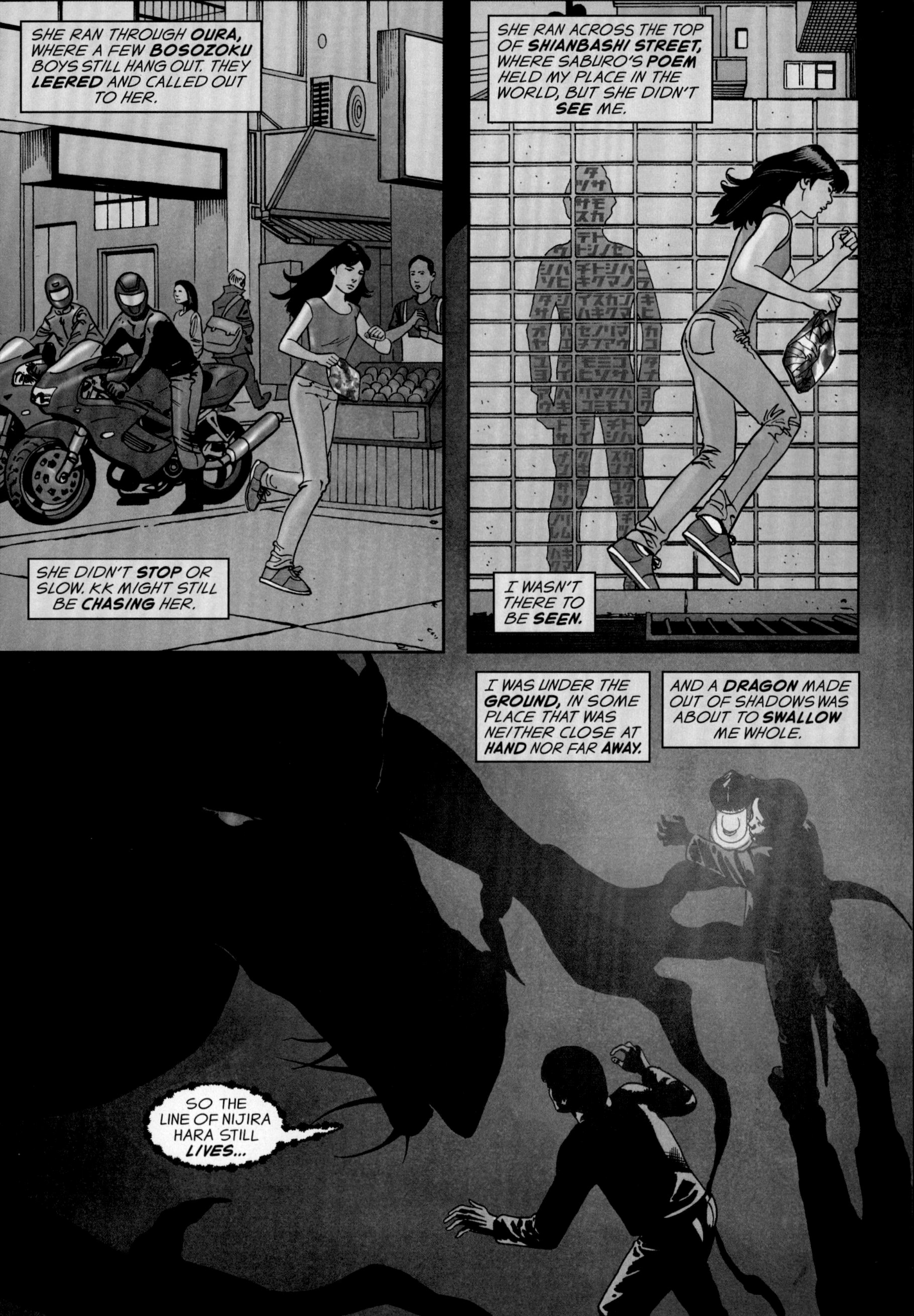
SHE RAN THROUGH OURA, WHERE A FEW BOSOZOKU BOYS STILL HANG OUT. THEY LEERED AND CALLED OUT TO HER.
SHE DIDN'T STOP OR SLOW. KK MIGHT STILL BE CHASING HER.
SHE RAN ACROSS THE TOP OF SHIANBASHI STREET, WHERE SABURO'S POEM HELD MY PLACE IN THE WORLD, BUT SHE DIDN'T SEE ME.
I WASN'T THERE TO BE SEEN.
I WAS UNDER THE GROUND, IN SOME PLACE THAT WAS NEITHER CLOSE AT HAND NOR FAR AWAY.
AND A DRAGON MADE OUT OF SHADOWS WAS ABOUT TO SWALLOW ME WHOLE.
SO THE LINE OF NIJIRA HARA STILL LIVES...

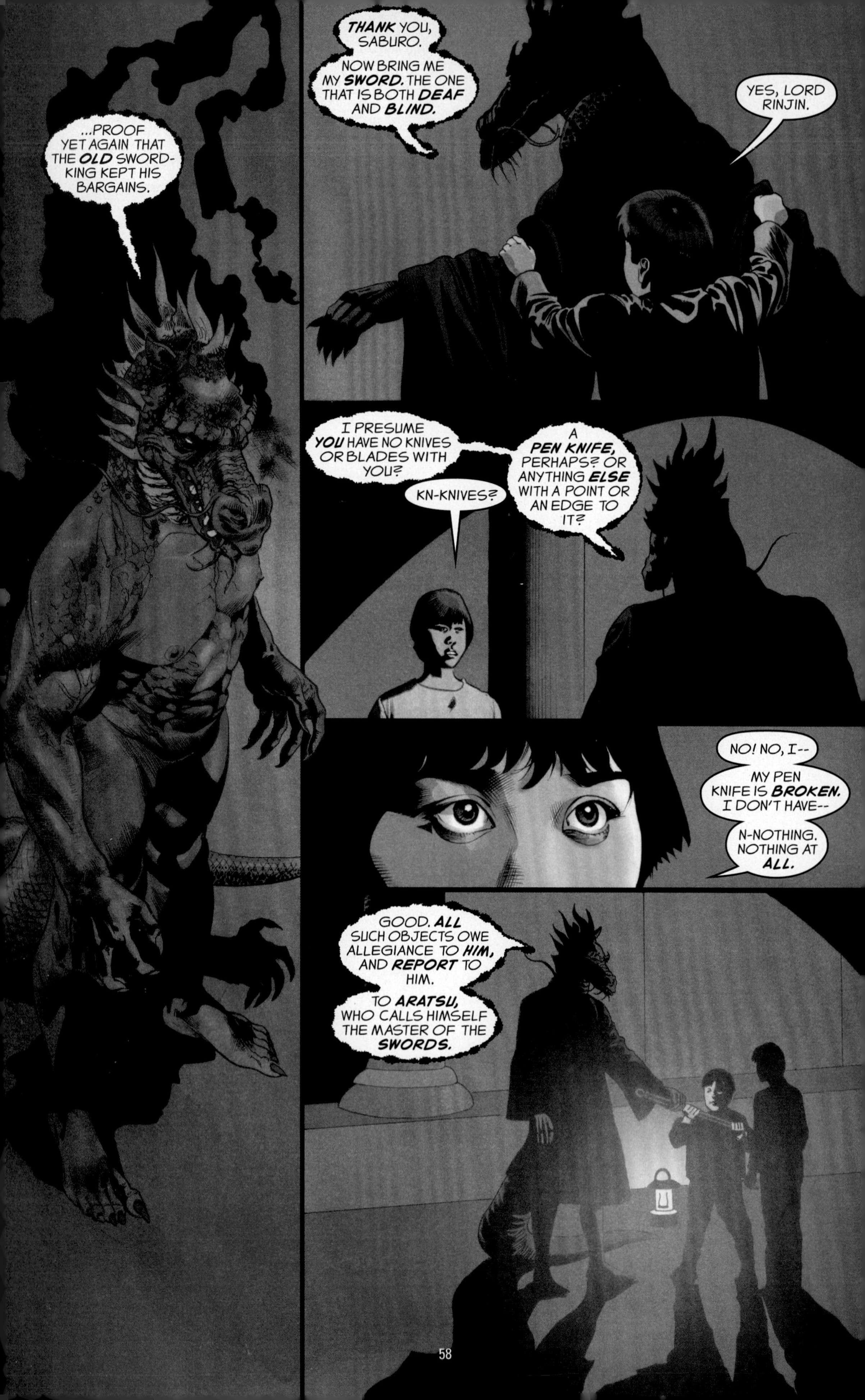
...PROOF YET AGAIN THAT THE OLD SWORD-KING KEPT HIS BARGAINS.
THANK YOU, SABURO.
NOW BRING ME MY SWORD. THE ONE THAT IS BOTH DEAF AND BLIND.
YES, LORD RINJIN.
I PRESUME YOU HAVE NO KNIVES OR BLADES WITH YOU?
KN-KNIVES?
A PEN KNIFE, PERHAPS? OR ANYTHING ELSE WITH A POINT OR AN EDGE TO IT?
NO! NO, I--
MY PEN KNIFE IS BROKEN. I DON'T HAVE--
N-NOTHING. NOTHING AT ALL.
GOOD. ALL SUCH OBJECTS OWE ALLEGIANCE TO HIM, AND REPORT TO HIM.
TO ARATSU, WHO CALLS HIMSELF THE MASTER OF THE SWORDS.

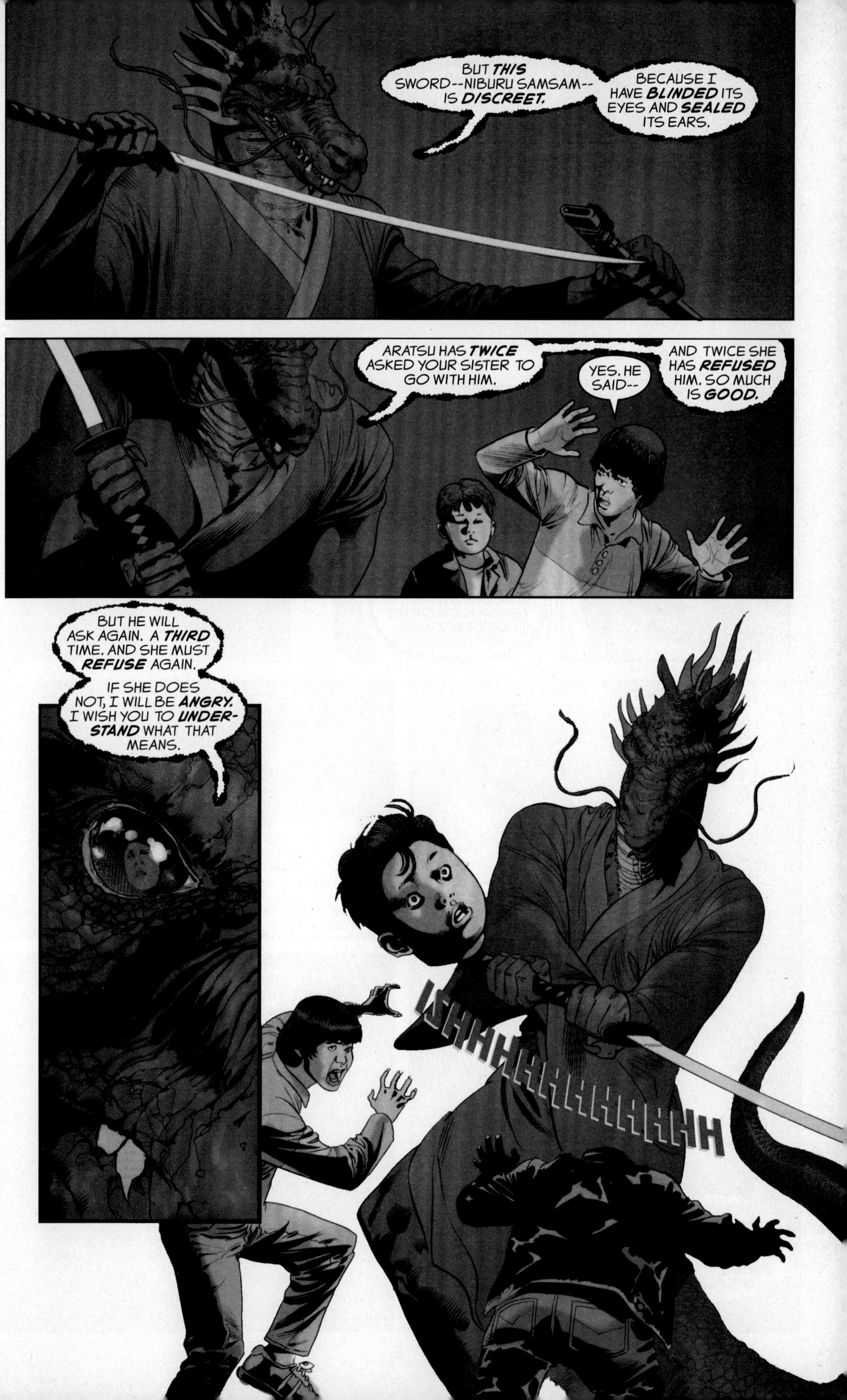
BUT THIS SWORD--NIBURU SAMSAM--IS DISCREET.
BECAUSE I HAVE BLINDED ITS EYES AND SEALED ITS EARS.
ARATSU HAS TWICE ASKED YOUR SISTER TO GO WITH HIM.
YES. HE SAID--
AND TWICE SHE HAS REFUSED HIM. SO MUCH IS GOOD.
BUT HE WILL ASK AGAIN. A THIRD TIME. AND SHE MUST REFUSE AGAIN.
IF SHE DOES NOT, I WILL BE ANGRY. I WISH YOU TO UNDERSTAND WHAT THAT MEANS.
SHHHHHHHHHHHHH

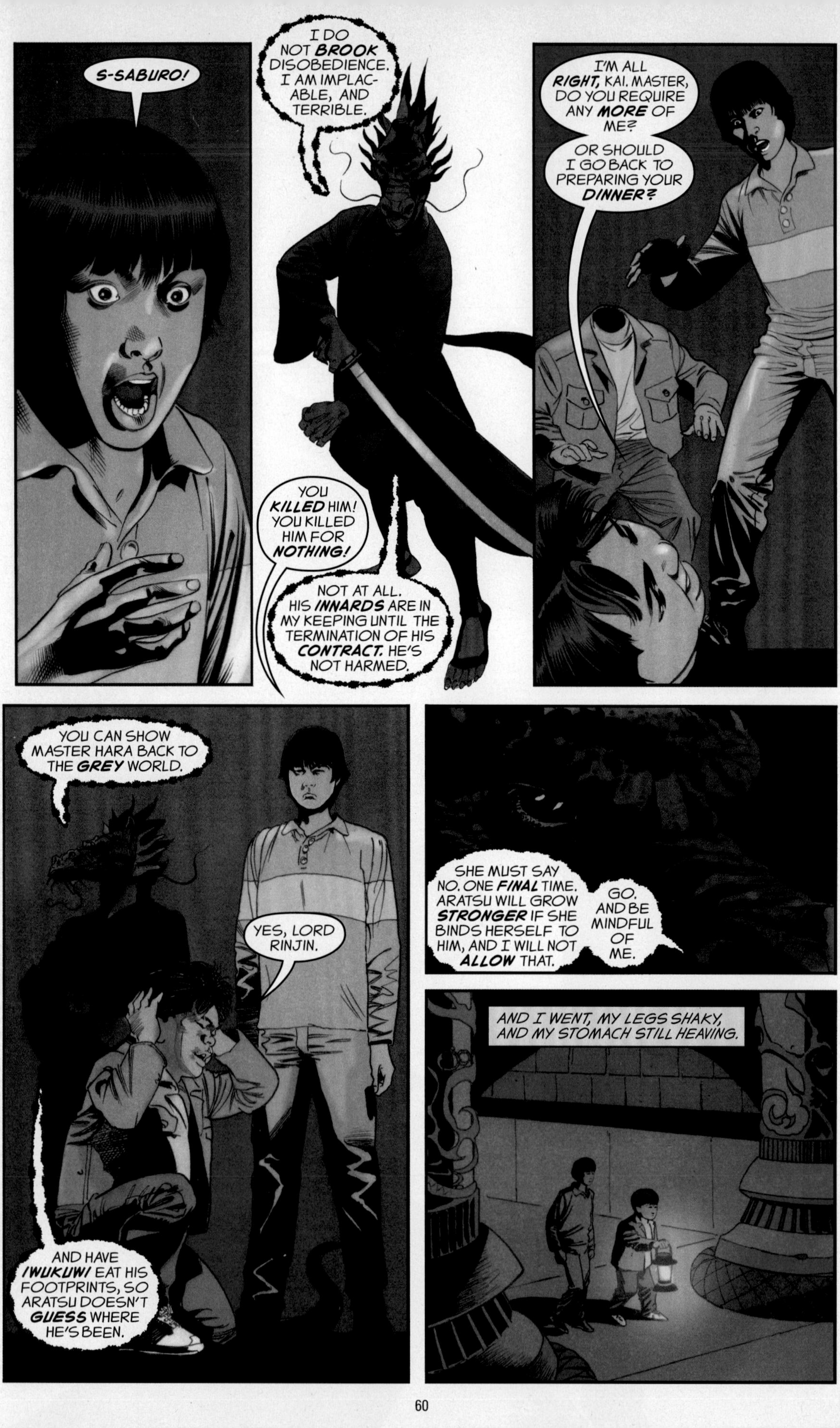
S-SABURO!
I DO NOT BROOK DISOBEDIENCE. I AM IMPLACABLE, AND TERRIBLE.
YOU KILLED HIM! YOU KILLED HIM FOR NOTHING!
NOT AT ALL. HIS INNARDS ARE IN MY KEEPING UNTIL THE TERMINATION OF HIS CONTRACT. HE'S NOT HARMED.
I'M ALL RIGHT, KAI. MASTER, DO YOU REQUIRE ANY MORE OF ME?
OR SHOULD I GO BACK TO PREPARING YOUR DINNER?
YOU CAN SHOW MASTER HARA BACK TO THE GREY WORLD.
AND HAVE IWUKUWI EAT HIS FOOTPRINTS, SO ARATSU DOESN'T GUESS WHERE HE'S BEEN.
YES, LORD RINJIN.
SHE MUST SAY NO. ONE FINAL TIME. ARATSU WILL GROW STRONGER IF SHE BINDS HERSELF TO HIM, AND I WILL NOT ALLOW THAT.
GO. AND BE MINDFUL OF ME.
AND I WENT, MY LEGS SHAKY, AND MY STOMACH STILL HEAVING.

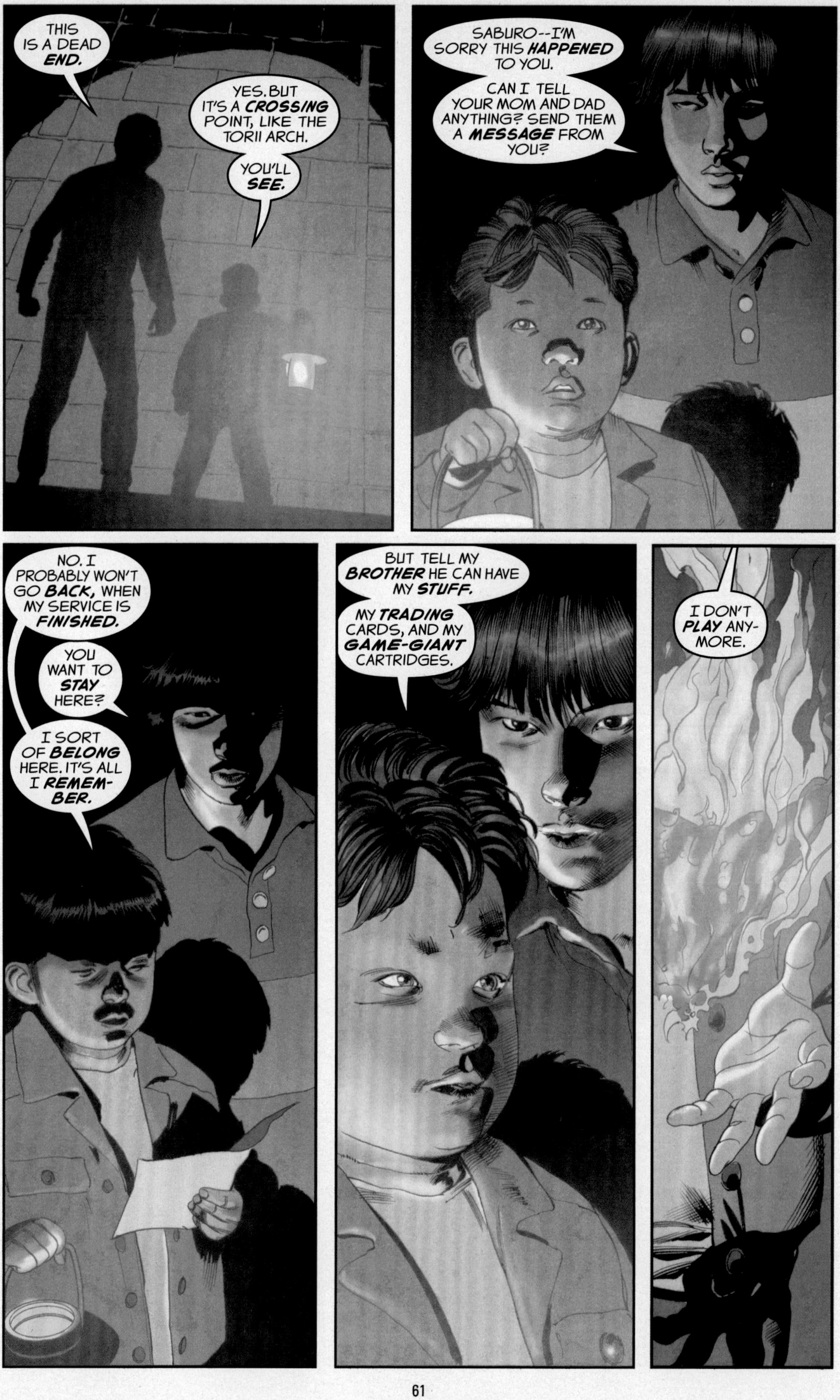
THIS IS A DEAD END.
YES. BUT IT'S A CROSSING POINT, LIKE THE TORII ARCH.
YOU'LL SEE.
SABURO--I'M SORRY THIS HAPPENED TO YOU.
CAN I TELL YOUR MOM AND DAD ANYTHING? SEND THEM A MESSAGE FROM YOU?
NO. I PROBABLY WON'T GO BACK, WHEN MY SERVICE IS FINISHED.
YOU WANT TO STAY HERE?
I SORT OF BELONG HERE. IT'S ALL I REMEMBER.
BUT TELL MY BROTHER HE CAN HAVE MY STUFF.
MY TRADING CARDS, AND MY GAME-GIANT CARTRIDGES.
I DON'T PLAY ANYMORE.

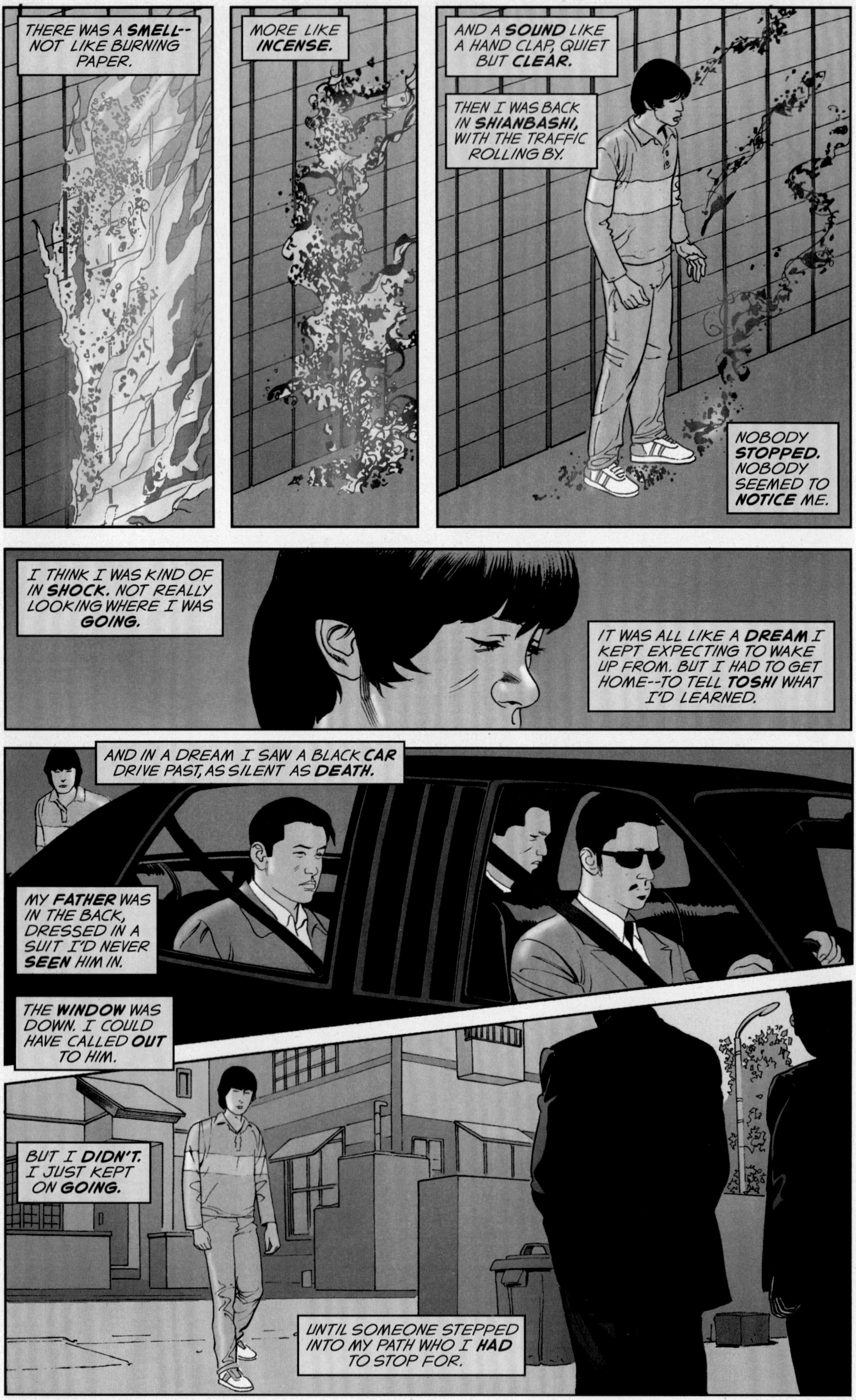
THERE WAS A SMELL--NOT LIKE BURNING PAPER.
MORE LIKE INCENSE.
AND A SOUND LIKE A HAND CLAP, QUIET BUT CLEAR.
THEN I WAS BACK IN SHIANBASHI, WITH THE TRAFFIC ROLLING BY.
NOBODY STOPPED. NOBODY SEEMED TO NOTICE ME.
I THINK I WAS KIND OF IN SHOCK. NOT REALLY LOOKING WHERE I WAS GOING.
IT WAS ALL LIKE A DREAM I KEPT EXPECTING TO WAKE UP FROM. BUT I HAD TO GET HOME--TO TELL TOSHI WHAT I'D LEARNED.
AND IN A DREAM I SAW A BLACK CAR DRIVE PAST, AS SILENT AS DEATH.
MY FATHER WAS IN THE BACK, DRESSED IN A SUIT I'D NEVER SEEN HIM IN.
THE WINDOW WAS DOWN. I COULD HAVE CALLED OUT TO HIM.
BUT I DIDN'T. I JUST KEPT ON GOING.
UNTIL SOMEONE STEPPED INTO MY PATH WHO I HAD TO STOP FOR.

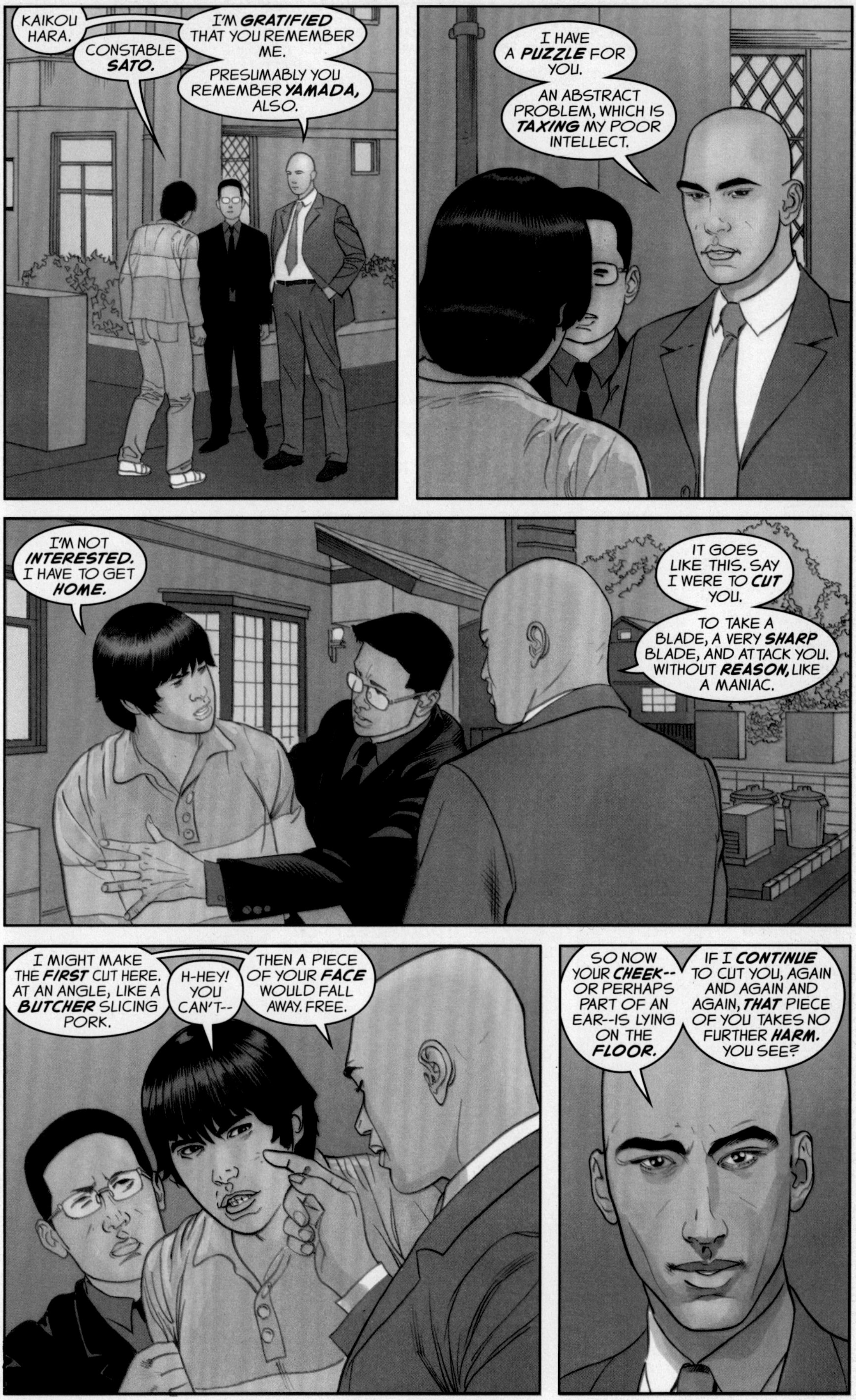
KAIKOU HARA.
CONSTABLE SATO.
I'M GRATIFIED THAT YOU REMEMBER ME.
PRESUMABLY YOU REMEMBER YAMADA, ALSO.
I HAVE A PUZZLE FOR YOU.
AN ABSTRACT PROBLEM, WHICH IS TAXING MY POOR INTELLECT.
I'M NOT INTERESTED. I HAVE TO GET HOME.
IT GOES LIKE THIS. SAY I WERE TO CUT YOU.
TO TAKE A BLADE, A VERY SHARP BLADE, AND ATTACK YOU. WITHOUT REASON, LIKE A MANIAC.
I MIGHT MAKE THE FIRST CUT HERE. AT AN ANGLE, LIKE A BUTCHER SLICING PORK.
H-HEY! YOU CAN'T--
THEN A PIECE OF YOUR FACE WOULD FALL AWAY. FREE.
SO NOW YOUR CHEEK--OR PERHAPS PART OF AN EAR--IS LYING ON THE FLOOR.
IF I CONTINUE TO CUT YOU, AGAIN AND AGAIN AND AGAIN, THAT PIECE OF YOU TAKES NO FURTHER HARM. YOU SEE?

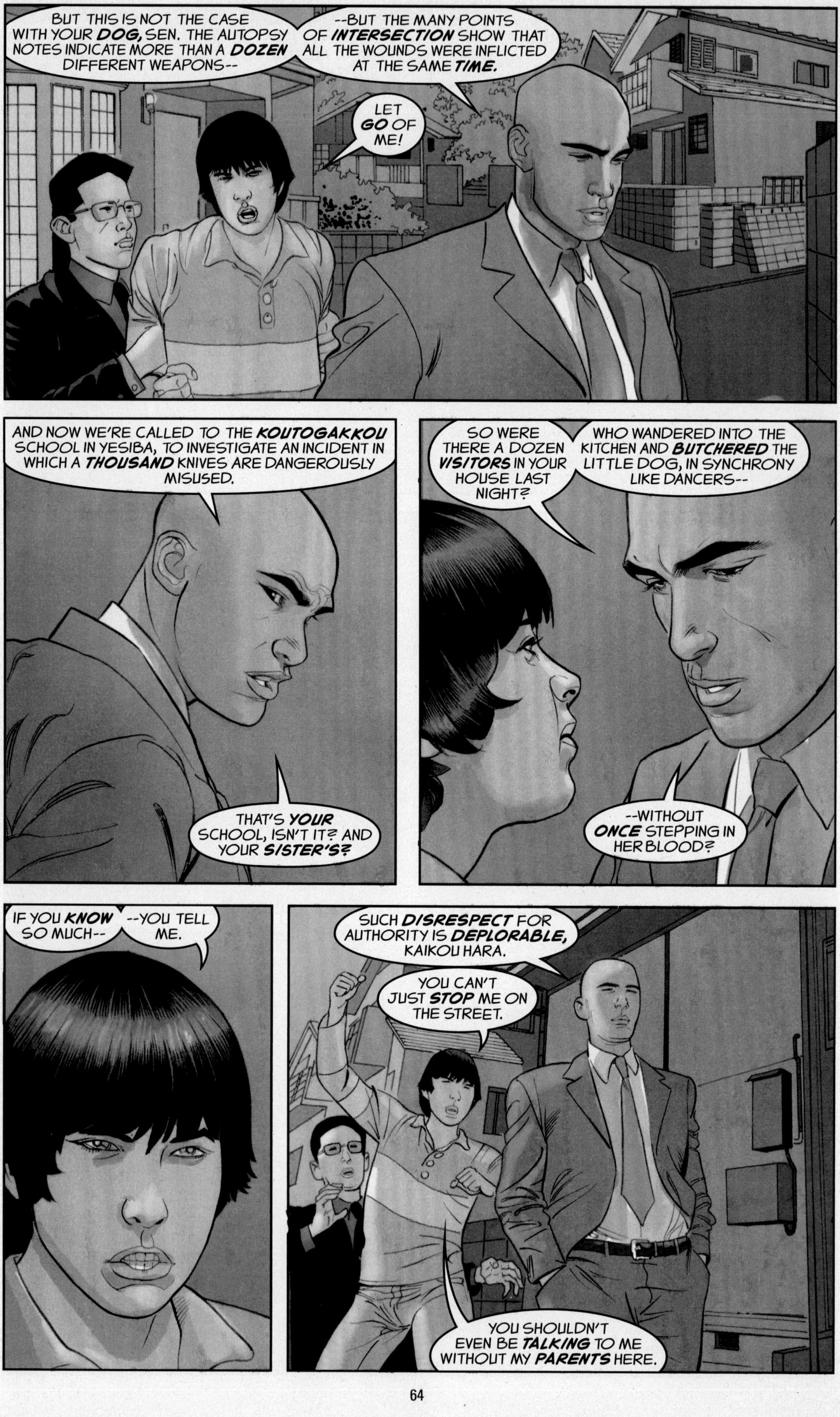
BUT THIS IS NOT THE CASE WITH YOUR DOG, SEN. THE AUTOPSY NOTES INDICATE MORE THAN A DOZEN DIFFERENT WEAPONS--
--BUT THE MANY POINTS OF INTERSECTION SHOW THAT ALL THE WOUNDS WERE INFLICTED AT THE SAME TIME.
LET GO OF ME!
AND NOW WE'RE CALLED TO THE KOUTOGAKKOU SCHOOL IN YESIBA, TO INVESTIGATE AN INCIDENT IN WHICH A THOUSAND KNIVES ARE DANGEROUSLY MISUSED.
THAT'S YOUR SCHOOL, ISN'T IT? AND YOUR SISTER'S?
SO WERE THERE A DOZEN VISITORS IN YOUR HOUSE LAST NIGHT?
WHO WANDERED INTO THE KITCHEN AND BUTCHERED THE LITTLE DOG, IN SYNCHRONY LIKE DANCERS--
--WITHOUT ONCE STEPPING IN HER BLOOD?
IF YOU KNOW SO MUCH--
--YOU TELL ME.
SUCH DISRESPECT FOR AUTHORITY IS DEPLORABLE, KAIKOU HARA.
YOU CAN'T JUST STOP ME ON THE STREET.
YOU SHOULDN'T EVEN BE TALKING TO ME WITHOUT MY PARENTS HERE.

IT WAS A **CHANCE** MEETING. WE HAPPENED TO BE TAKING A **STROLL** HERE.

GIVE MASTER HARA MY **CARD**, YAMADA. HE'LL WANT TO **USE** IT AT SOME POINT.

YOU'LL CHANGE YOUR **MIND** ABOUT TALKING TO ME, KAIKOU.

YOU'LL FIND THE **ALTERNATIVES** FAR MORE **DISRUPTIVE** TO YOUR PEACE OF MIND.

I'VE GOT NOTHING TO **SAY**.

OF COURSE, OF COURSE. WE'LL **SEE**.

I DIDN'T **KILL** SEN! AND I DON'T **APPRECIATE** BEING--

...?

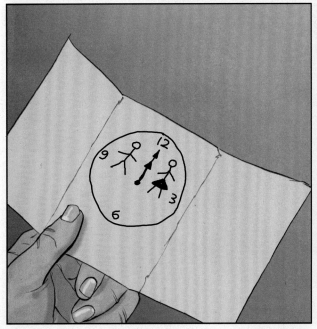

EVERY PICTURE TELLS A **STORY**.

THIS ONE I ALREADY **KNEW**.

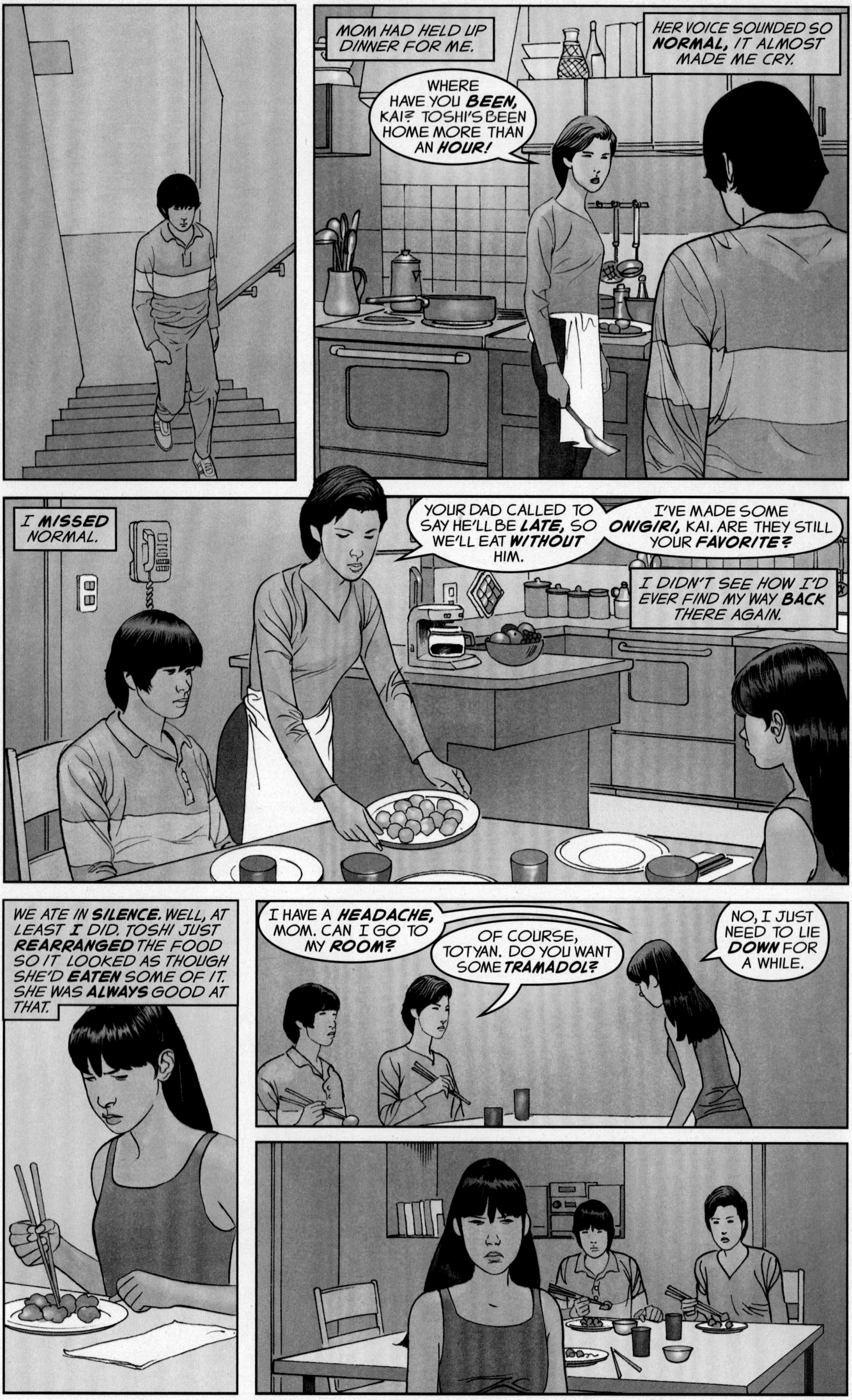
MOM HAD HELD UP DINNER FOR ME.
HER VOICE SOUNDED SO NORMAL, IT ALMOST MADE ME CRY.
WHERE HAVE YOU BEEN, KAI? TOSHI'S BEEN HOME MORE THAN AN HOUR!
I MISSED NORMAL.
YOUR DAD CALLED TO SAY HE'LL BE LATE, SO WE'LL EAT WITHOUT HIM.
I'VE MADE SOME ONIGIRI, KAI. ARE THEY STILL YOUR FAVORITE?
I DIDN'T SEE HOW I'D EVER FIND MY WAY BACK THERE AGAIN.
WE ATE IN SILENCE. WELL, AT LEAST I DID. TOSHI JUST REARRANGED THE FOOD SO IT LOOKED AS THOUGH SHE'D EATEN SOME OF IT. SHE WAS ALWAYS GOOD AT THAT.
I HAVE A HEADACHE, MOM. CAN I GO TO MY ROOM?
OF COURSE, TOTYAN. DO YOU WANT SOME TRAMADOL?
NO, I JUST NEED TO LIE DOWN FOR A WHILE.

I TRIED TO PRETEND IT WAS ALL BUSINESS AS USUAL. BUT TIME WAS PASSING SO SLOWLY--

--IT WAS AS IF I COULD **SEE** EACH BIG FAT SECOND SLOUCHING PAST.

JUST BEFORE MIDNIGHT, MOM DOZED OFF. I MOVED QUIETLY, SO AS NOT TO WAKE HER.

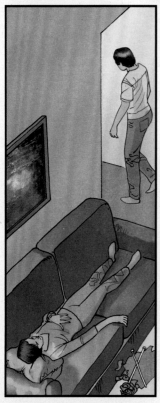

I **SO** DIDN'T WANT HER TO GET SUCKED INTO THIS.

TOSHI--

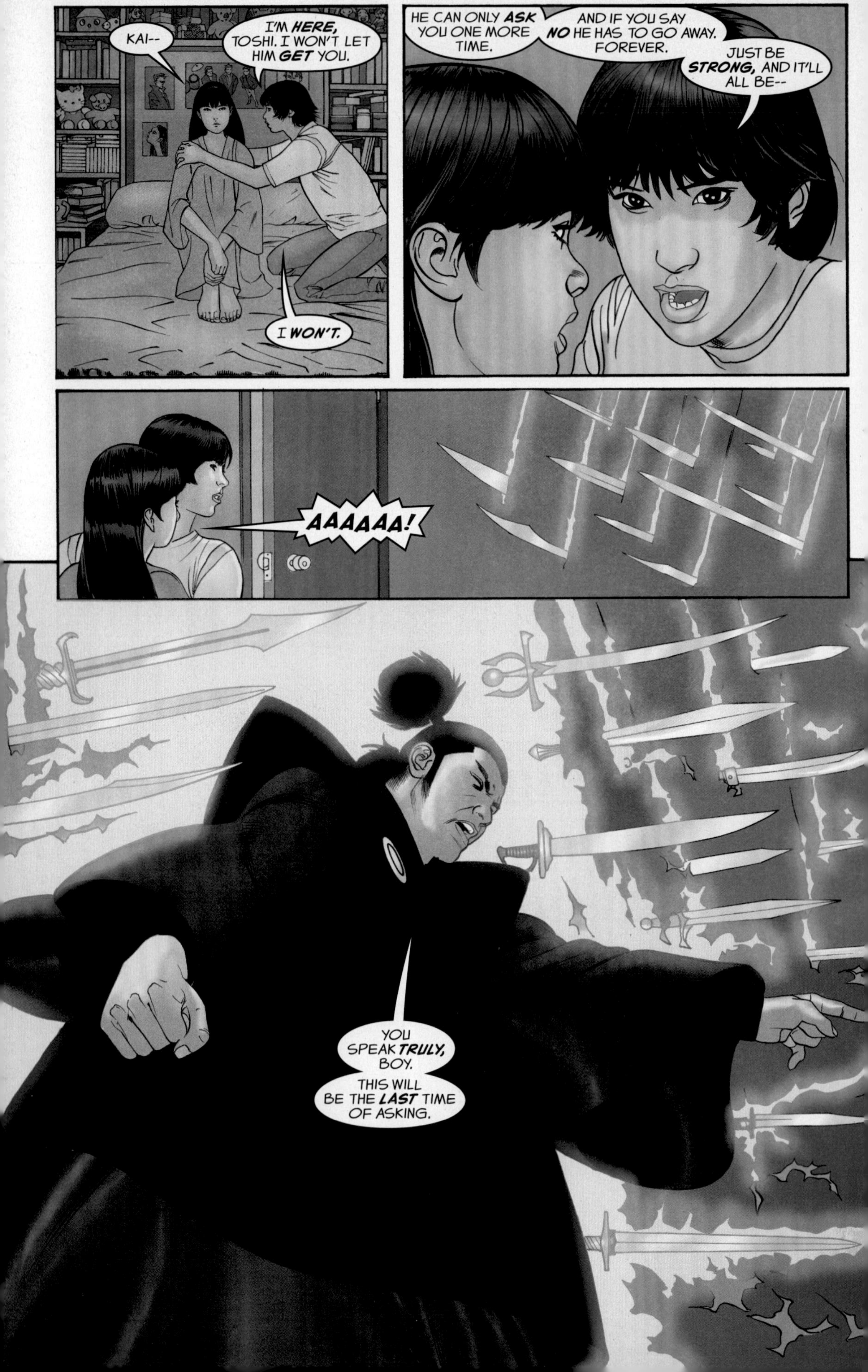
KAI--
I'M HERE, TOSHI. I WON'T LET HIM GET YOU.
I WON'T.
HE CAN ONLY ASK YOU ONE MORE TIME.
AND IF YOU SAY NO HE HAS TO GO AWAY. FOREVER.
JUST BE STRONG, AND IT'LL ALL BE--
AAAAAA!
YOU SPEAK TRULY, BOY.
THIS WILL BE THE LAST TIME OF ASKING.

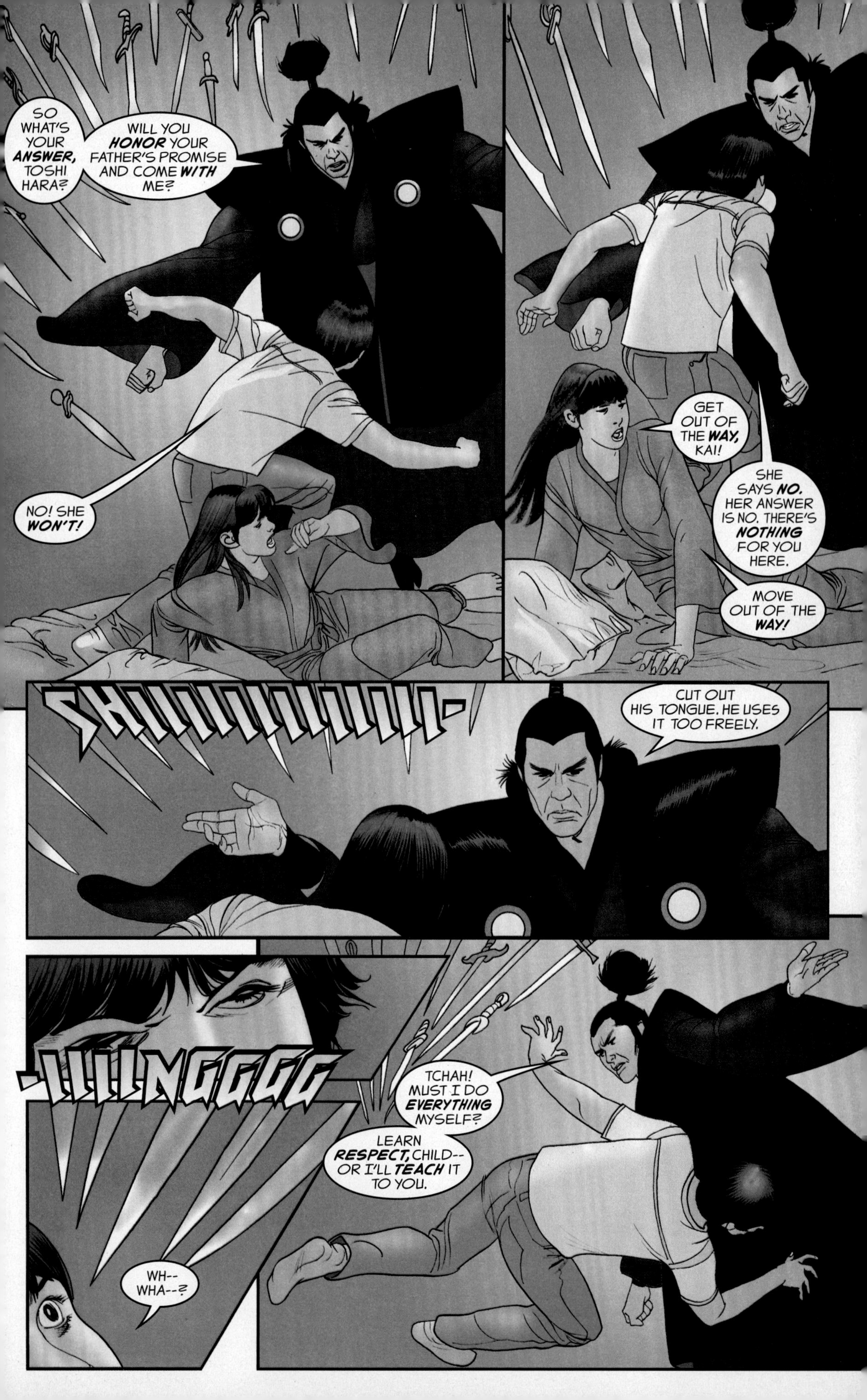
SO WHAT'S YOUR ANSWER, TOSHI HARA?
WILL YOU HONOR YOUR FATHER'S PROMISE AND COME WITH ME?
NO! SHE WON'T!
GET OUT OF THE WAY, KAI!
SHE SAYS NO. HER ANSWER IS NO. THERE'S NOTHING FOR YOU HERE.
MOVE OUT OF THE WAY!
SHIIIIIIIIIIII-
CUT OUT HIS TONGUE. HE USES IT TOO FREELY.
-IIIINGGGG
TCHAH! MUST I DO EVERYTHING MYSELF?
LEARN RESPECT, CHILD-- OR I'LL TEACH IT TO YOU.
WH-- WHA--?

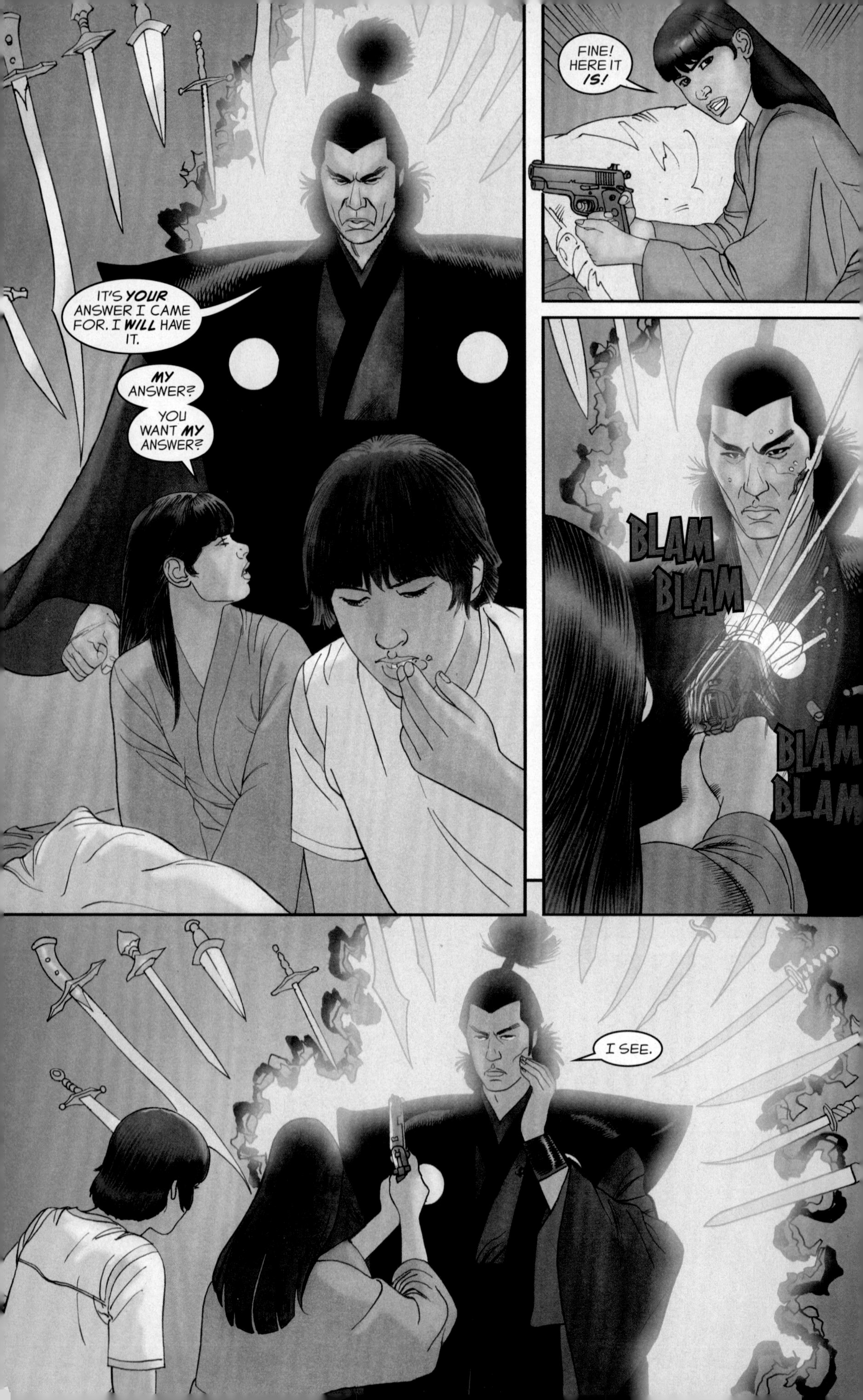
IT'S **YOUR** ANSWER I CAME FOR. I **WILL** HAVE IT.
MY ANSWER?
YOU WANT **MY** ANSWER?
FINE! HERE IT **IS!**
BLAM BLAM
BLAM BLAM
I SEE.

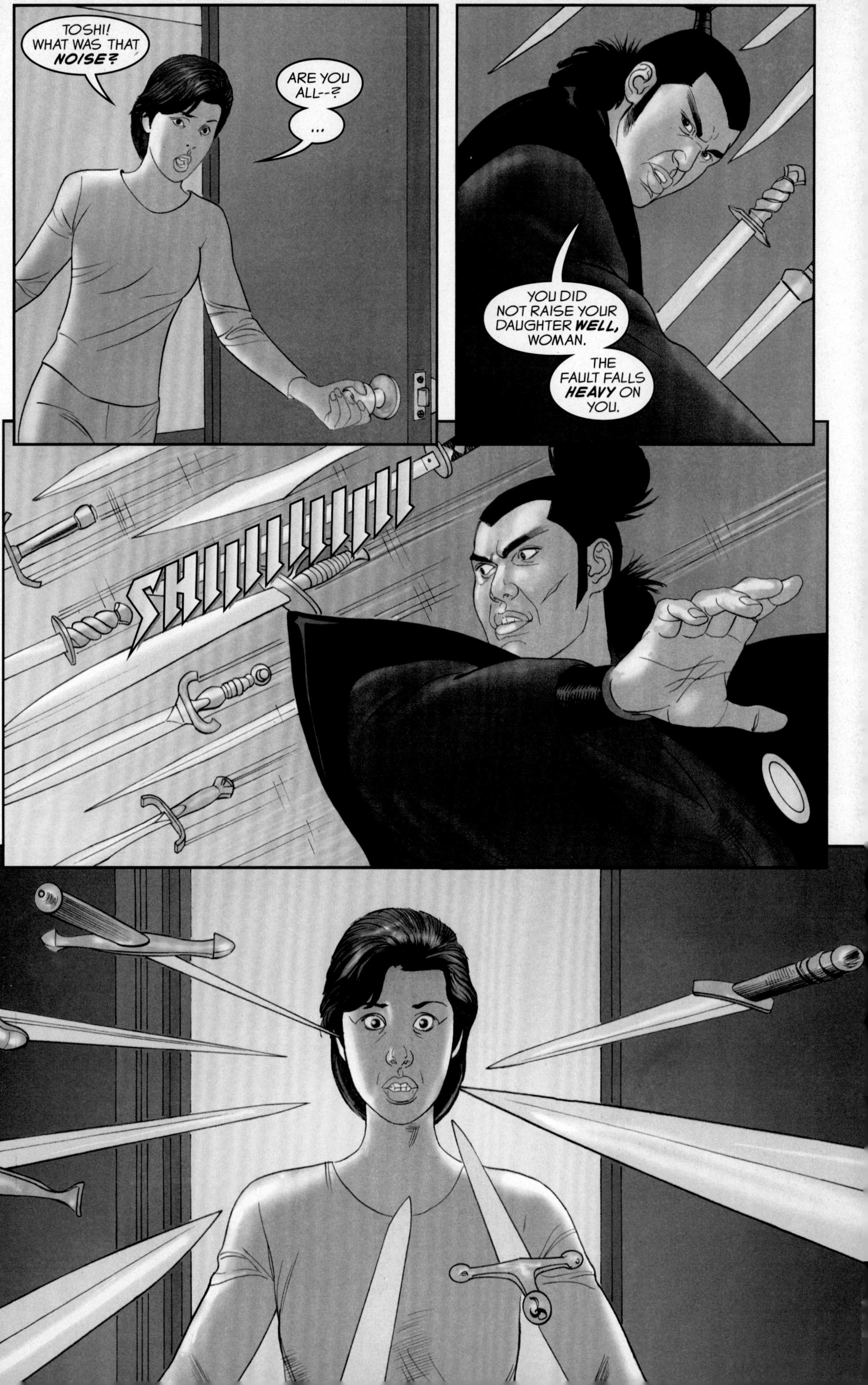
TOSHI! WHAT WAS THAT NOISE?
ARE YOU ALL--?
...
YOU DID NOT RAISE YOUR DAUGHTER WELL, WOMAN.
THE FAULT FALLS HEAVY ON YOU.
SHIIIIIIIIII

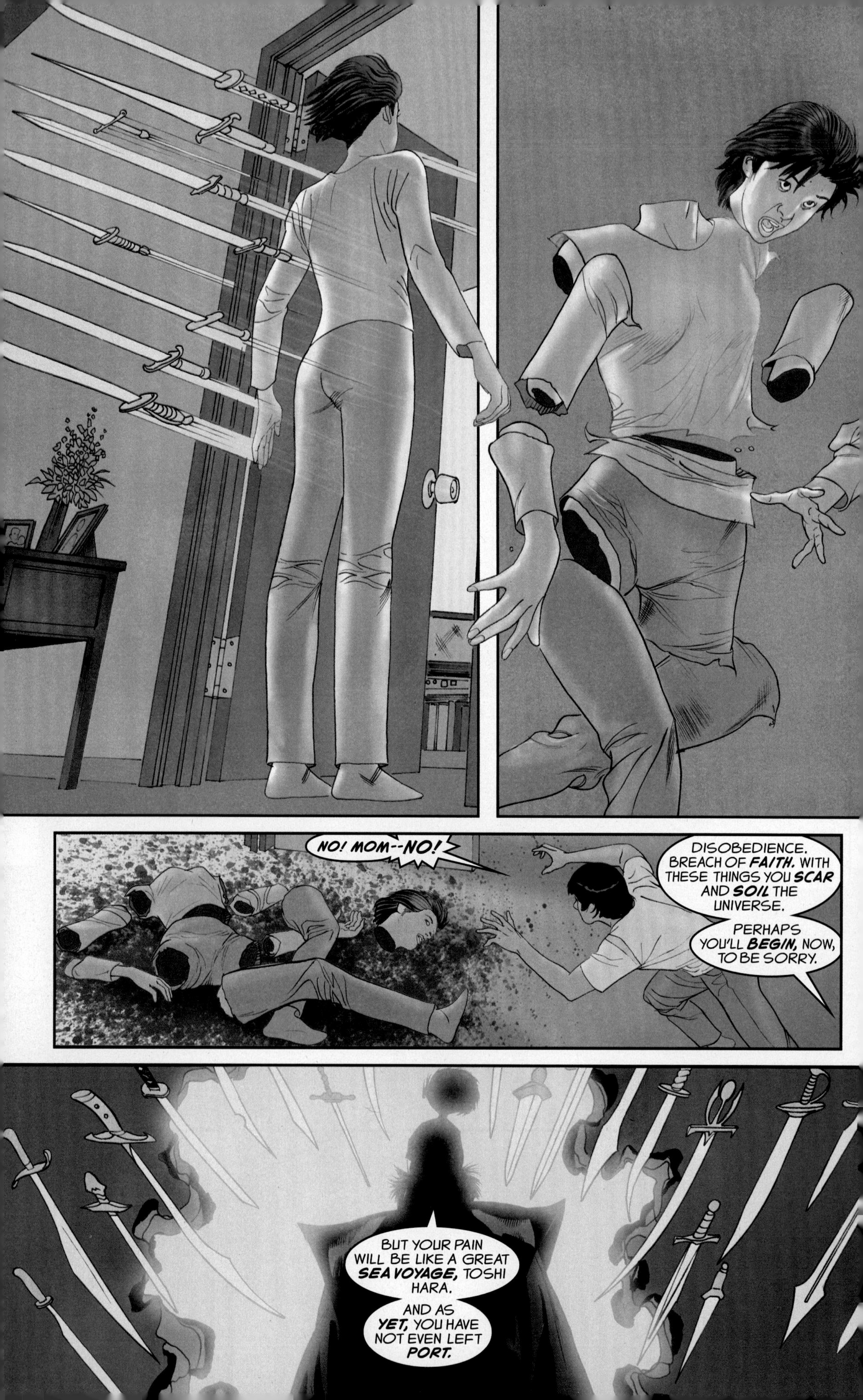
NO! MOM--NO!
DISOBEDIENCE. BREACH OF FAITH. WITH THESE THINGS YOU SCAR AND SOIL THE UNIVERSE.
PERHAPS YOU'LL BEGIN, NOW, TO BE SORRY.
BUT YOUR PAIN WILL BE LIKE A GREAT SEA VOYAGE, TOSHI HARA.
AND AS YET, YOU HAVE NOT EVEN LEFT PORT.

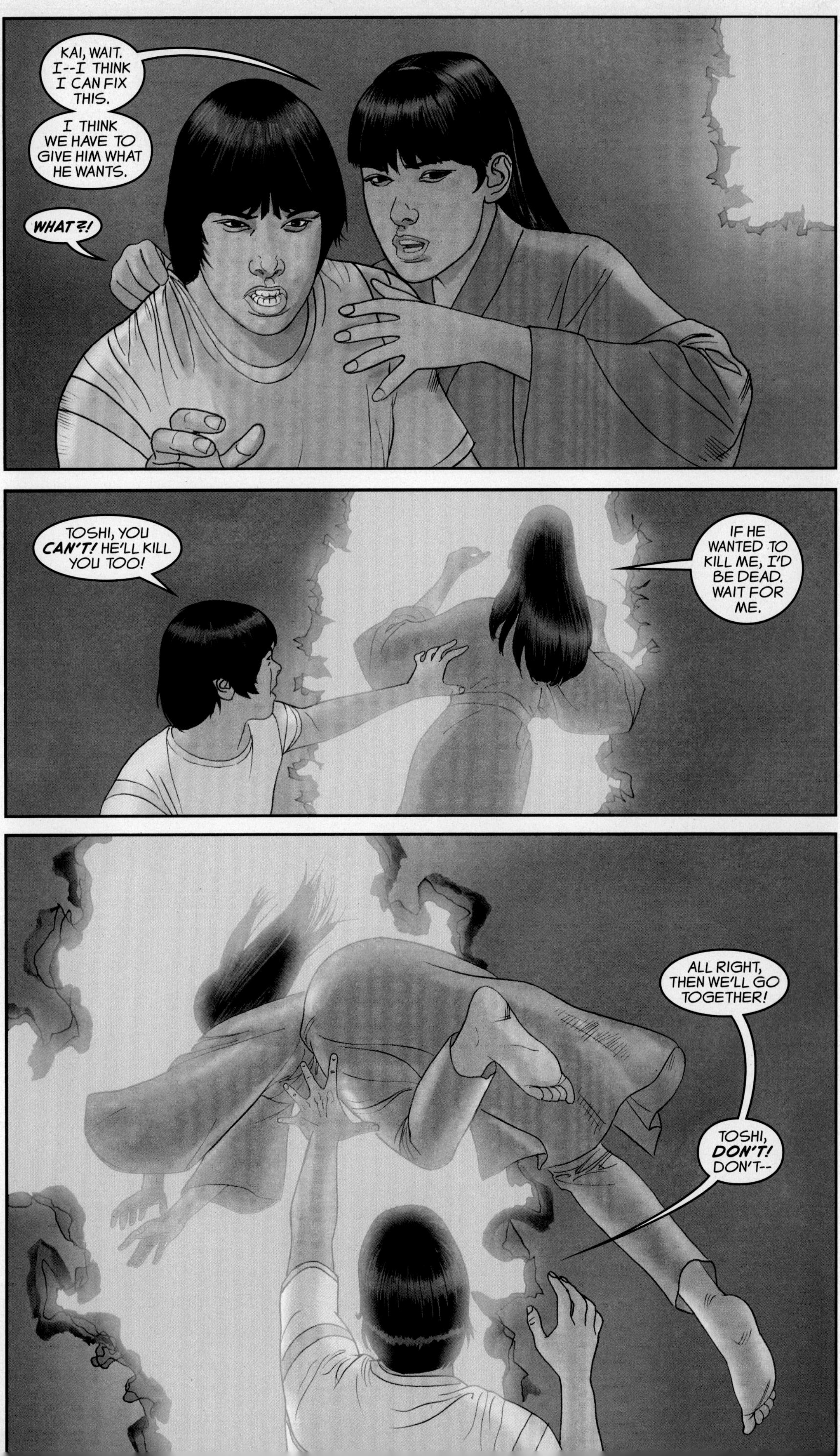
KAI, WAIT. I--I THINK I CAN FIX THIS.
I THINK WE HAVE TO GIVE HIM WHAT HE WANTS.
WHAT?!
TOSHI, YOU **CAN'T!** HE'LL KILL YOU TOO!
IF HE WANTED TO KILL ME, I'D BE DEAD. WAIT FOR ME.
ALL RIGHT, THEN WE'LL GO TOGETHER!
TOSHI, **DON'T!** DON'T--

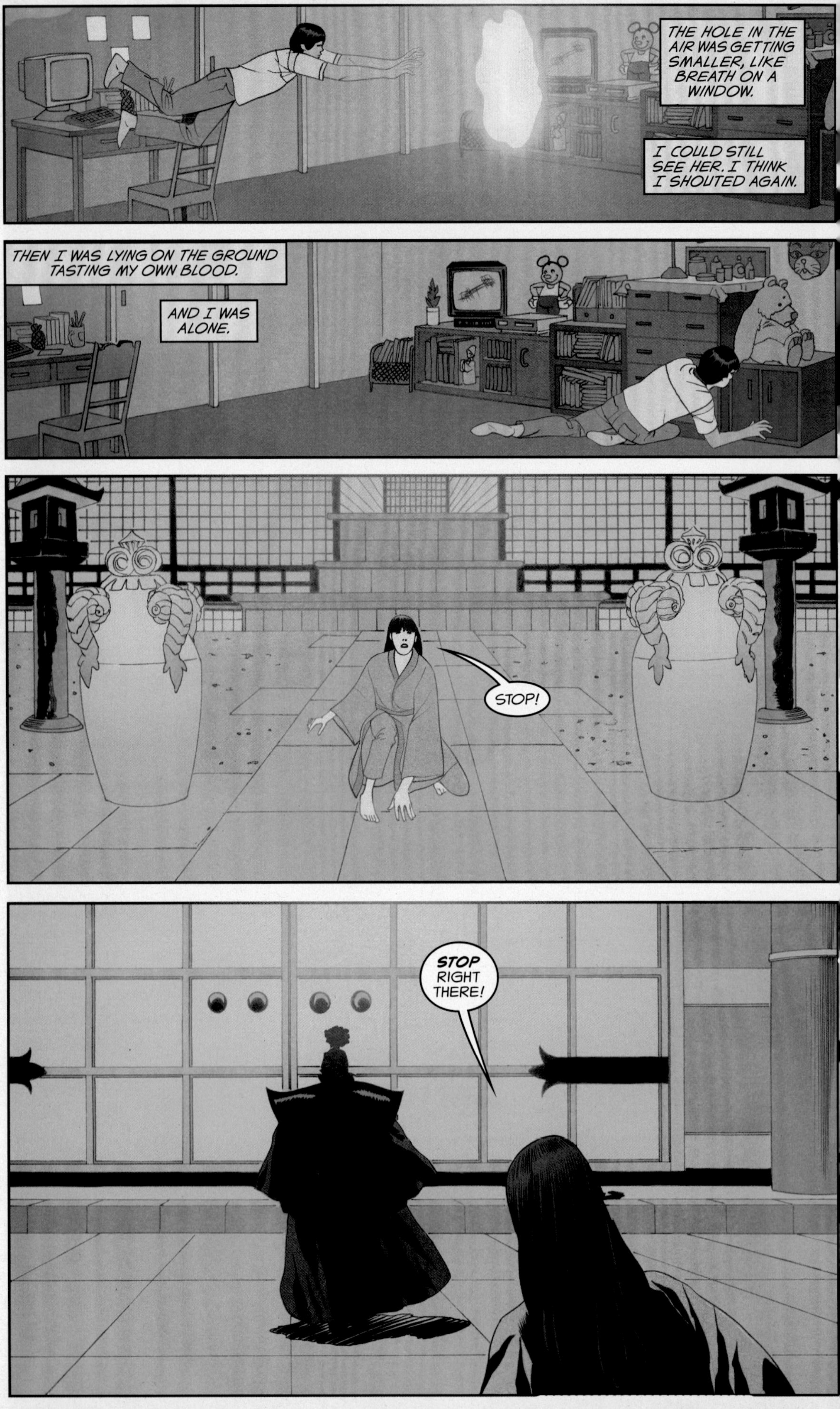
THE HOLE IN THE AIR WAS GETTING SMALLER, LIKE BREATH ON A WINDOW.
I COULD STILL SEE HER. I THINK I SHOUTED AGAIN.
THEN I WAS LYING ON THE GROUND TASTING MY OWN BLOOD.
AND I WAS ALONE.
STOP!
STOP RIGHT THERE!

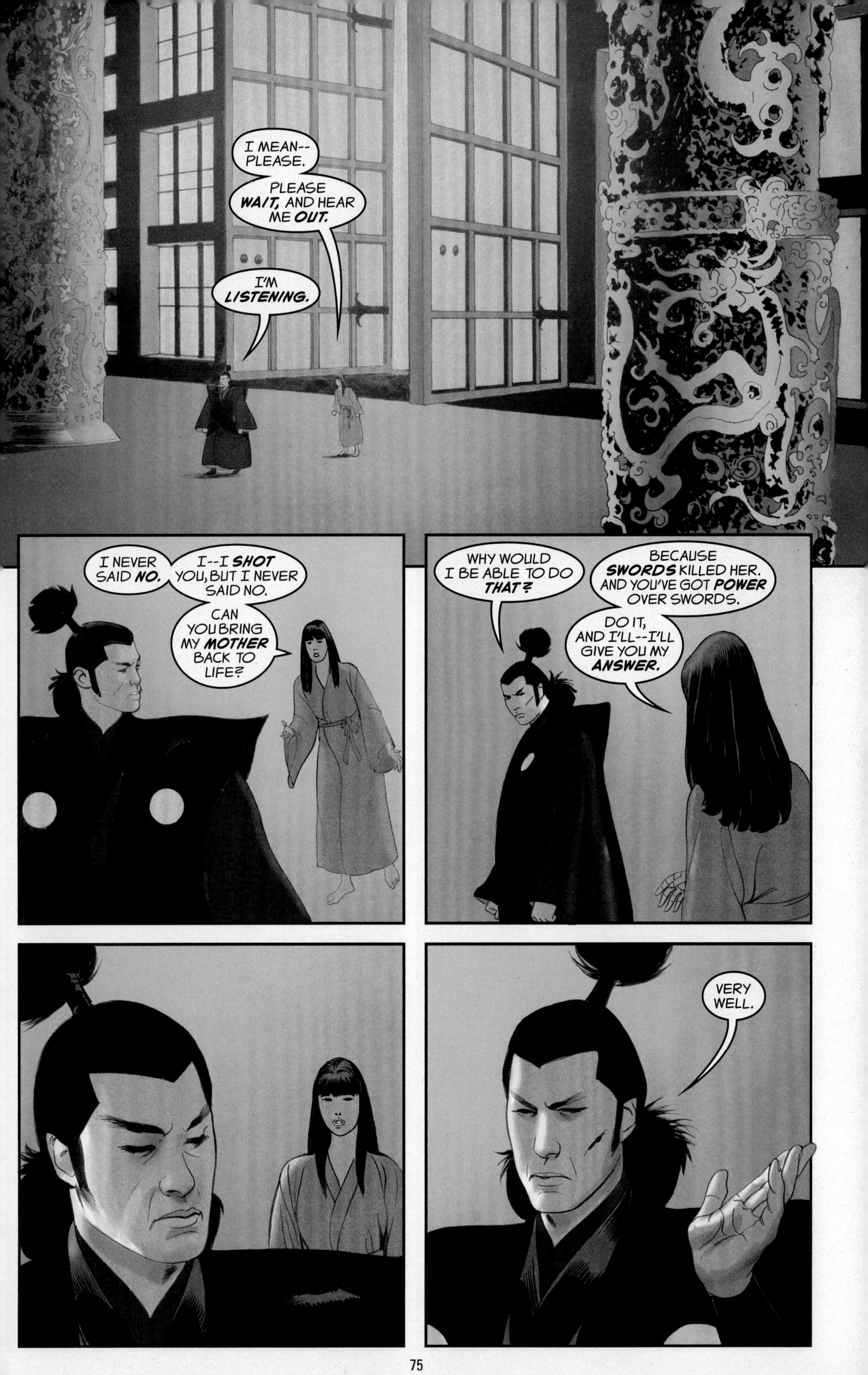
I MEAN-- PLEASE.
PLEASE WAIT, AND HEAR ME OUT.
I'M LISTENING.
I NEVER SAID NO.
I--I SHOT YOU, BUT I NEVER SAID NO.
CAN YOU BRING MY MOTHER BACK TO LIFE?
WHY WOULD I BE ABLE TO DO THAT?
BECAUSE SWORDS KILLED HER. AND YOU'VE GOT POWER OVER SWORDS.
DO IT, AND I'LL--I'LL GIVE YOU MY ANSWER.
VERY WELL.

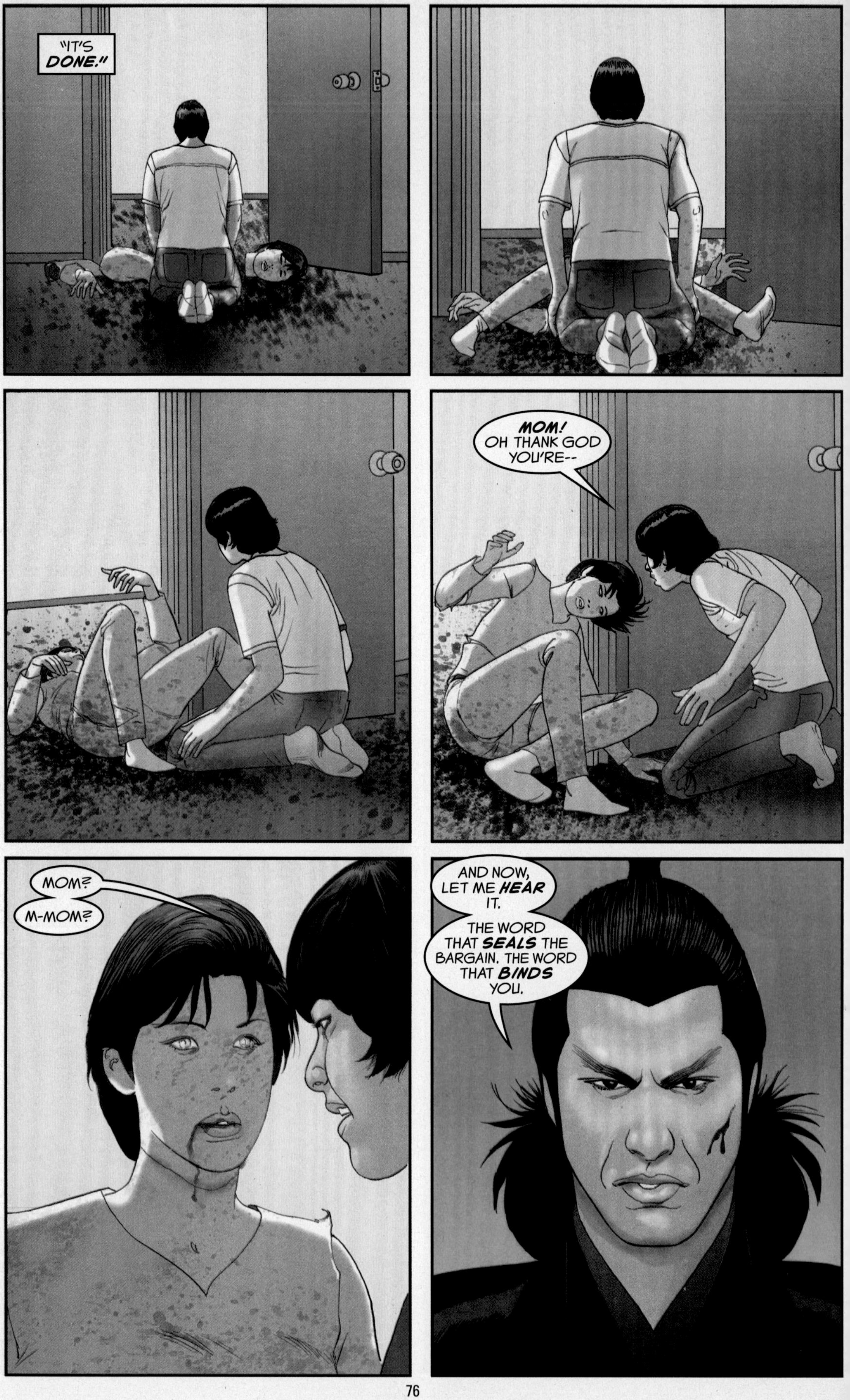
"IT'S DONE."
MOM! OH THANK GOD YOU'RE--
MOM?
M-MOM?
AND NOW, LET ME HEAR IT.
THE WORD THAT SEALS THE BARGAIN. THE WORD THAT BINDS YOU.

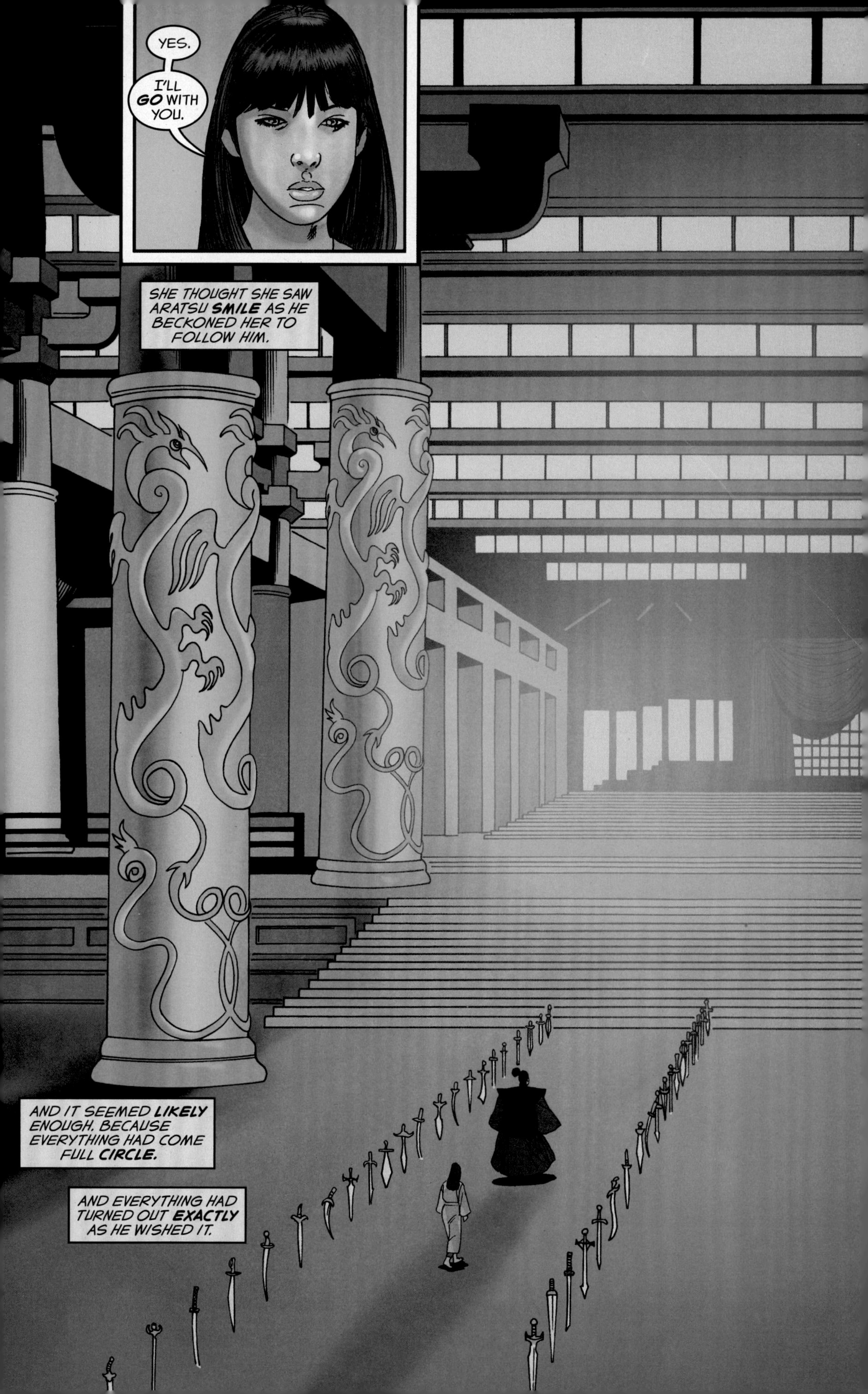
YES.
I'LL **GO** WITH YOU.
SHE THOUGHT SHE SAW ARATSU **SMILE** AS HE BECKONED HER TO FOLLOW HIM.
AND IT SEEMED **LIKELY** ENOUGH. BECAUSE EVERYTHING HAD COME FULL **CIRCLE.**
AND EVERYTHING HAD TURNED OUT **EXACTLY** AS HE WISHED IT.

chapter four

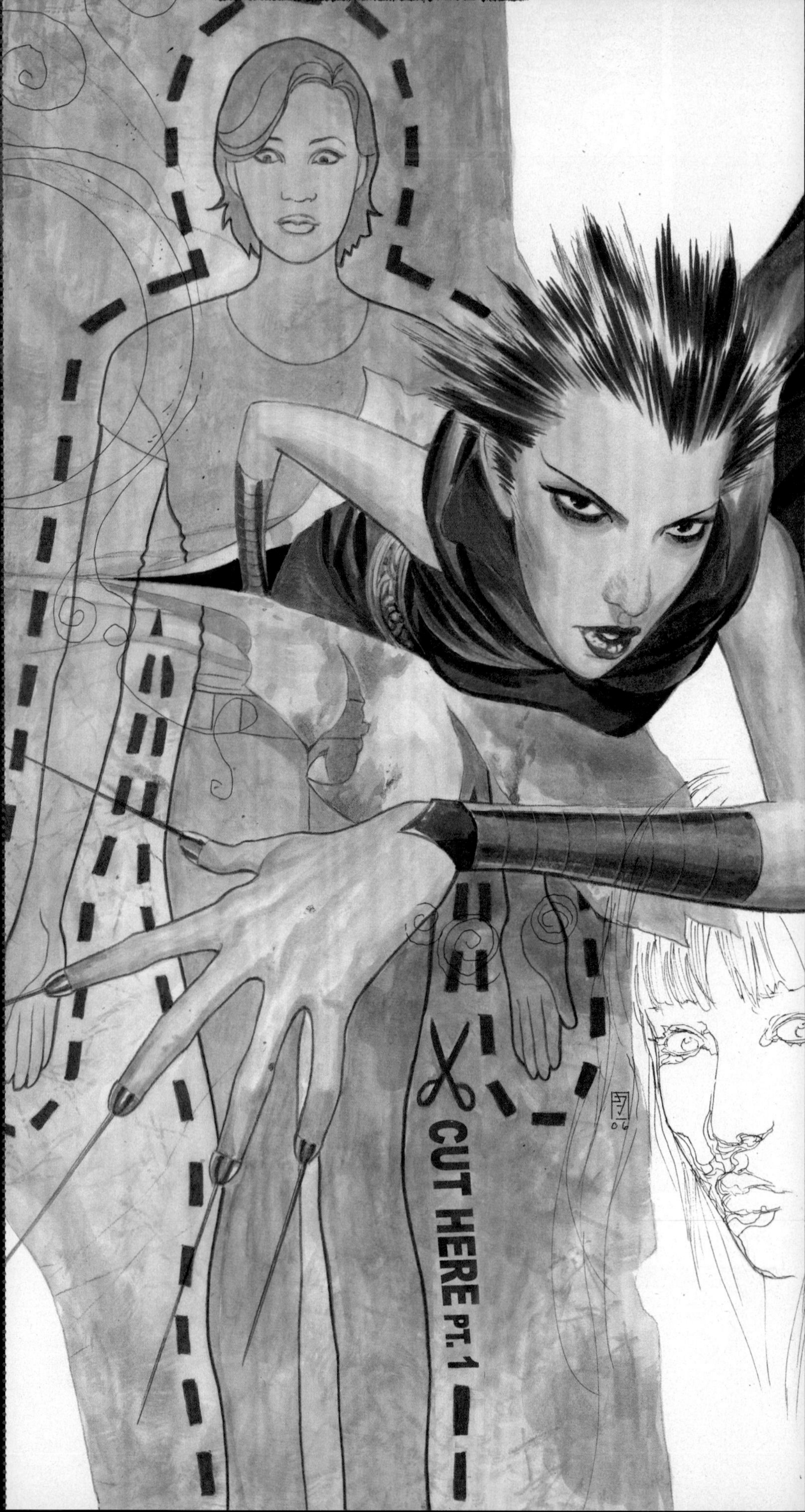
CUT HERE PT. 1

The swords are so *graceful*. Like birds.

Like silent *birds*.

Like *kingfishers* in Glover Garden in the summer *heat*.

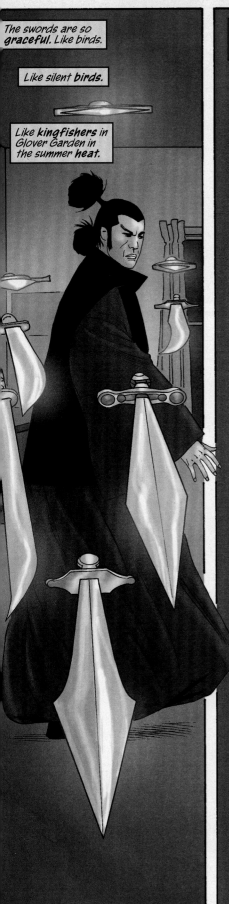

And when they dip, oh! The flash of *light* along their wings, into the air...

The *sun* broken into brilliant sparks.

Oh *please* come back.

Then *gone*.

Gone while you're blinking your *eyes*, and you think, oh please--

And it *does*. A little of the light *does* come back.

In the *wake* on the water. In the *ripples* that breed and break.

I CAN'T *BELIEVE* IT. YOU DREW MY *PICTURE*!

NOT JUST *YOU*, MISTER BIGHEAD.

BUT IT WAS ME YOU WERE *REALLY* LOOKING AT, WASN'T IT?

MIYA, MIYA *TANAKA*, HER CLOTHES ARE TORN AND *DIRTY*! HOLD YOUR BREATH WHEN SHE WALKS BY, AND COUNT RIGHT UP TO *THIRTY*!

SEE? *NOTHING* IN THE SHOE CHEST.

THERE WAS A *MONSTER*!

TOSHI, GO TO *SLEEP* NOW.

ART COLLEGE? WHY WOULD *YOU* GO TO ART COLLEGE?

WHAT WILL THEY *TEACH* YOU? HOW TO HOLD A *PENCIL*?

YOU NEED A *HUSBAND*, GIRL. A HUSBAND AND A *FAMILY*.

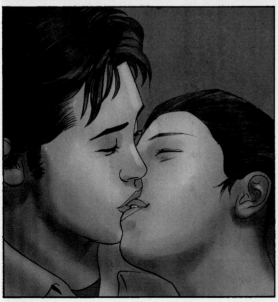

I--I'M AT A LOSS TO *EXPLAIN*--THERE WAS ONLY *ONE* FETAL HEARTBEAT!

PERHAPS THEY'VE JUST GOT THE ONE *HEART* BETWEEN THEM, THEN.

THE ONE *SOUL*.

YOU'RE THE **SON,** IS THAT RIGHT?

KITO? KITO HARA?

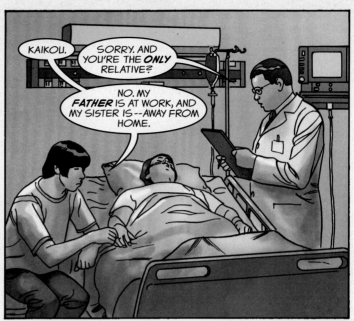

KAIKOU.

SORRY. AND YOU'RE THE **ONLY** RELATIVE?

NO. MY **FATHER** IS AT WORK, AND MY SISTER IS--AWAY FROM HOME.

CAN YOU EXPLAIN TO ME WHAT EXACTLY **HAPPENED?**

SHE--MOM-- SHE PASSED **OUT.** THAT'S ALL.

AND NOW SHE WON'T WAKE UP.

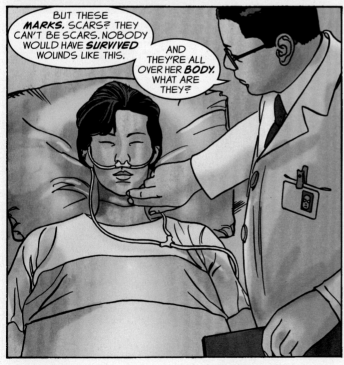

BUT THESE **MARKS.** SCARS? THEY CAN'T BE SCARS. NOBODY WOULD HAVE **SURVIVED** WOUNDS LIKE THIS.

AND THEY'RE ALL OVER HER **BODY.** WHAT ARE THEY?

THEY'RE...THEY'RE JUST **BIRTHMARKS.**

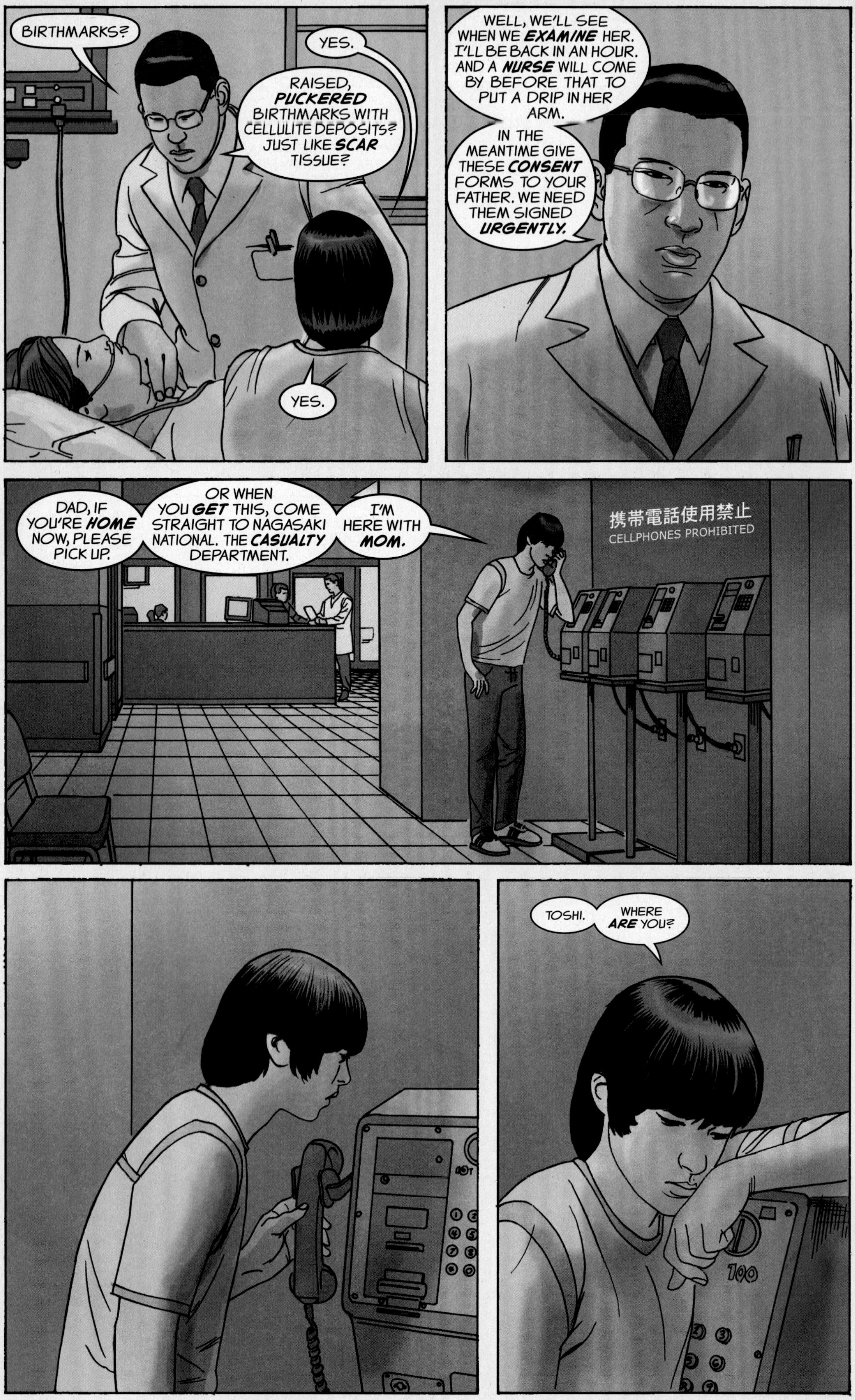
BIRTHMARKS?
YES.
RAISED, PUCKERED BIRTHMARKS WITH CELLULITE DEPOSITS? JUST LIKE SCAR TISSUE?
YES.
WELL, WE'LL SEE WHEN WE EXAMINE HER. I'LL BE BACK IN AN HOUR. AND A NURSE WILL COME BY BEFORE THAT TO PUT A DRIP IN HER ARM.
IN THE MEANTIME GIVE THESE CONSENT FORMS TO YOUR FATHER. WE NEED THEM SIGNED URGENTLY.
DAD, IF YOU'RE HOME NOW, PLEASE PICK UP.
OR WHEN YOU GET THIS, COME STRAIGHT TO NAGASAKI NATIONAL. THE CASUALTY DEPARTMENT.
I'M HERE WITH MOM.
携帯電話使用禁止
CELLPHONES PROHIBITED
TOSHI.
WHERE ARE YOU?

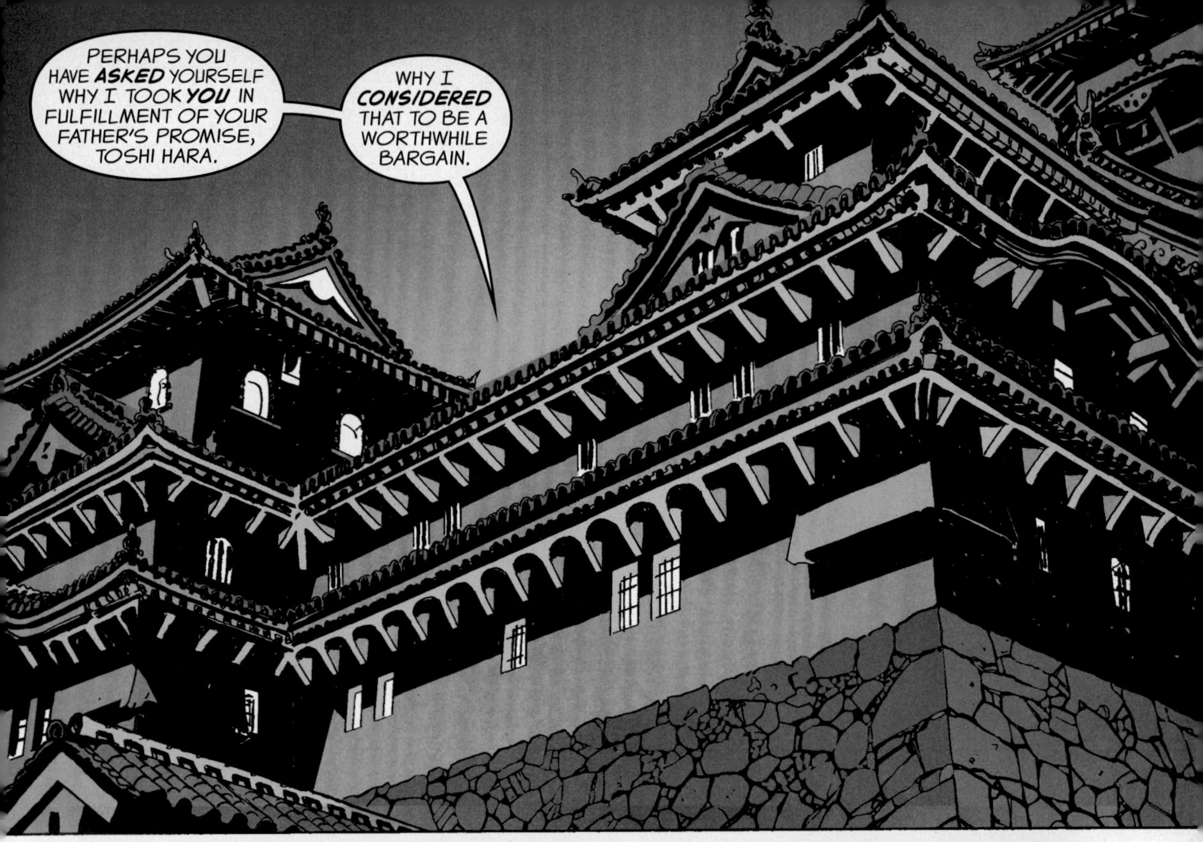
PERHAPS YOU HAVE ASKED YOURSELF WHY I TOOK YOU IN FULFILLMENT OF YOUR FATHER'S PROMISE, TOSHI HARA.
WHY I CONSIDERED THAT TO BE A WORTHWHILE BARGAIN.

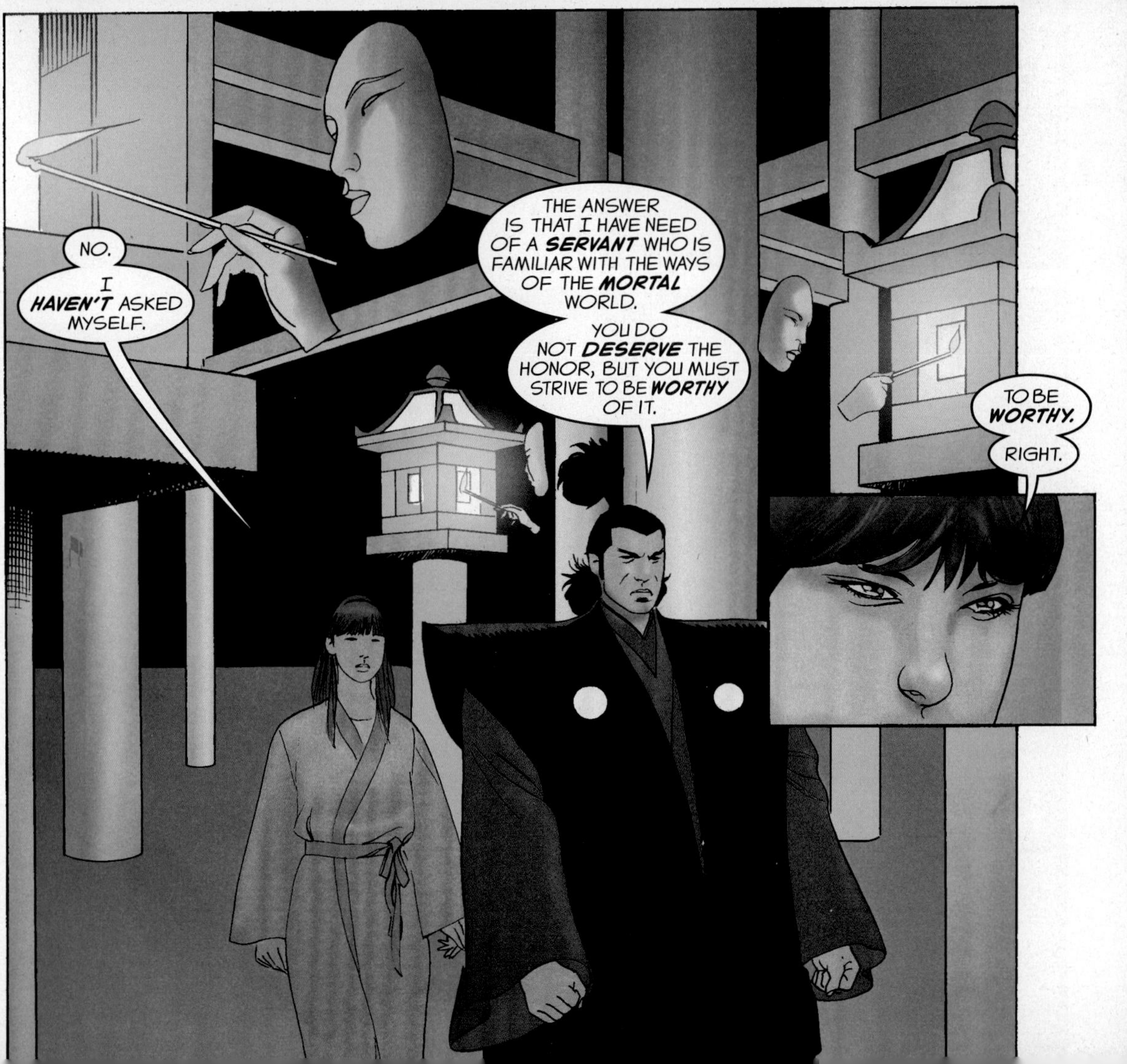
NO.
I HAVEN'T ASKED MYSELF.
THE ANSWER IS THAT I HAVE NEED OF A SERVANT WHO IS FAMILIAR WITH THE WAYS OF THE MORTAL WORLD.
YOU DO NOT DESERVE THE HONOR, BUT YOU MUST STRIVE TO BE WORTHY OF IT.
TO BE WORTHY.
RIGHT.

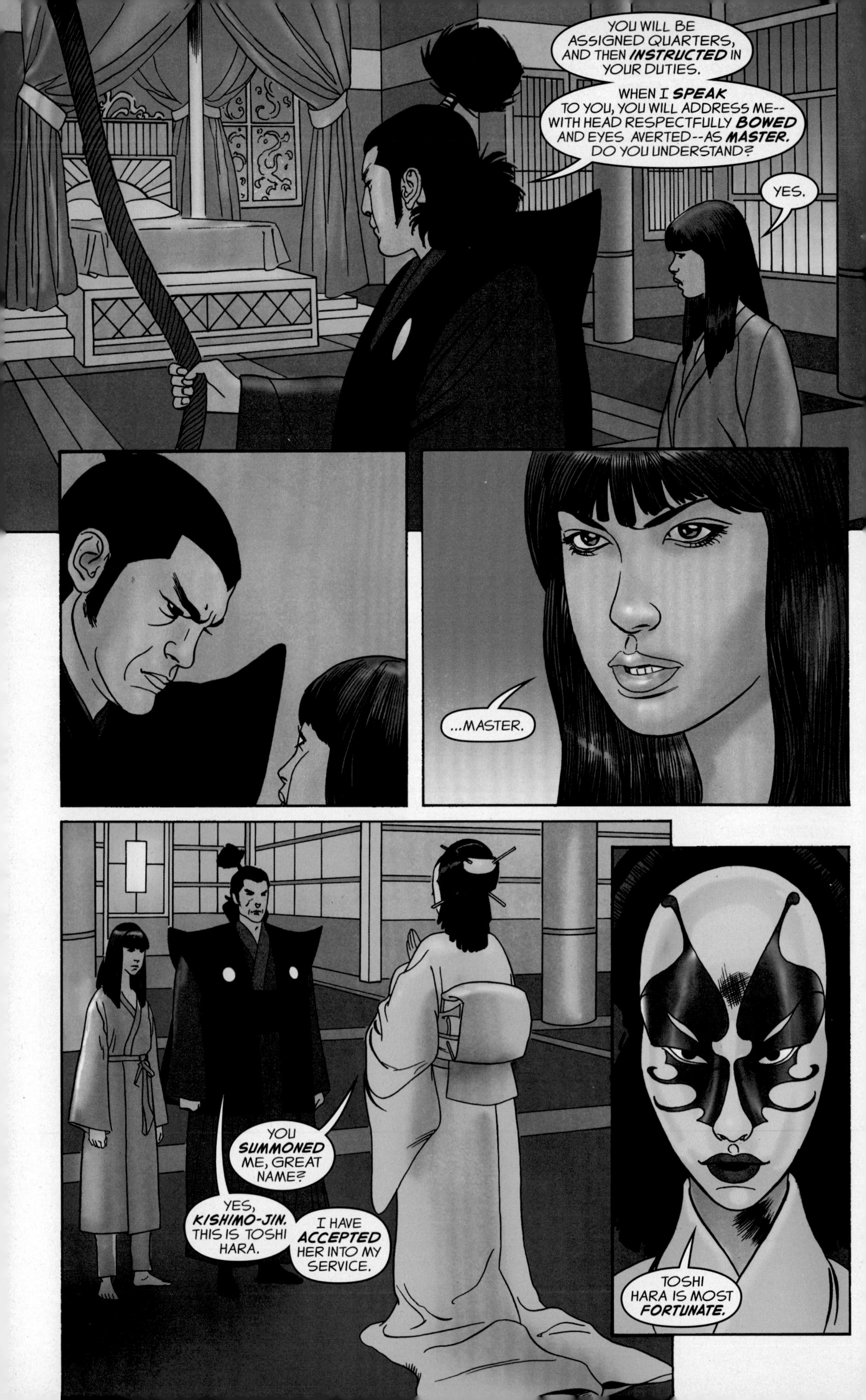
YOU WILL BE ASSIGNED QUARTERS, AND THEN *INSTRUCTED* IN YOUR DUTIES.
WHEN I *SPEAK* TO YOU, YOU WILL ADDRESS ME-- WITH HEAD RESPECTFULLY *BOWED* AND EYES AVERTED--AS *MASTER.* DO YOU UNDERSTAND?
YES.
...MASTER.
YOU *SUMMONED* ME, GREAT NAME?
YES, *KISHIMO-JIN.* THIS IS TOSHI HARA.
I HAVE *ACCEPTED* HER INTO MY SERVICE.
TOSHI HARA IS MOST *FORTUNATE.*

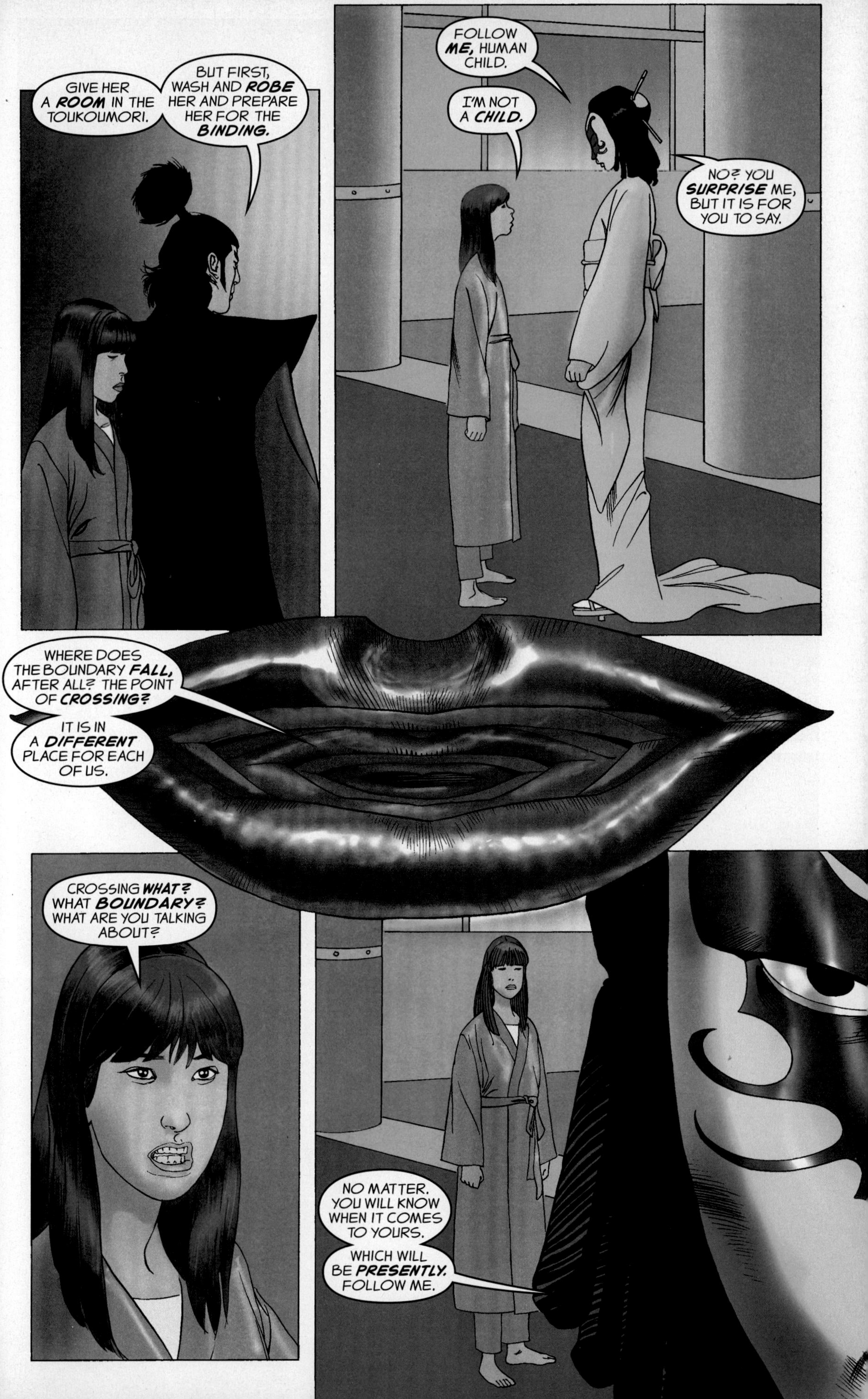
GIVE HER A ROOM IN THE TOUKOUMORI.
BUT FIRST, WASH AND ROBE HER AND PREPARE HER FOR THE BINDING.
FOLLOW ME, HUMAN CHILD.
I'M NOT A CHILD.
NO? YOU SURPRISE ME, BUT IT IS FOR YOU TO SAY.
WHERE DOES THE BOUNDARY FALL, AFTER ALL? THE POINT OF CROSSING?
IT IS IN A DIFFERENT PLACE FOR EACH OF US.
CROSSING WHAT? WHAT BOUNDARY? WHAT ARE YOU TALKING ABOUT?
NO MATTER. YOU WILL KNOW WHEN IT COMES TO YOURS.
WHICH WILL BE PRESENTLY. FOLLOW ME.

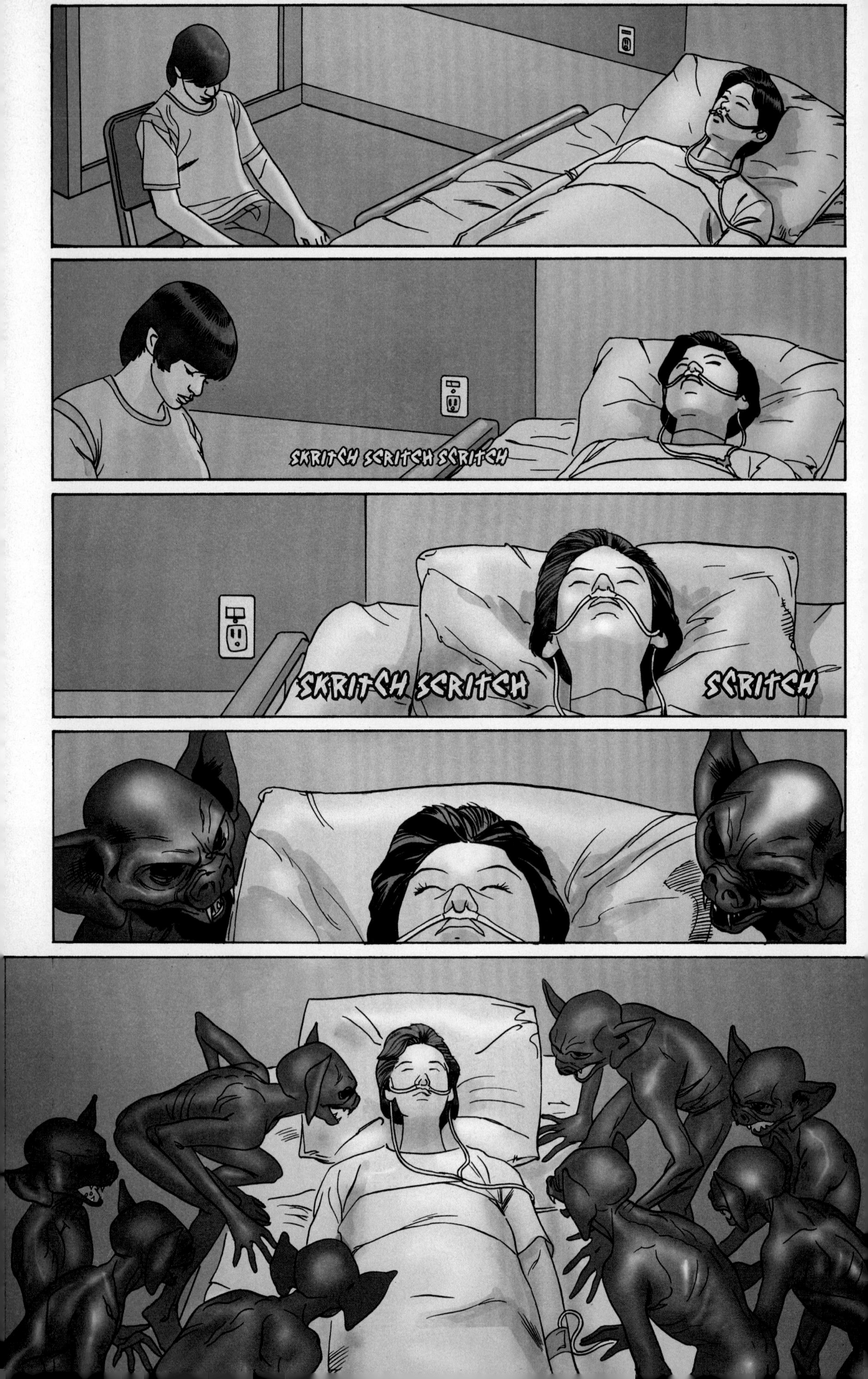
SKRITCH SCRITCH SCRITCH
SKRITCH SCRITCH
SCRITCH

Toshi was such a *tomboy*. Such a--a *bruiser*.

Nothing *ever* frightened her. Why couldn't *I* be that brave? That *heed-less* of the rules?

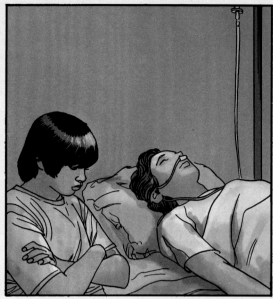

At Nagoya I had a *teacher*--Mr. *Wing*--whose Korean accent was so strong we called him *Wee-ung*. Two syllables.

He had nice *eyes*, though. Blue, blue eyes. He must have had a European *mother*.

MMMWH--

GET *AWAY* FROM HER!

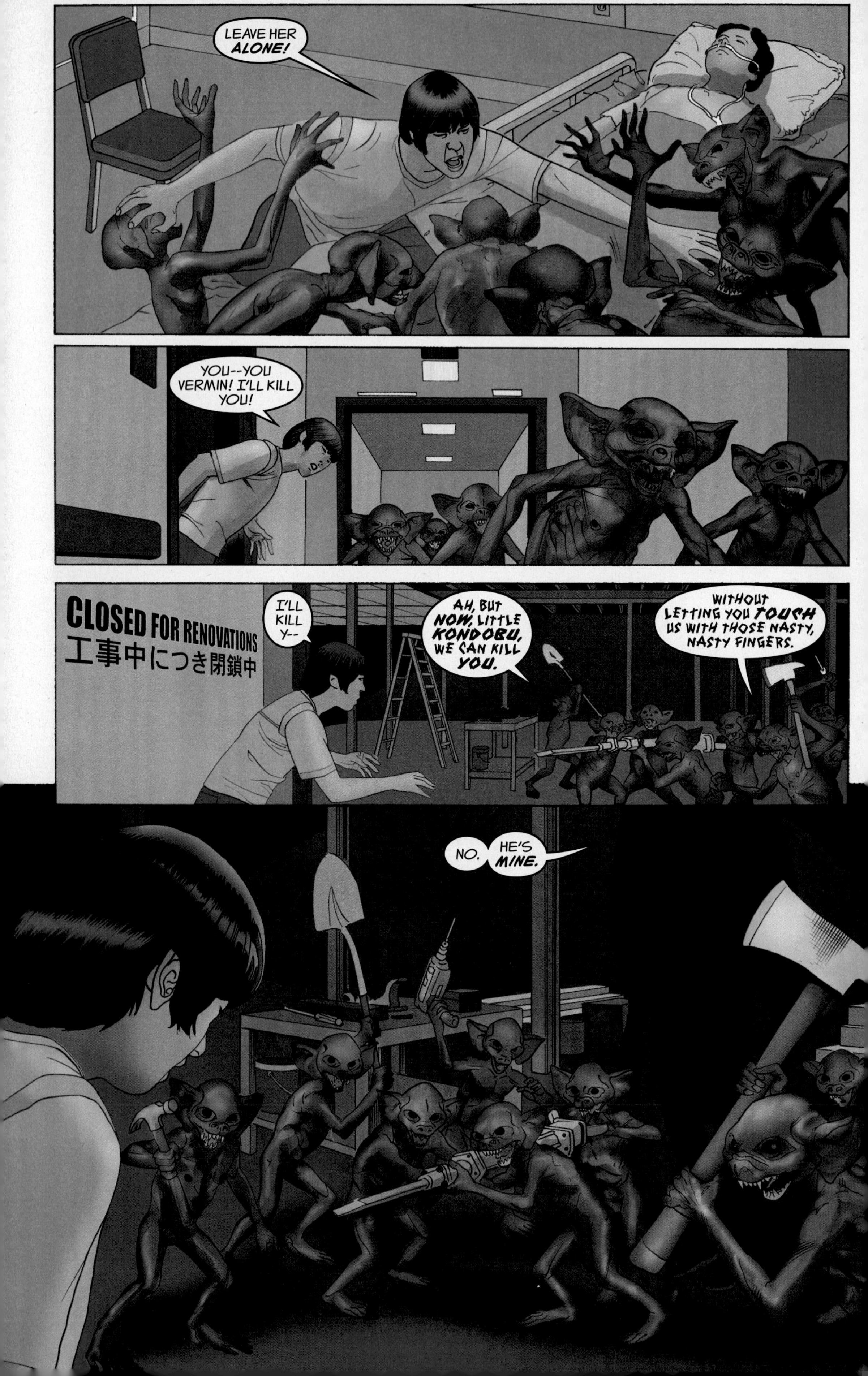
LEAVE HER ALONE!
YOU--YOU VERMIN! I'LL KILL YOU!
CLOSED FOR RENOVATIONS
工事中につき閉鎖中
I'LL KILL Y--
AH, BUT NOW, LITTLE KONDOBU, WE CAN KILL YOU.
WITHOUT LETTING YOU TOUCH US WITH THOSE NASTY, NASTY FINGERS.
NO.
HE'S MINE.

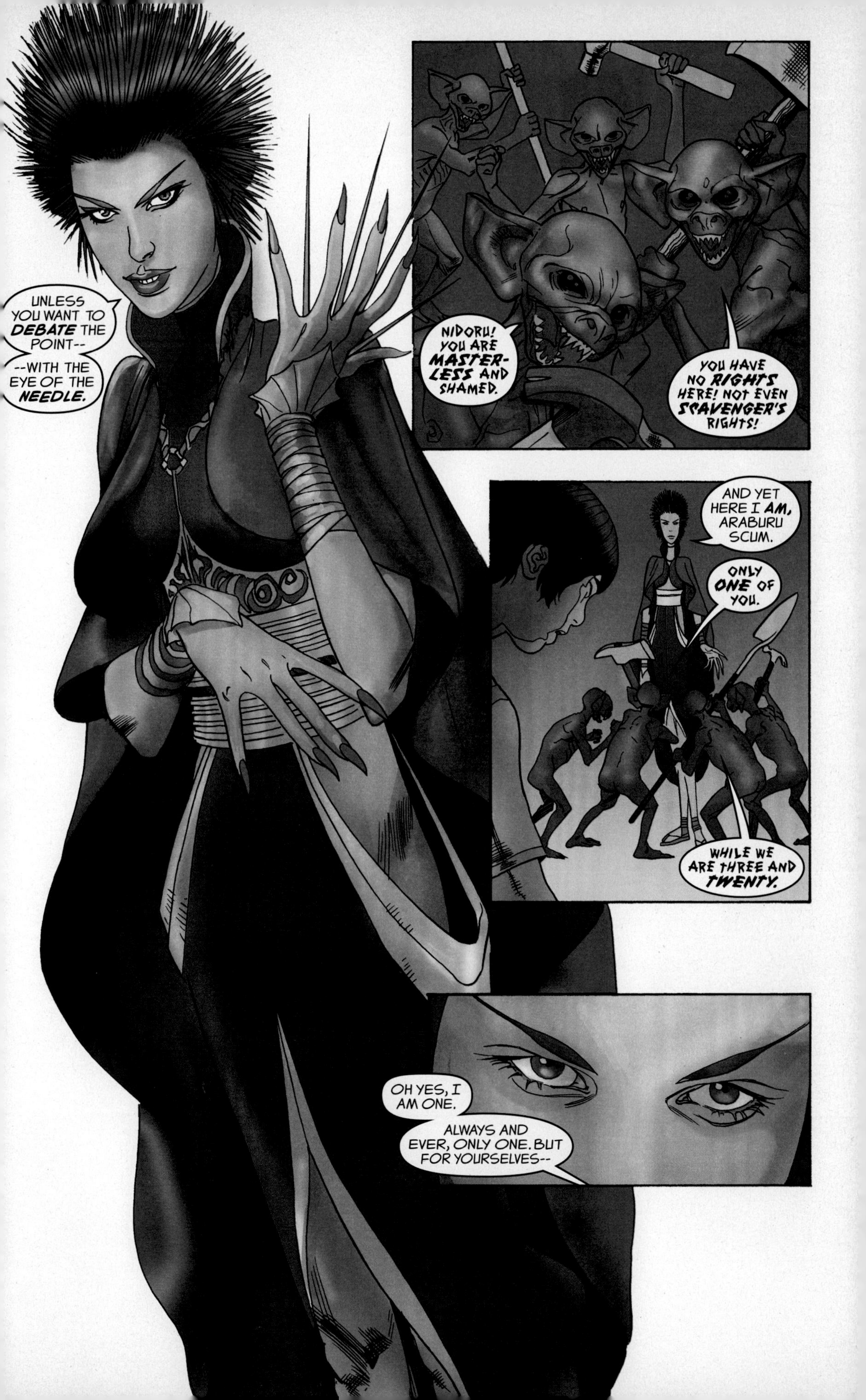
UNLESS YOU WANT TO DEBATE THE POINT--
--WITH THE EYE OF THE NEEDLE.
NIDORU! YOU ARE MASTER-LESS AND SHAMED.
YOU HAVE NO RIGHTS HERE! NOT EVEN SCAVENGER'S RIGHTS!
AND YET HERE I AM, ARABURU SCUM.
ONLY ONE OF YOU.
WHILE WE ARE THREE AND TWENTY.
OH YES, I AM ONE.
ALWAYS AND EVER, ONLY ONE. BUT FOR YOURSELVES--

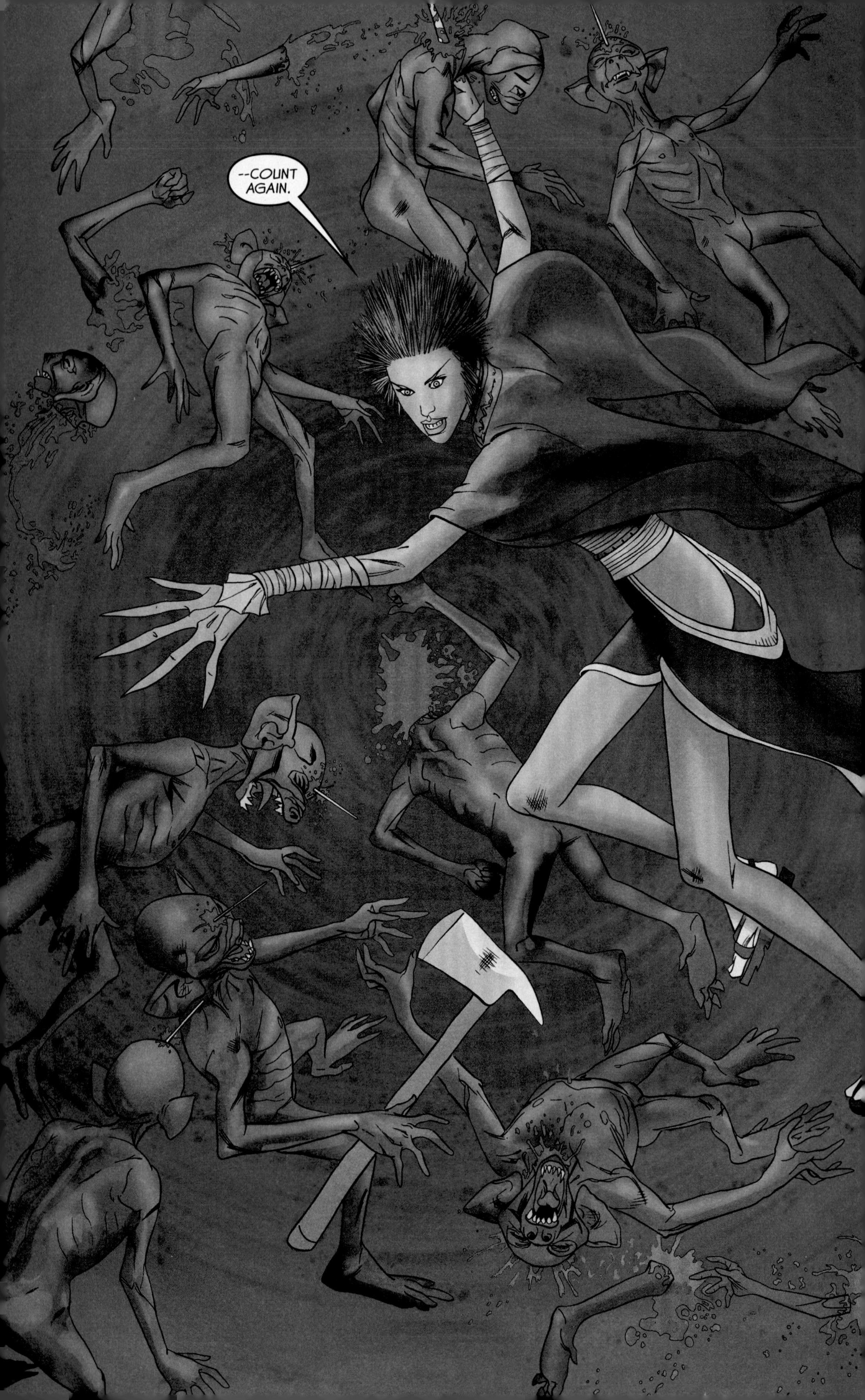
--COUNT AGAIN.

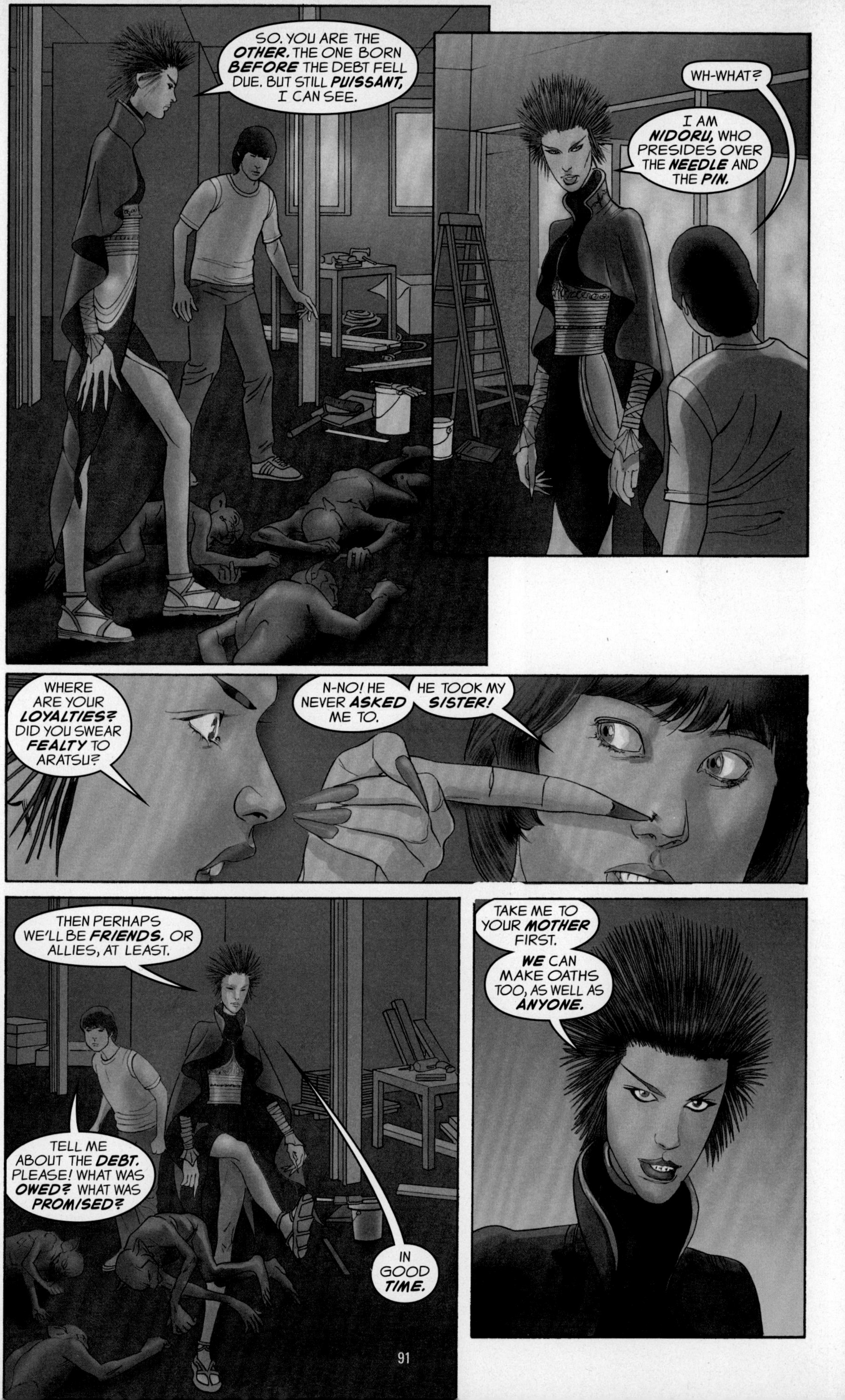
SO. YOU ARE THE OTHER. THE ONE BORN BEFORE THE DEBT FELL DUE. BUT STILL PUISSANT, I CAN SEE.
WH-WHAT?
I AM NIDORU, WHO PRESIDES OVER THE NEEDLE AND THE PIN.
WHERE ARE YOUR LOYALTIES? DID YOU SWEAR FEALTY TO ARATSU?
N-NO! HE NEVER ASKED ME TO.
HE TOOK MY SISTER!
THEN PERHAPS WE'LL BE FRIENDS. OR ALLIES, AT LEAST.
TELL ME ABOUT THE DEBT. PLEASE! WHAT WAS OWED? WHAT WAS PROMISED?
IN GOOD TIME.
TAKE ME TO YOUR MOTHER FIRST.
WE CAN MAKE OATHS TOO, AS WELL AS ANYONE.

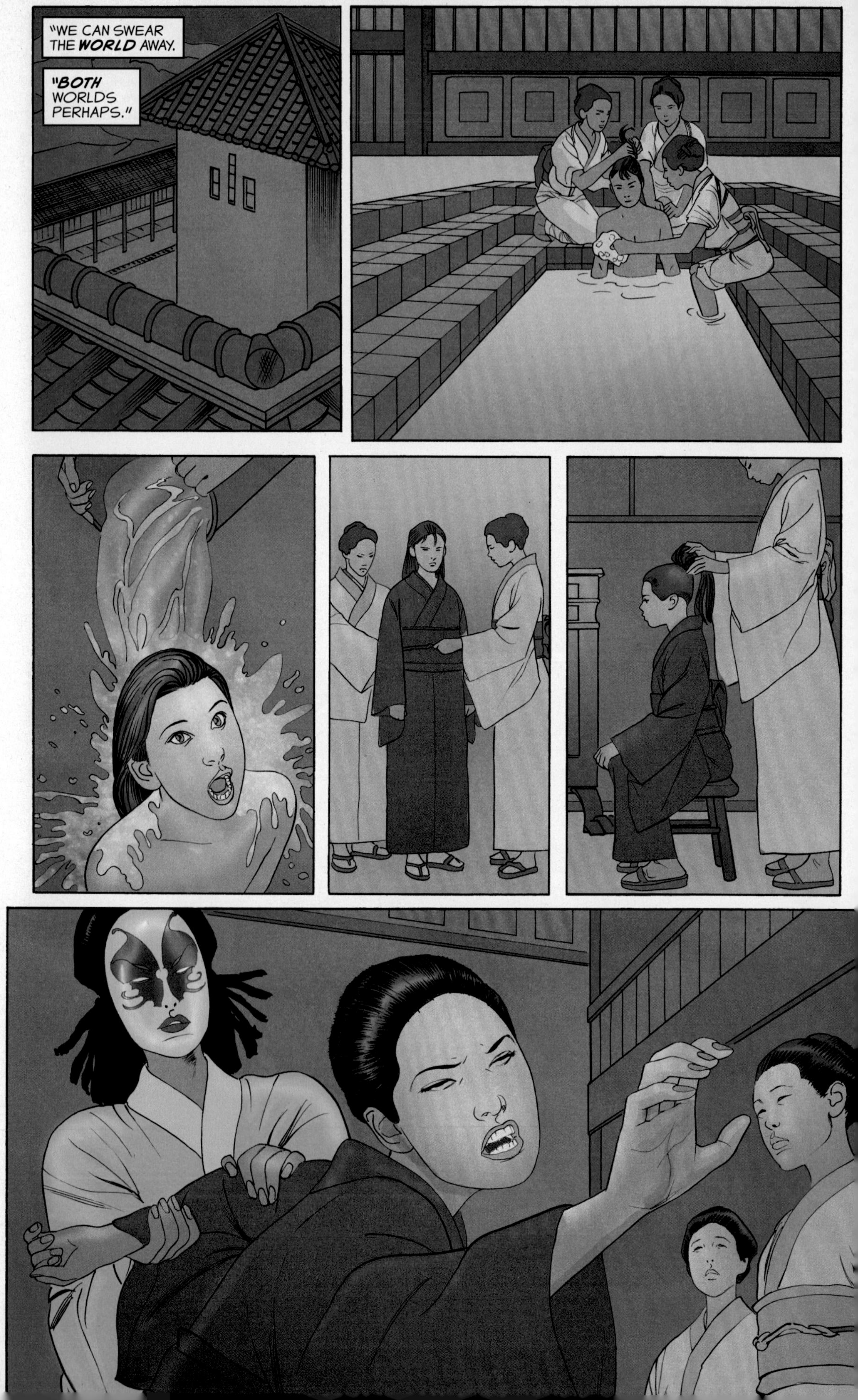
"WE CAN SWEAR THE WORLD AWAY.
"BOTH WORLDS PERHAPS."

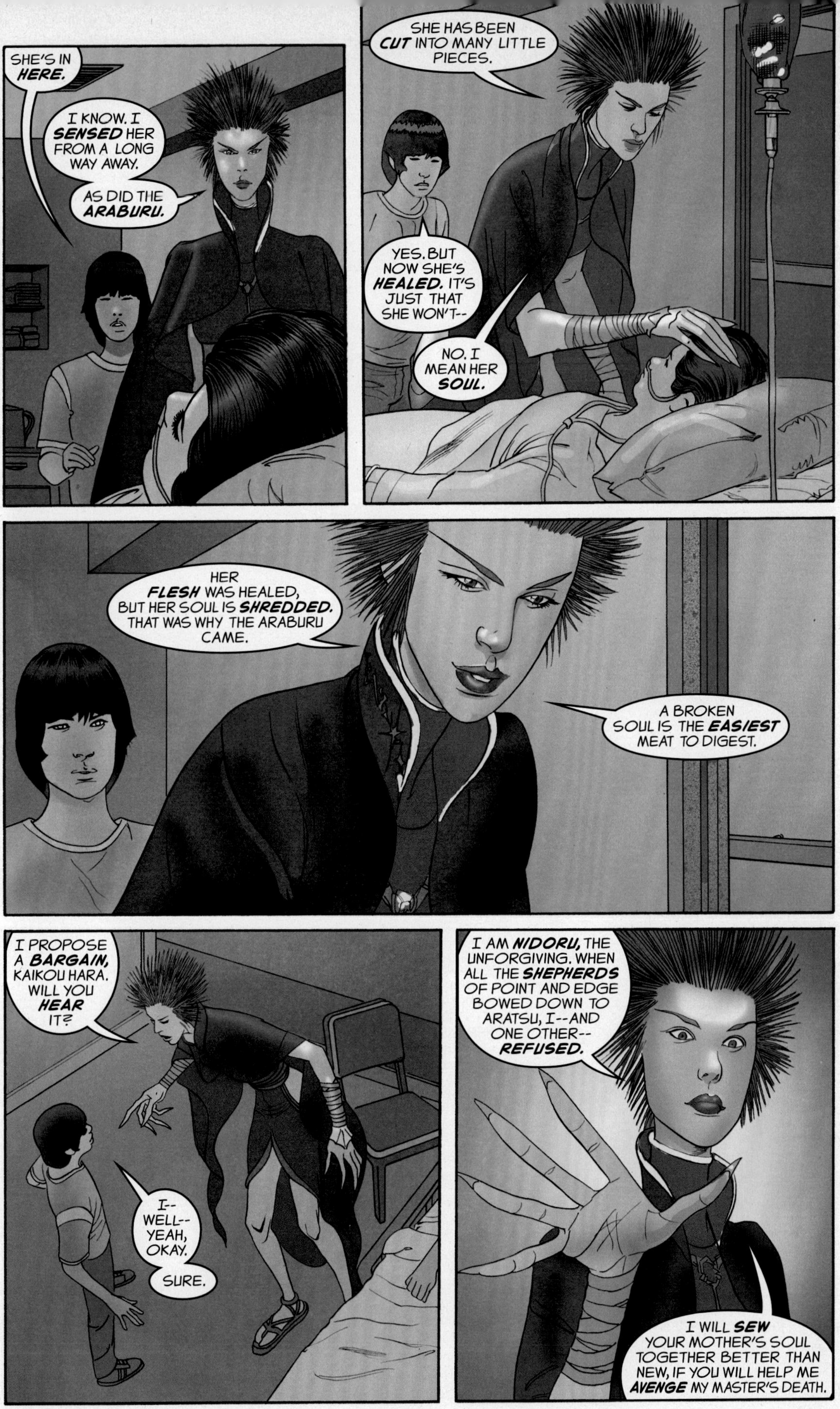
SHE'S IN HERE.
I KNOW. I SENSED HER FROM A LONG WAY AWAY.
AS DID THE ARABURU.
SHE HAS BEEN CUT INTO MANY LITTLE PIECES.
YES. BUT NOW SHE'S HEALED. IT'S JUST THAT SHE WON'T--
NO. I MEAN HER SOUL.
HER FLESH WAS HEALED, BUT HER SOUL IS SHREDDED. THAT WAS WHY THE ARABURU CAME.
A BROKEN SOUL IS THE EASIEST MEAT TO DIGEST.
I PROPOSE A BARGAIN, KAIKOU HARA. WILL YOU HEAR IT?
I-- WELL-- YEAH, OKAY.
SURE.
I AM NIDORU, THE UNFORGIVING. WHEN ALL THE SHEPHERDS OF POINT AND EDGE BOWED DOWN TO ARATSU, I--AND ONE OTHER-- REFUSED.
I WILL SEW YOUR MOTHER'S SOUL TOGETHER BETTER THAN NEW, IF YOU WILL HELP ME AVENGE MY MASTER'S DEATH.

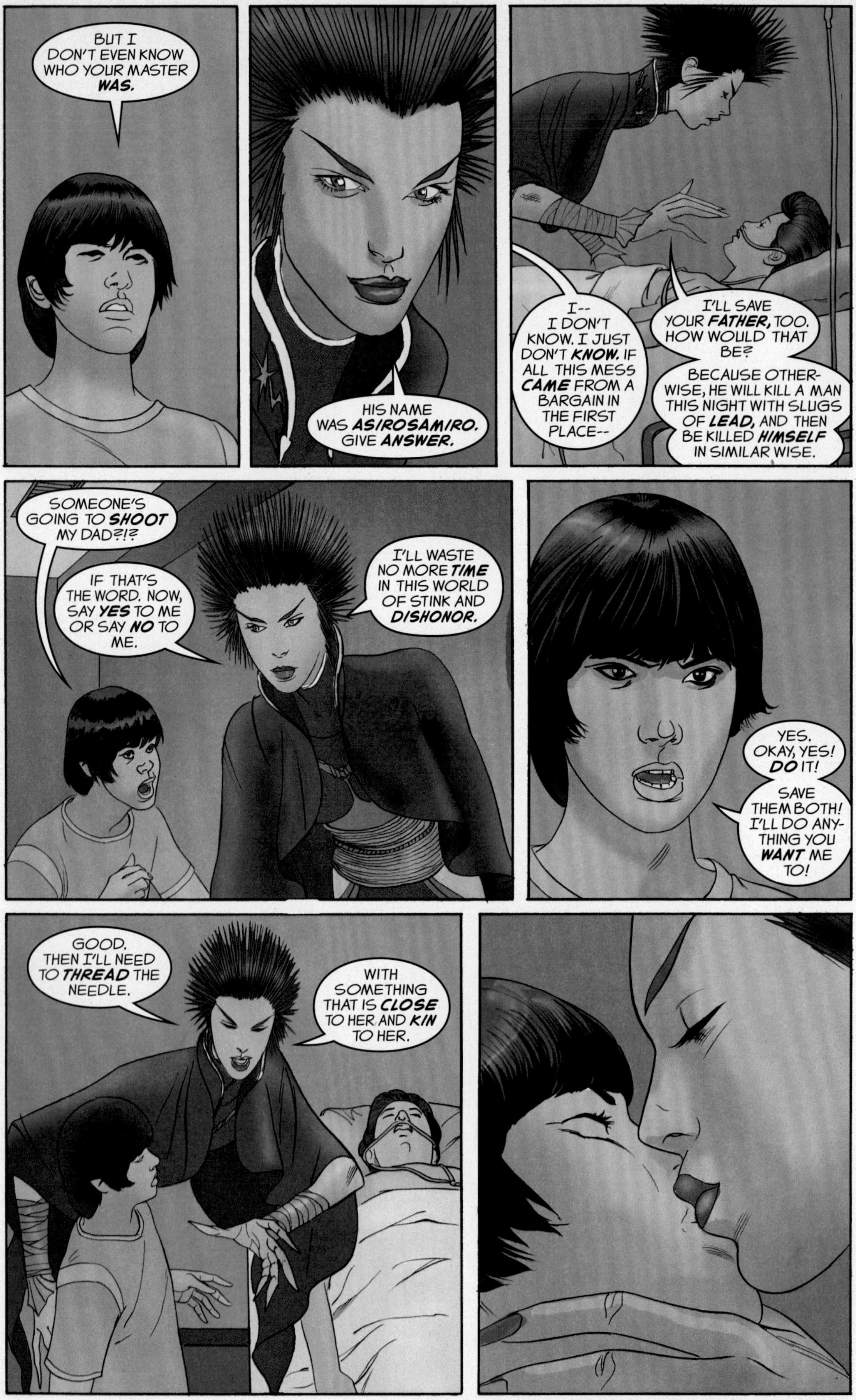
BUT I DON'T EVEN KNOW WHO YOUR MASTER WAS.
HIS NAME WAS ASIROSAMIRO. GIVE ANSWER.
I-- I DON'T KNOW. I JUST DON'T KNOW. IF ALL THIS MESS CAME FROM A BARGAIN IN THE FIRST PLACE--
I'LL SAVE YOUR FATHER, TOO. HOW WOULD THAT BE?
BECAUSE OTHERWISE, HE WILL KILL A MAN THIS NIGHT WITH SLUGS OF LEAD, AND THEN BE KILLED HIMSELF IN SIMILAR WISE.
SOMEONE'S GOING TO SHOOT MY DAD?!?
IF THAT'S THE WORD. NOW, SAY YES TO ME OR SAY NO TO ME.
I'LL WASTE NO MORE TIME IN THIS WORLD OF STINK AND DISHONOR.
YES. OKAY, YES! DO IT!
SAVE THEM BOTH! I'LL DO ANYTHING YOU WANT ME TO!
GOOD. THEN I'LL NEED TO THREAD THE NEEDLE.
WITH SOMETHING THAT IS CLOSE TO HER AND KIN TO HER.

OW!

WHY DID YOU--?

EXCELLENT! YOUR *BLOOD* WILL BE THE THREAD.

KEEP *WATCH*, KAIKOU HARA. YOUR MOTHER'S SPOOR MAY BRING ON *MORE* OF THE CARRION-EATERS.

AND I'D AS SOON NOT BE *INTERRUPTED* AS I WORK.

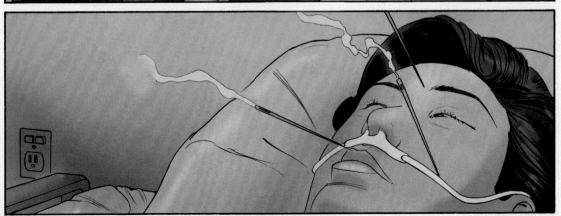

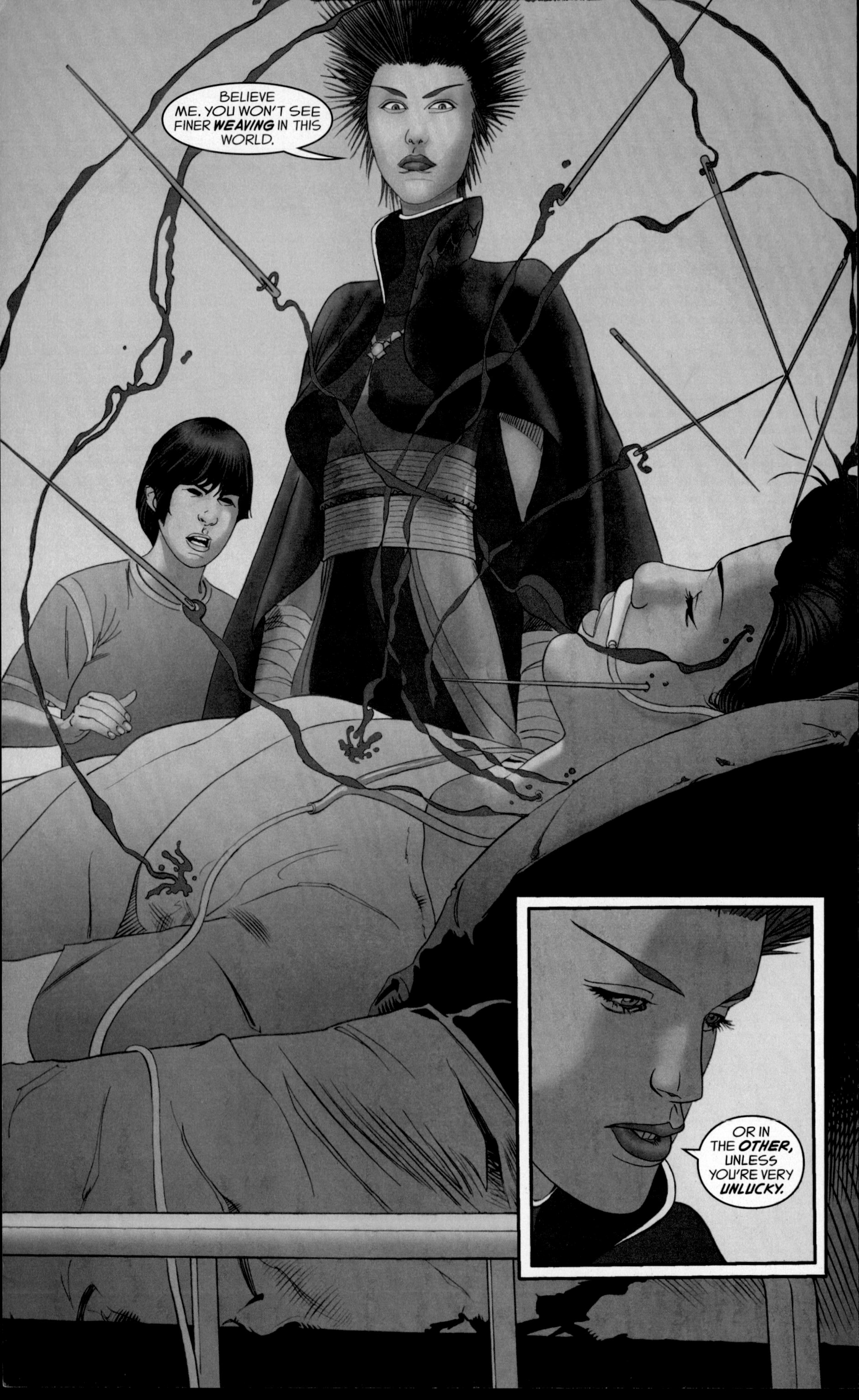
BELIEVE ME. YOU WON'T SEE FINER WEAVING IN THIS WORLD.
OR IN THE OTHER, UNLESS YOU'RE VERY UNLUCKY.

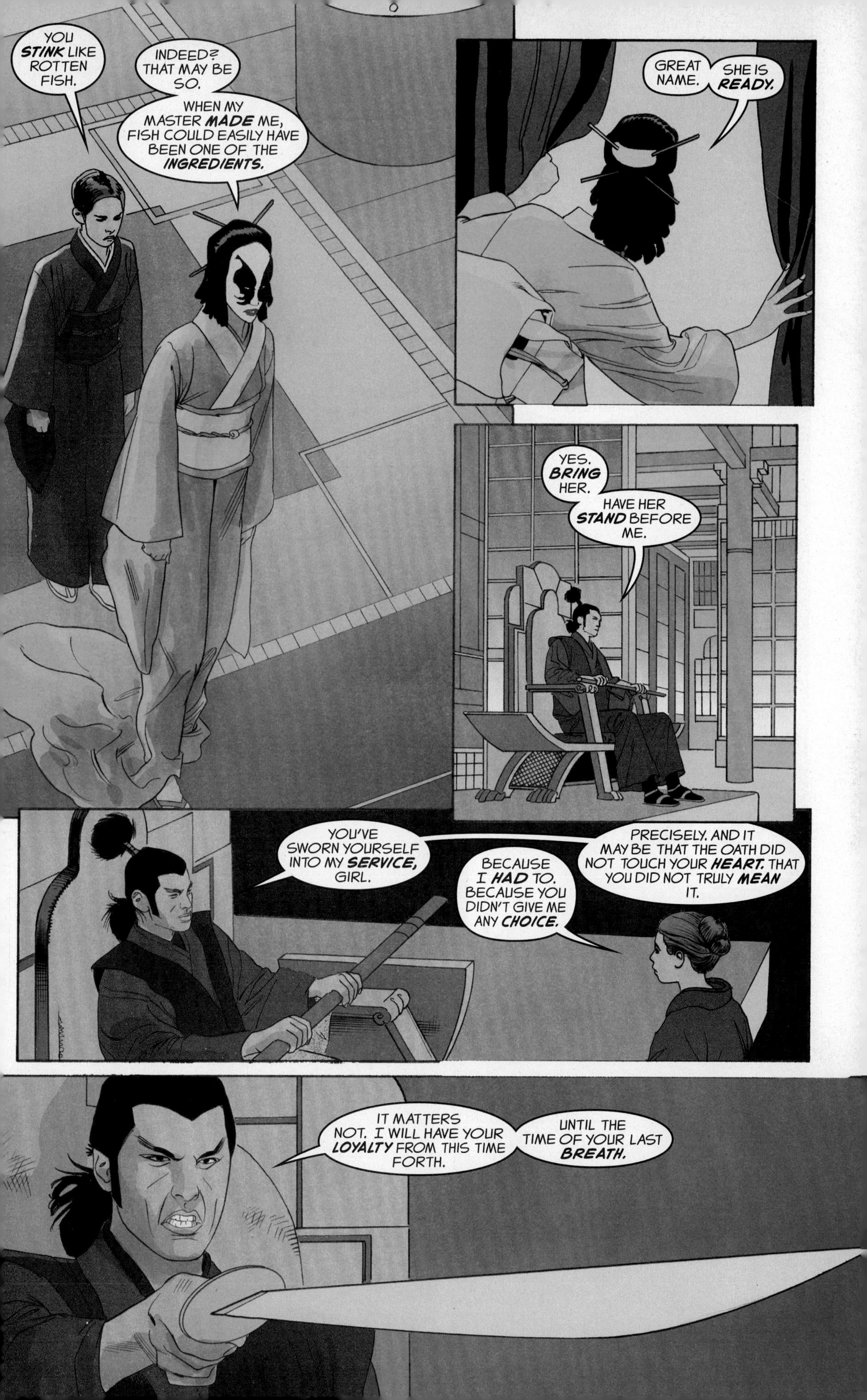
YOU STINK LIKE ROTTEN FISH.
INDEED? THAT MAY BE SO.
WHEN MY MASTER MADE ME, FISH COULD EASILY HAVE BEEN ONE OF THE INGREDIENTS.
GREAT NAME.
SHE IS READY.
YES. BRING HER.
HAVE HER STAND BEFORE ME.
YOU'VE SWORN YOURSELF INTO MY SERVICE, GIRL.
BECAUSE I HAD TO. BECAUSE YOU DIDN'T GIVE ME ANY CHOICE.
PRECISELY. AND IT MAY BE THAT THE OATH DID NOT TOUCH YOUR HEART. THAT YOU DID NOT TRULY MEAN IT.
IT MATTERS NOT. I WILL HAVE YOUR LOYALTY FROM THIS TIME FORTH.
UNTIL THE TIME OF YOUR LAST BREATH.

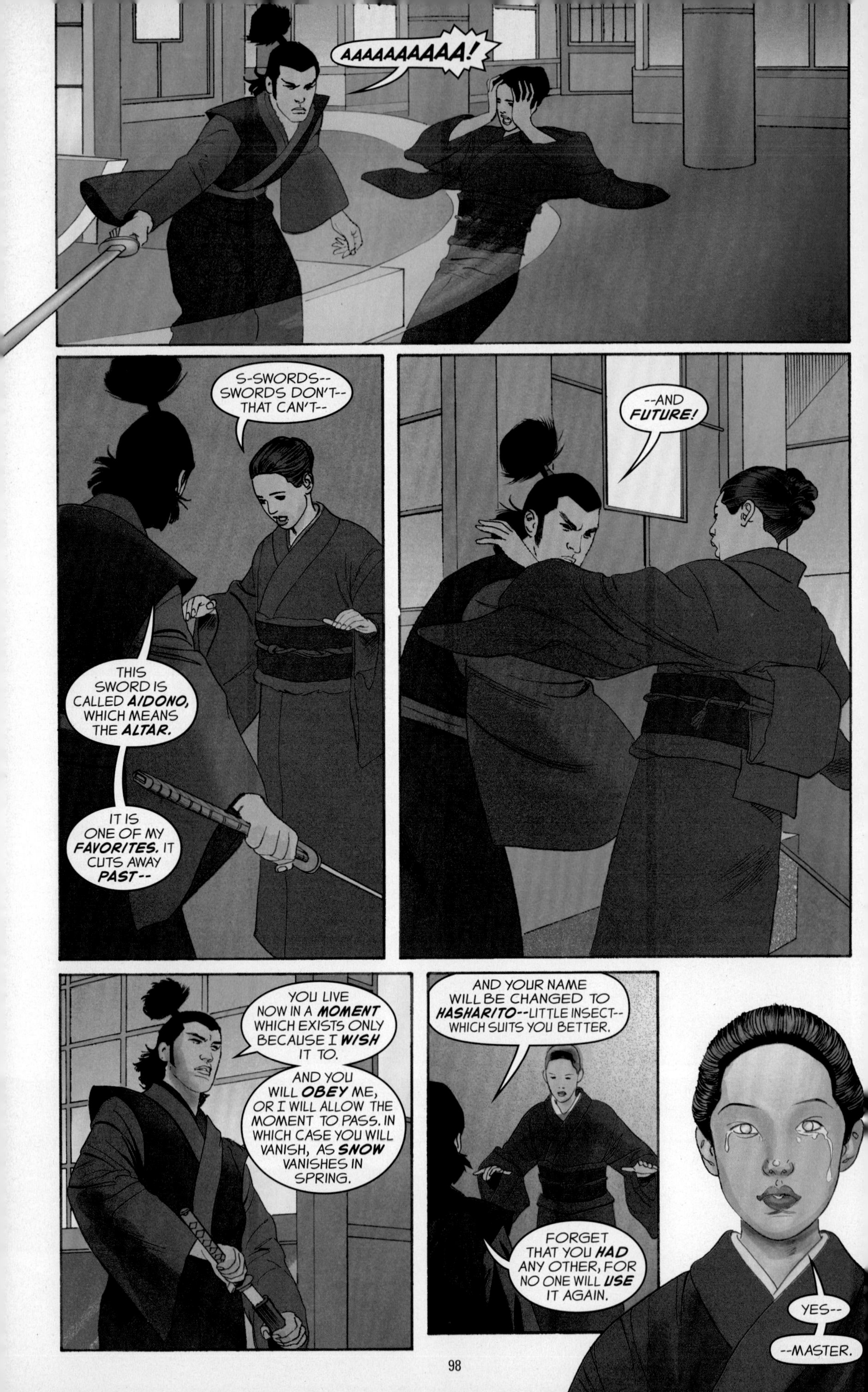
AAAAAAAAAA!
S-SWORDS-- SWORDS DON'T-- THAT CAN'T--
THIS SWORD IS CALLED AIDONO, WHICH MEANS THE ALTAR.
IT IS ONE OF MY FAVORITES. IT CUTS AWAY PAST--
--AND FUTURE!
YOU LIVE NOW IN A MOMENT WHICH EXISTS ONLY BECAUSE I WISH IT TO.
AND YOU WILL OBEY ME, OR I WILL ALLOW THE MOMENT TO PASS. IN WHICH CASE YOU WILL VANISH, AS SNOW VANISHES IN SPRING.
AND YOUR NAME WILL BE CHANGED TO HASHARITO--LITTLE INSECT-- WHICH SUITS YOU BETTER.
FORGET THAT YOU HAD ANY OTHER, FOR NO ONE WILL USE IT AGAIN.
YES--
--MASTER.

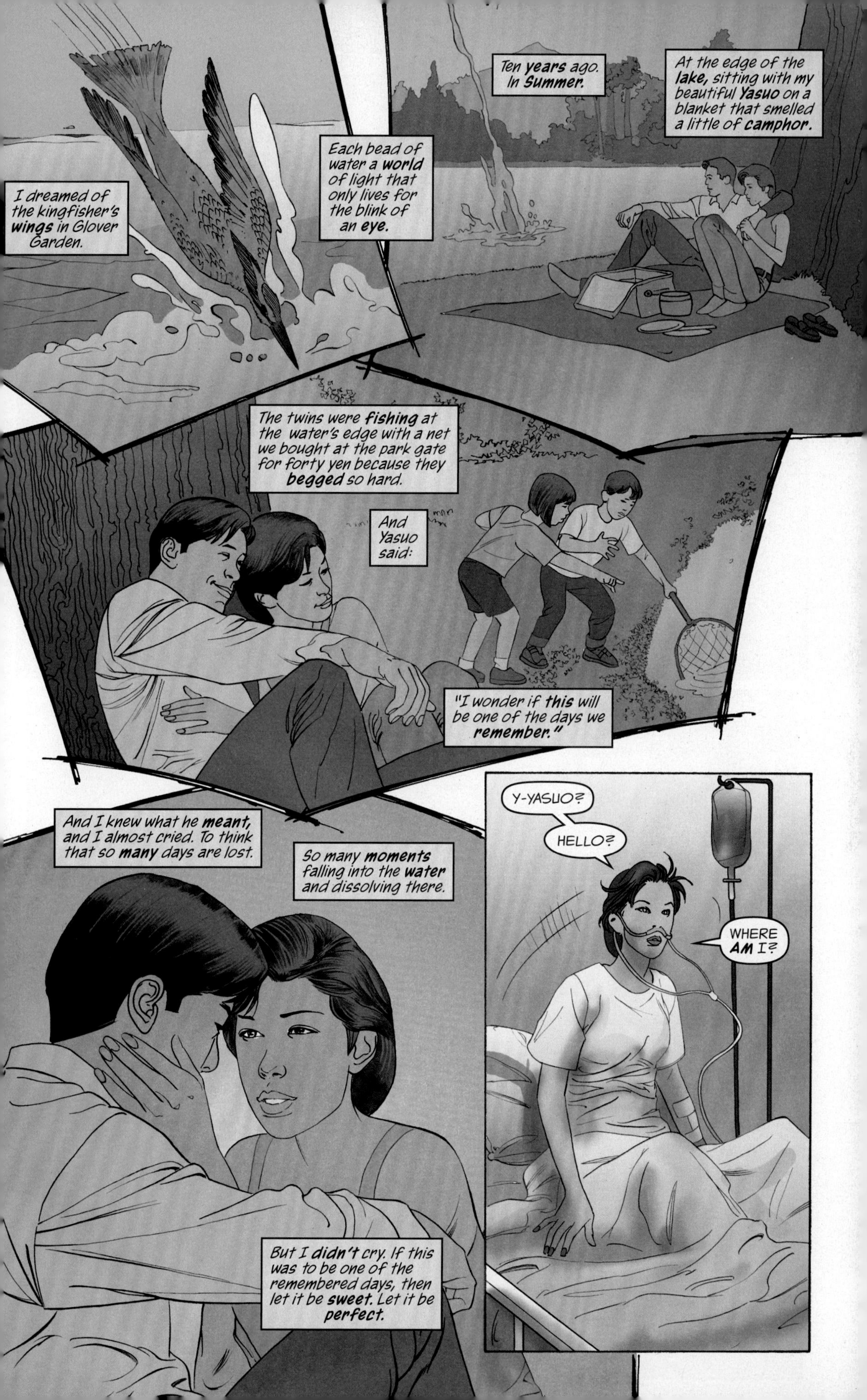
I dreamed of the kingfisher's wings in Glover Garden.
Each bead of water a world of light that only lives for the blink of an eye.
Ten years ago. In Summer.
At the edge of the lake, sitting with my beautiful Yasuo on a blanket that smelled a little of camphor.
The twins were fishing at the water's edge with a net we bought at the park gate for forty yen because they begged so hard.
And Yasuo said:
"I wonder if this will be one of the days we remember."
And I knew what he meant, and I almost cried. To think that so many days are lost.
So many moments falling into the water and dissolving there.
But I didn't cry. If this was to be one of the remembered days, then let it be sweet. Let it be perfect.
Y-YASUO?
HELLO?
WHERE AM I?

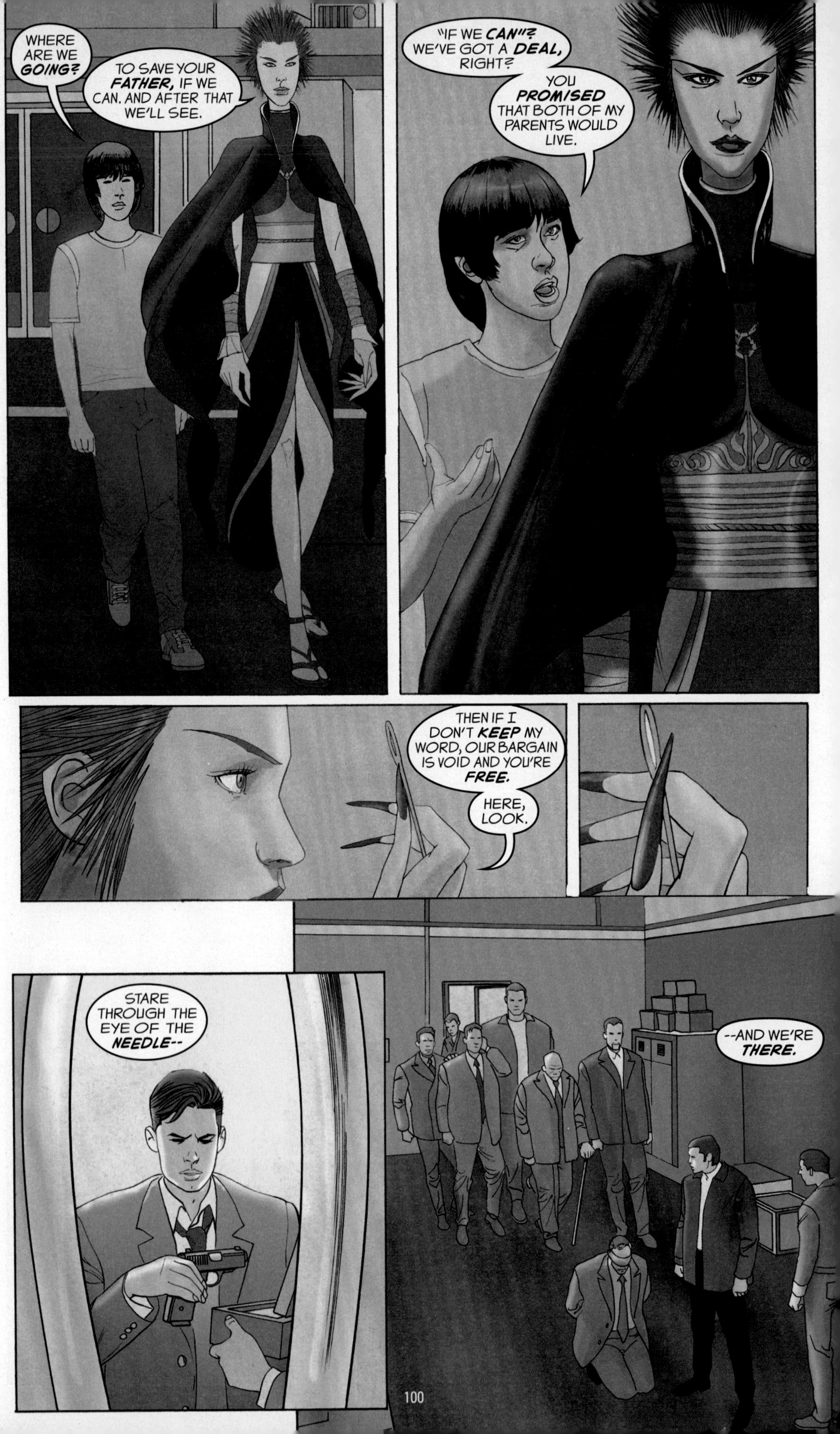
WHERE ARE WE GOING?
TO SAVE YOUR FATHER, IF WE CAN. AND AFTER THAT WE'LL SEE.
"IF WE CAN"? WE'VE GOT A DEAL, RIGHT?
YOU PROMISED THAT BOTH OF MY PARENTS WOULD LIVE.
THEN IF I DON'T KEEP MY WORD, OUR BARGAIN IS VOID AND YOU'RE FREE.
HERE, LOOK.
STARE THROUGH THE EYE OF THE NEEDLE--
--AND WE'RE THERE.

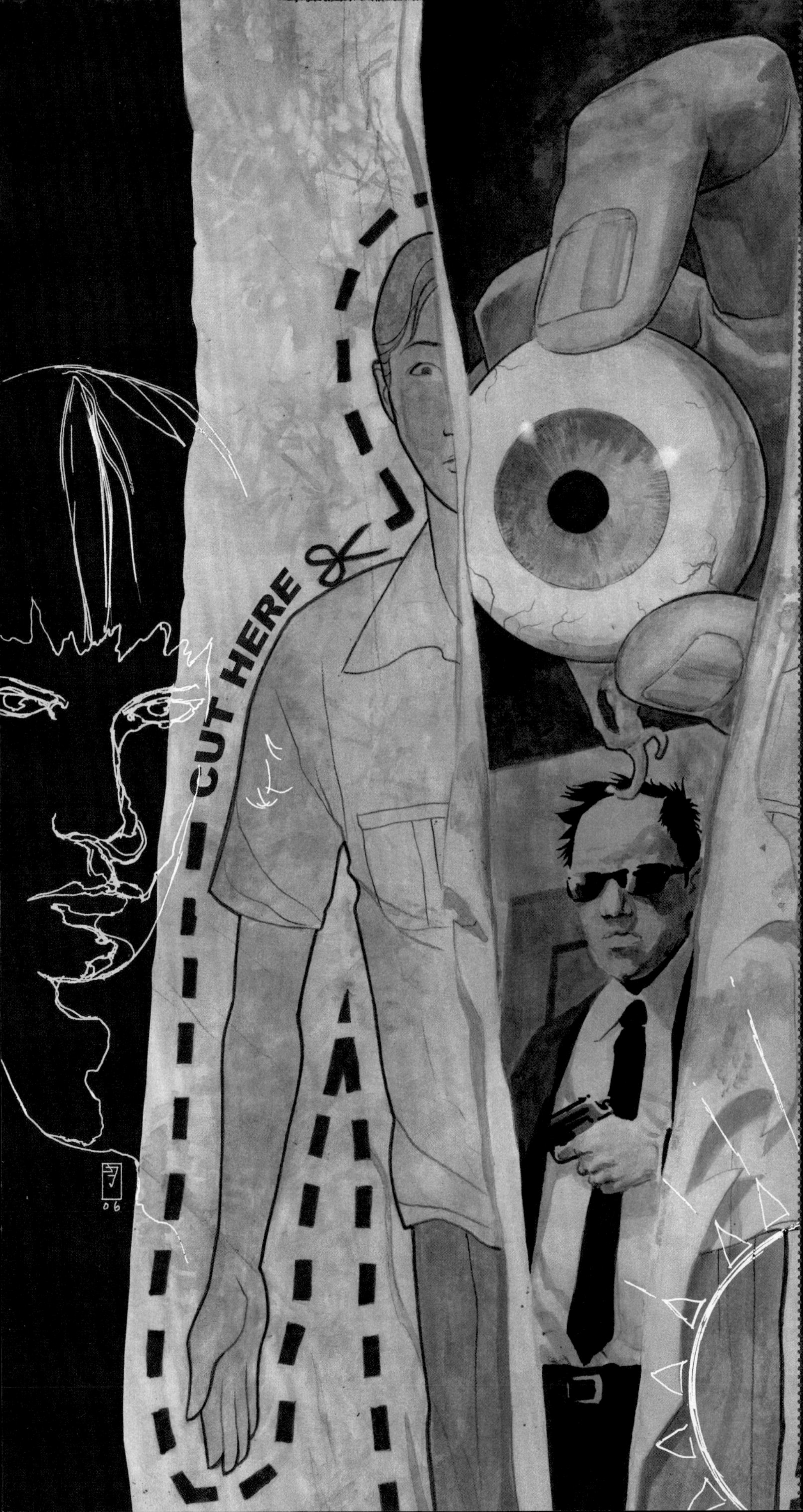
CUT HERE

chapter five

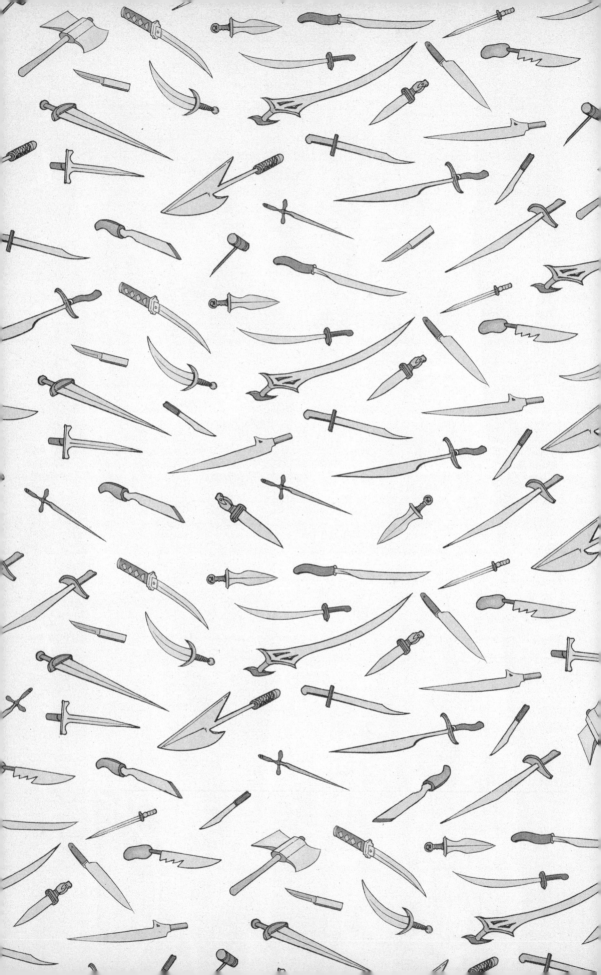

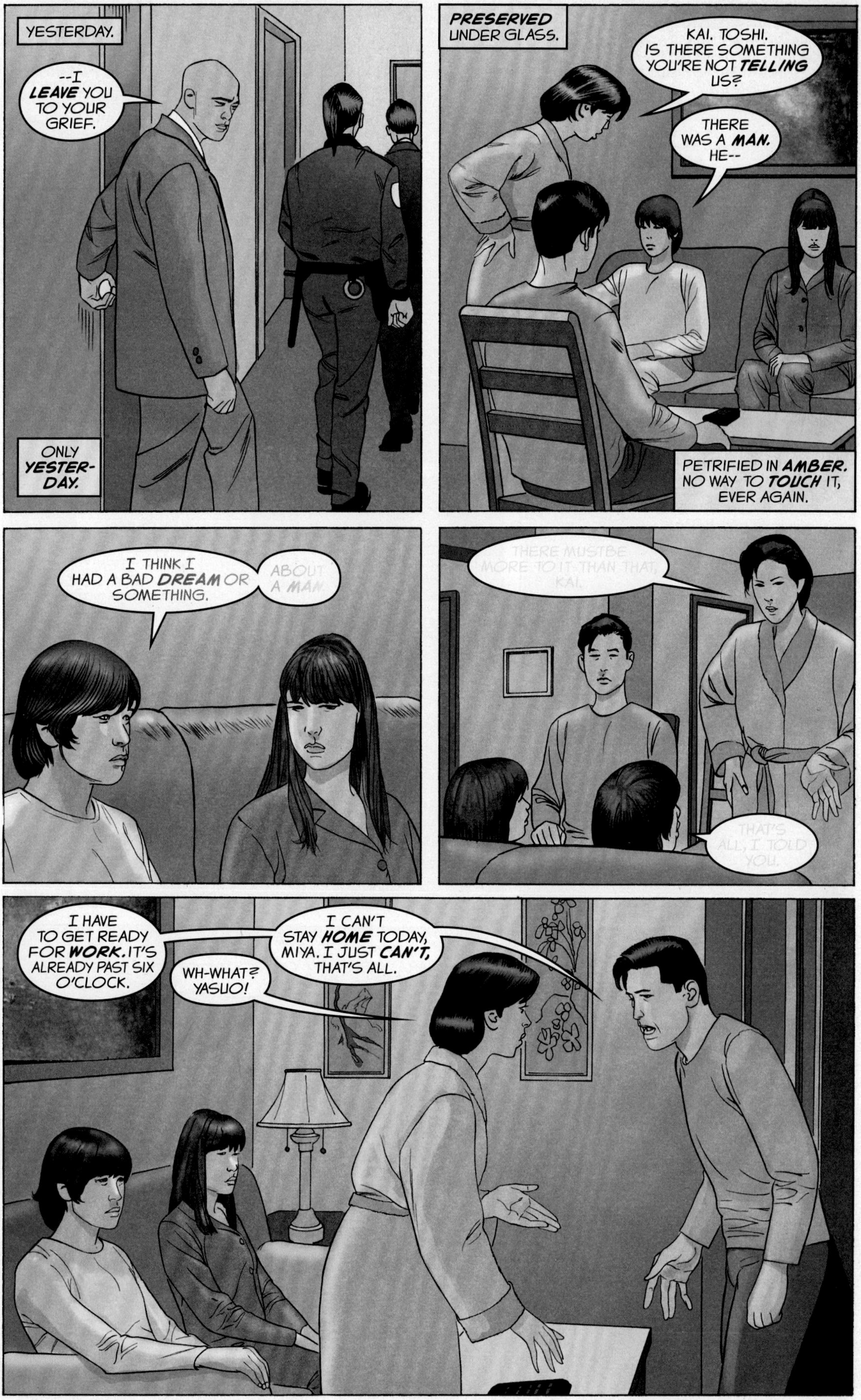
YESTERDAY.
--I LEAVE YOU TO YOUR GRIEF.
ONLY YESTER-DAY.
PRESERVED UNDER GLASS.
KAI. TOSHI. IS THERE SOMETHING YOU'RE NOT TELLING US?
THERE WAS A MAN. HE--
PETRIFIED IN AMBER. NO WAY TO TOUCH IT, EVER AGAIN.
I THINK I HAD A BAD DREAM OR SOMETHING.
ABOUT A MAN
THERE MUSTBE MORE TO IT THAN THAT, KAI.
THAT'S ALL, I TOLD YOU.
I HAVE TO GET READY FOR WORK. IT'S ALREADY PAST SIX O'CLOCK.
WH-WHAT? YASUO!
I CAN'T STAY HOME TODAY, MIYA. I JUST CAN'T, THAT'S ALL.

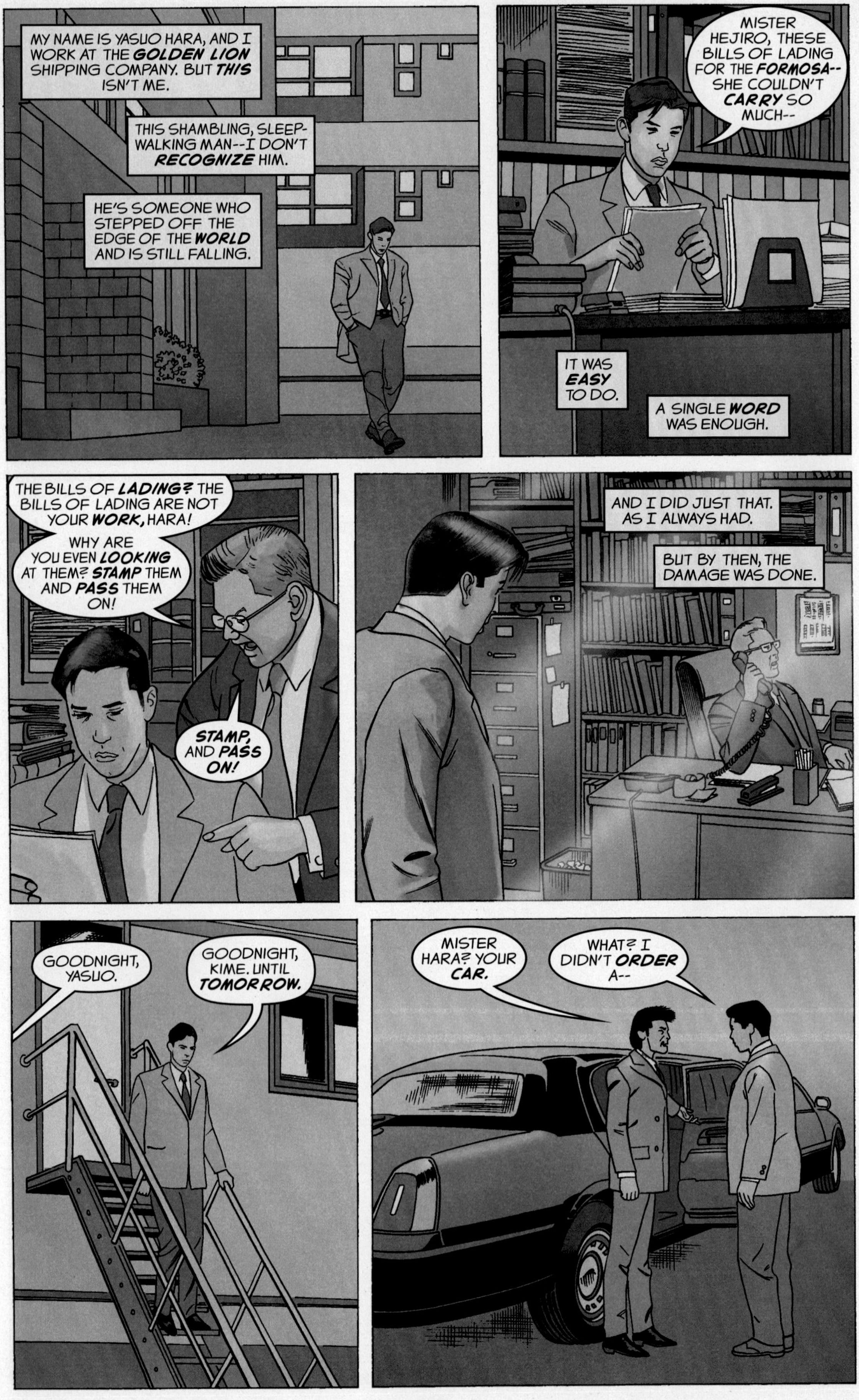

MY NAME IS YASUO HARA, AND I WORK AT THE GOLDEN LION SHIPPING COMPANY. BUT THIS ISN'T ME.
THIS SHAMBLING, SLEEP-WALKING MAN--I DON'T RECOGNIZE HIM.
HE'S SOMEONE WHO STEPPED OFF THE EDGE OF THE WORLD AND IS STILL FALLING.
MISTER HEJIRO, THESE BILLS OF LADING FOR THE FORMOSA--SHE COULDN'T CARRY SO MUCH--
IT WAS EASY TO DO.
A SINGLE WORD WAS ENOUGH.
THE BILLS OF LADING? THE BILLS OF LADING ARE NOT YOUR WORK, HARA!
WHY ARE YOU EVEN LOOKING AT THEM? STAMP THEM AND PASS THEM ON!
STAMP, AND PASS ON!
AND I DID JUST THAT. AS I ALWAYS HAD.
BUT BY THEN, THE DAMAGE WAS DONE.
GOODNIGHT, YASUO.
GOODNIGHT, KIME. UNTIL TOMORROW.
MISTER HARA? YOUR CAR.
WHAT? I DIDN'T ORDER A--

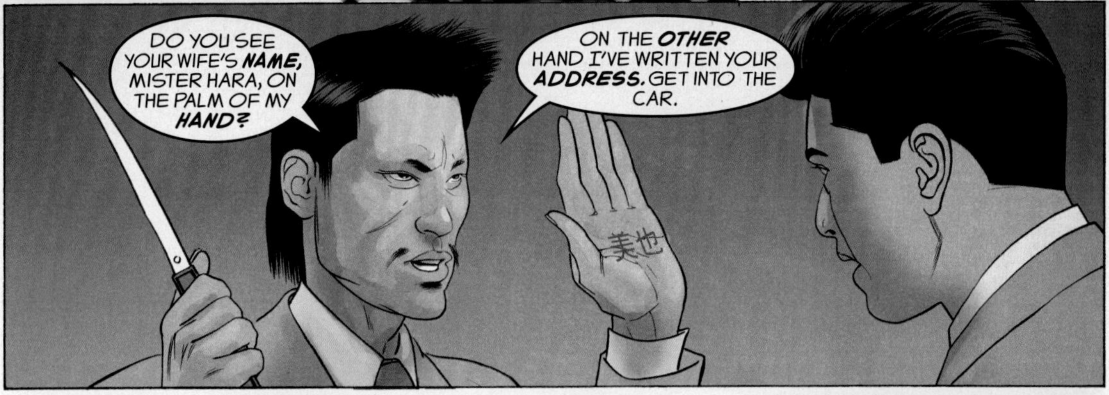
DO YOU SEE YOUR WIFE'S NAME, MISTER HARA, ON THE PALM OF MY HAND?
美也
ON THE OTHER HAND I'VE WRITTEN YOUR ADDRESS. GET INTO THE CAR.

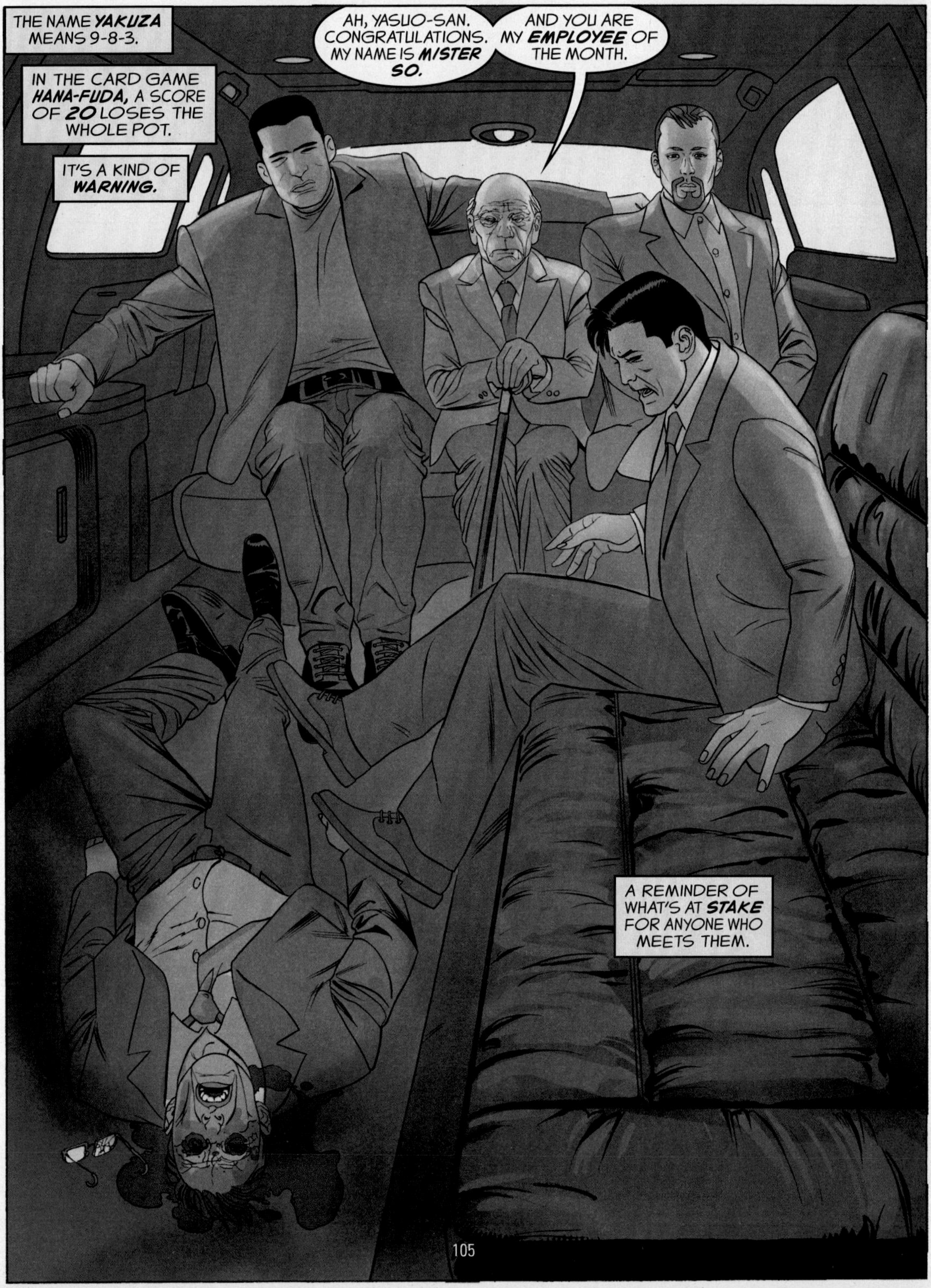
THE NAME YAKUZA MEANS 9-8-3.
IN THE CARD GAME HANA-FUDA, A SCORE OF 20 LOSES THE WHOLE POT.
IT'S A KIND OF WARNING.
AH, YASUO-SAN. CONGRATULATIONS. MY NAME IS MISTER SO.
AND YOU ARE MY EMPLOYEE OF THE MONTH.
A REMINDER OF WHAT'S AT STAKE FOR ANYONE WHO MEETS THEM.

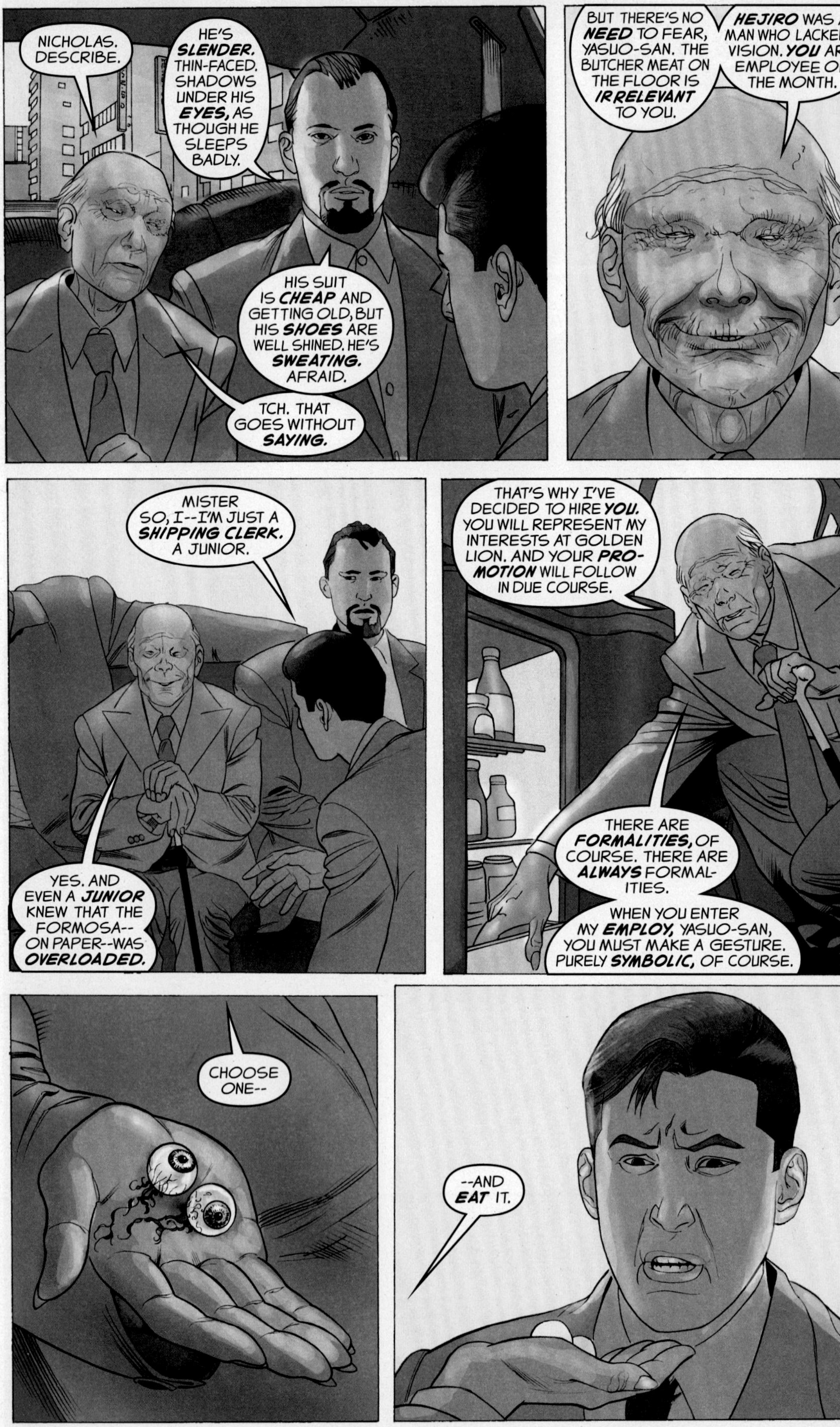
NICHOLAS. DESCRIBE.
HE'S SLENDER. THIN-FACED. SHADOWS UNDER HIS EYES, AS THOUGH HE SLEEPS BADLY.
HIS SUIT IS CHEAP AND GETTING OLD, BUT HIS SHOES ARE WELL SHINED. HE'S SWEATING. AFRAID.
TCH. THAT GOES WITHOUT SAYING.
BUT THERE'S NO NEED TO FEAR, YASUO-SAN. THE BUTCHER MEAT ON THE FLOOR IS IRRELEVANT TO YOU.
HEJIRO WAS A MAN WHO LACKED... VISION. YOU ARE EMPLOYEE OF THE MONTH.
MISTER SO, I--I'M JUST A SHIPPING CLERK. A JUNIOR.
YES. AND EVEN A JUNIOR KNEW THAT THE FORMOSA--ON PAPER--WAS OVERLOADED.
THAT'S WHY I'VE DECIDED TO HIRE YOU. YOU WILL REPRESENT MY INTERESTS AT GOLDEN LION. AND YOUR PROMOTION WILL FOLLOW IN DUE COURSE.
THERE ARE FORMALITIES, OF COURSE. THERE ARE ALWAYS FORMALITIES.
WHEN YOU ENTER MY EMPLOY, YASUO-SAN, YOU MUST MAKE A GESTURE. PURELY SYMBOLIC, OF COURSE.
CHOOSE ONE--
--AND EAT IT.

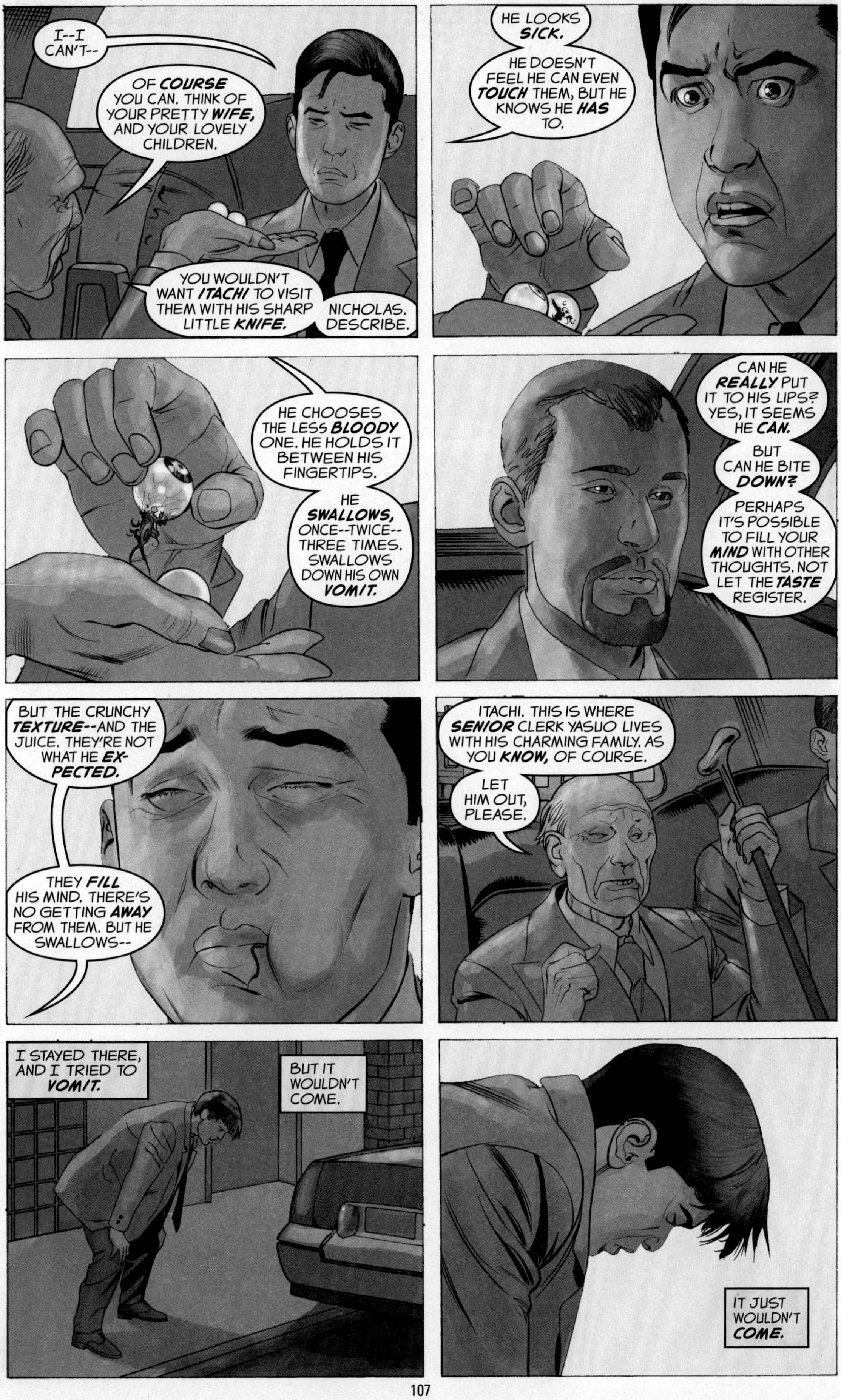
I--I CAN'T--
OF COURSE YOU CAN. THINK OF YOUR PRETTY WIFE, AND YOUR LOVELY CHILDREN.
YOU WOULDN'T WANT ITACHI TO VISIT THEM WITH HIS SHARP LITTLE KNIFE.
NICHOLAS. DESCRIBE.
HE LOOKS SICK.
HE DOESN'T FEEL HE CAN EVEN TOUCH THEM, BUT HE KNOWS HE HAS TO.
HE CHOOSES THE LESS BLOODY ONE. HE HOLDS IT BETWEEN HIS FINGERTIPS.
HE SWALLOWS, ONCE--TWICE--THREE TIMES. SWALLOWS DOWN HIS OWN VOMIT.
CAN HE REALLY PUT IT TO HIS LIPS? YES, IT SEEMS HE CAN.
BUT CAN HE BITE DOWN?
PERHAPS IT'S POSSIBLE TO FILL YOUR MIND WITH OTHER THOUGHTS. NOT LET THE TASTE REGISTER.
BUT THE CRUNCHY TEXTURE--AND THE JUICE. THEY'RE NOT WHAT HE EX-PECTED.
THEY FILL HIS MIND. THERE'S NO GETTING AWAY FROM THEM. BUT HE SWALLOWS--
ITACHI. THIS IS WHERE SENIOR CLERK YASUO LIVES WITH HIS CHARMING FAMILY. AS YOU KNOW, OF COURSE.
LET HIM OUT, PLEASE.
I STAYED THERE, AND I TRIED TO VOMIT.
BUT IT WOULDN'T COME.
IT JUST WOULDN'T COME.

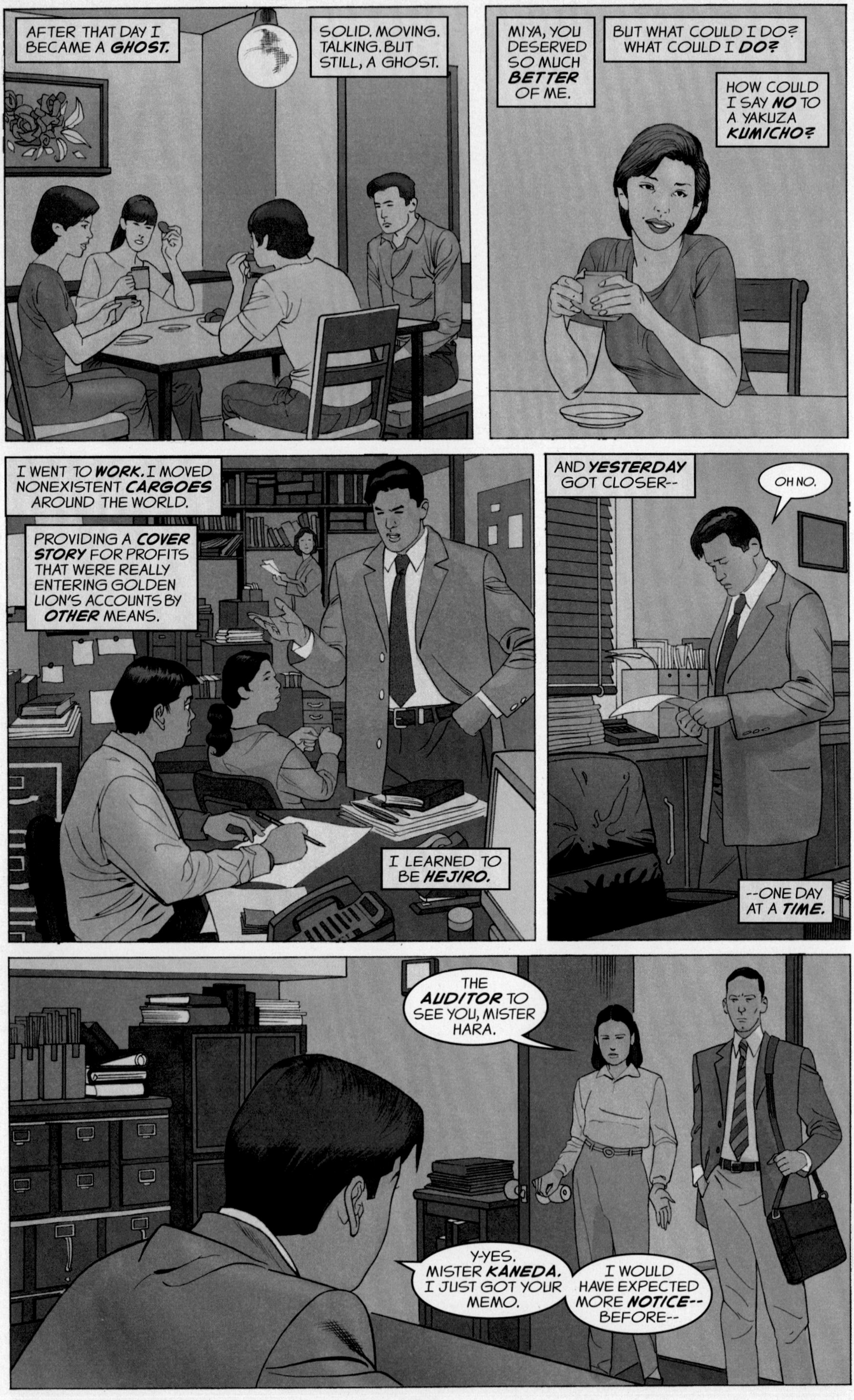
AFTER THAT DAY I BECAME A GHOST.
SOLID. MOVING. TALKING. BUT STILL, A GHOST.
MIYA, YOU DESERVED SO MUCH BETTER OF ME.
BUT WHAT COULD I DO? WHAT COULD I DO?
HOW COULD I SAY NO TO A YAKUZA KUMICHO?
I WENT TO WORK. I MOVED NONEXISTENT CARGOES AROUND THE WORLD.
PROVIDING A COVER STORY FOR PROFITS THAT WERE REALLY ENTERING GOLDEN LION'S ACCOUNTS BY OTHER MEANS.
I LEARNED TO BE HEJIRO.
AND YESTERDAY GOT CLOSER--
OH NO.
--ONE DAY AT A TIME.
THE AUDITOR TO SEE YOU, MISTER HARA.
Y-YES. MISTER KANEDA. I JUST GOT YOUR MEMO.
I WOULD HAVE EXPECTED MORE NOTICE-- BEFORE--

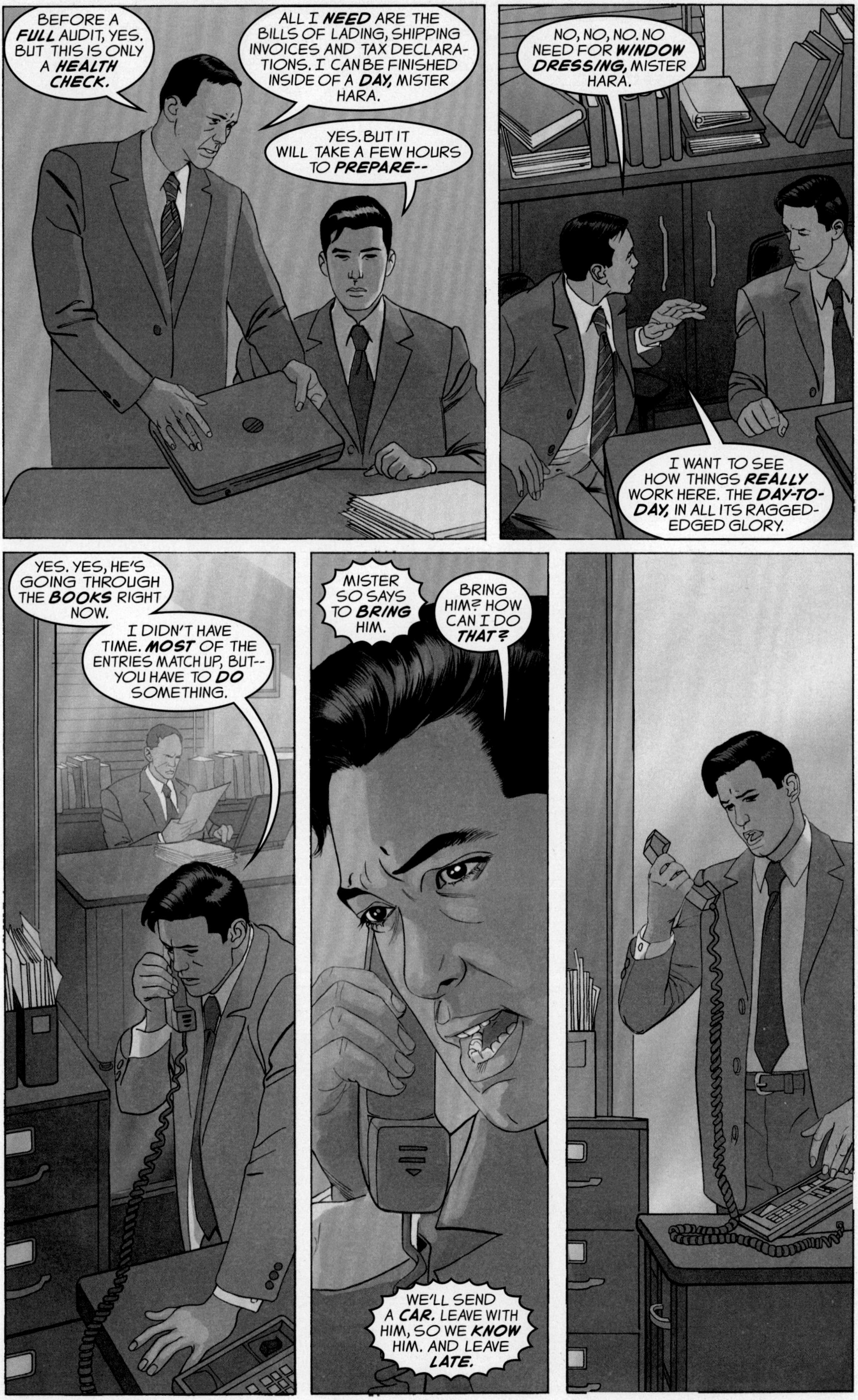
BEFORE A FULL AUDIT, YES. BUT THIS IS ONLY A HEALTH CHECK.
ALL I NEED ARE THE BILLS OF LADING, SHIPPING INVOICES AND TAX DECLARATIONS. I CAN BE FINISHED INSIDE OF A DAY, MISTER HARA.
YES. BUT IT WILL TAKE A FEW HOURS TO PREPARE--
NO, NO, NO. NO NEED FOR WINDOW DRESSING, MISTER HARA.
I WANT TO SEE HOW THINGS REALLY WORK HERE. THE DAY-TO-DAY, IN ALL ITS RAGGED-EDGED GLORY.
YES. YES, HE'S GOING THROUGH THE BOOKS RIGHT NOW.
I DIDN'T HAVE TIME. MOST OF THE ENTRIES MATCH UP, BUT-- YOU HAVE TO DO SOMETHING.
MISTER SO SAYS TO BRING HIM.
BRING HIM? HOW CAN I DO THAT?
WE'LL SEND A CAR. LEAVE WITH HIM, SO WE KNOW HIM. AND LEAVE LATE.

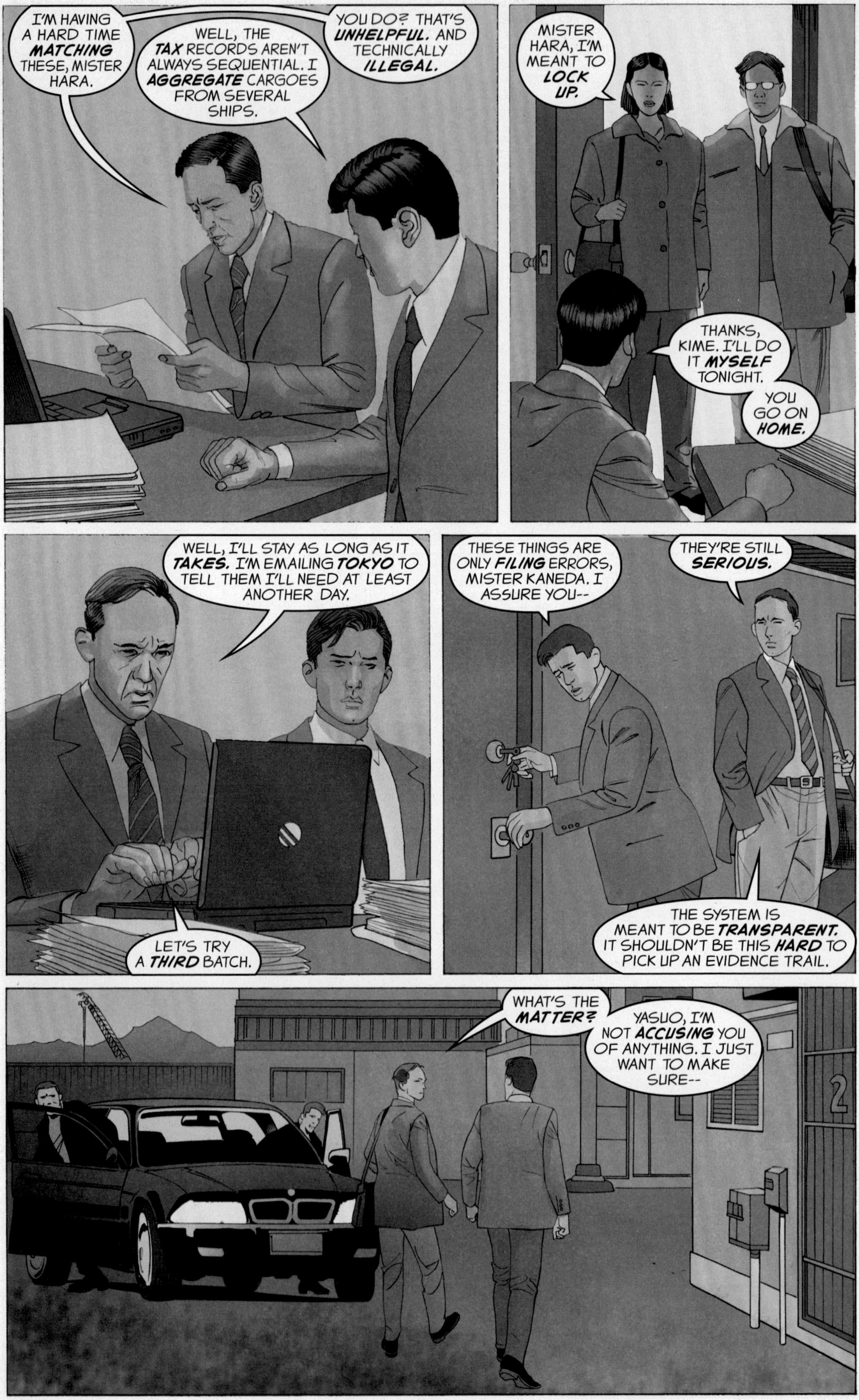
I'M HAVING A HARD TIME MATCHING THESE, MISTER HARA.
WELL, THE TAX RECORDS AREN'T ALWAYS SEQUENTIAL. I AGGREGATE CARGOES FROM SEVERAL SHIPS.
YOU DO? THAT'S UNHELPFUL. AND TECHNICALLY ILLEGAL.
MISTER HARA, I'M MEANT TO LOCK UP.
THANKS, KIME. I'LL DO IT MYSELF TONIGHT.
YOU GO ON HOME.
WELL, I'LL STAY AS LONG AS IT TAKES. I'M EMAILING TOKYO TO TELL THEM I'LL NEED AT LEAST ANOTHER DAY.
LET'S TRY A THIRD BATCH.
THESE THINGS ARE ONLY FILING ERRORS, MISTER KANEDA. I ASSURE YOU--
THEY'RE STILL SERIOUS.
THE SYSTEM IS MEANT TO BE TRANSPARENT. IT SHOULDN'T BE THIS HARD TO PICK UP AN EVIDENCE TRAIL.
WHAT'S THE MATTER?
YASUO, I'M NOT ACCUSING YOU OF ANYTHING. I JUST WANT TO MAKE SURE--
2

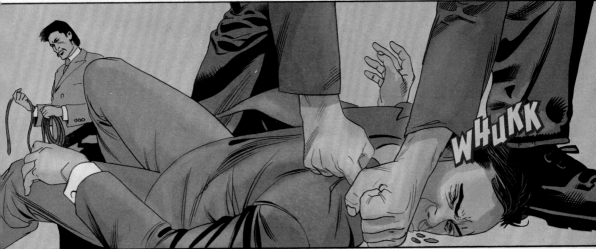

WHUKK

LITTLE *TURD* LANDED ONE ON MY CHIN. I'LL *MAIM* HIM FOR THAT.

COME ON, HARA. MISTER SO WANTS TO SEE *BOTH* OF YOU.

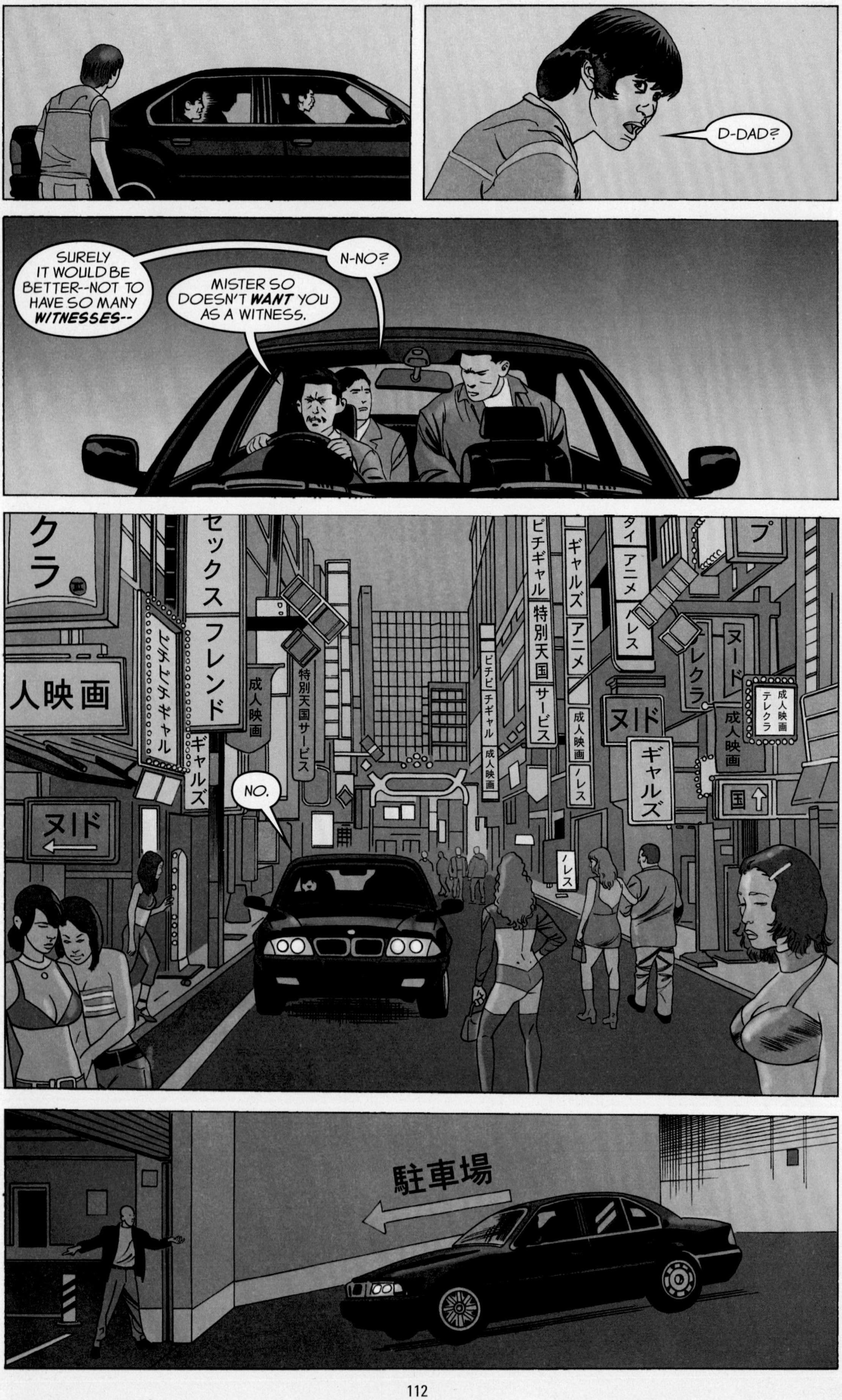
D-DAD?
SURELY IT WOULD BE BETTER--NOT TO HAVE SO MANY WITNESSES--
N-NO?
MISTER SO DOESN'T WANT YOU AS A WITNESS.
セックスフレンド
ピチピチギャル
特別天国サービス
成人映画
ギャルズ
ヌード
NO.
駐車場

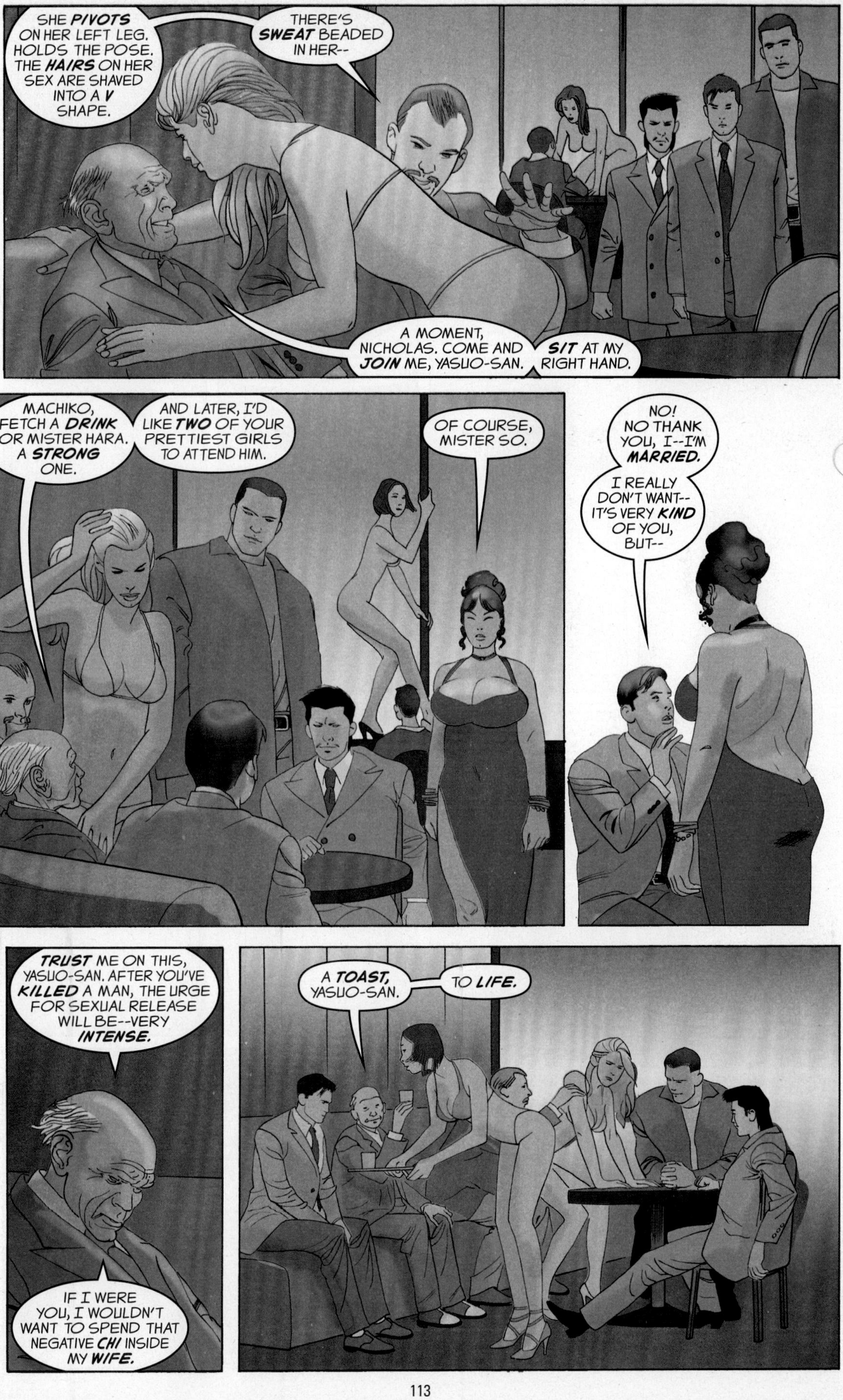

SHE PIVOTS ON HER LEFT LEG. HOLDS THE POSE. THE HAIRS ON HER SEX ARE SHAVED INTO A V SHAPE.
THERE'S SWEAT BEADED IN HER--
A MOMENT, NICHOLAS. COME AND JOIN ME, YASUO-SAN.
SIT AT MY RIGHT HAND.
MACHIKO, FETCH A DRINK FOR MISTER HARA. A STRONG ONE.
AND LATER, I'D LIKE TWO OF YOUR PRETTIEST GIRLS TO ATTEND HIM.
OF COURSE, MISTER SO.
NO! NO THANK YOU, I--I'M MARRIED.
I REALLY DON'T WANT-- IT'S VERY KIND OF YOU, BUT--
TRUST ME ON THIS, YASUO-SAN. AFTER YOU'VE KILLED A MAN, THE URGE FOR SEXUAL RELEASE WILL BE--VERY INTENSE.
IF I WERE YOU, I WOULDN'T WANT TO SPEND THAT NEGATIVE CHI INSIDE MY WIFE.
A TOAST, YASUO-SAN.
TO LIFE.

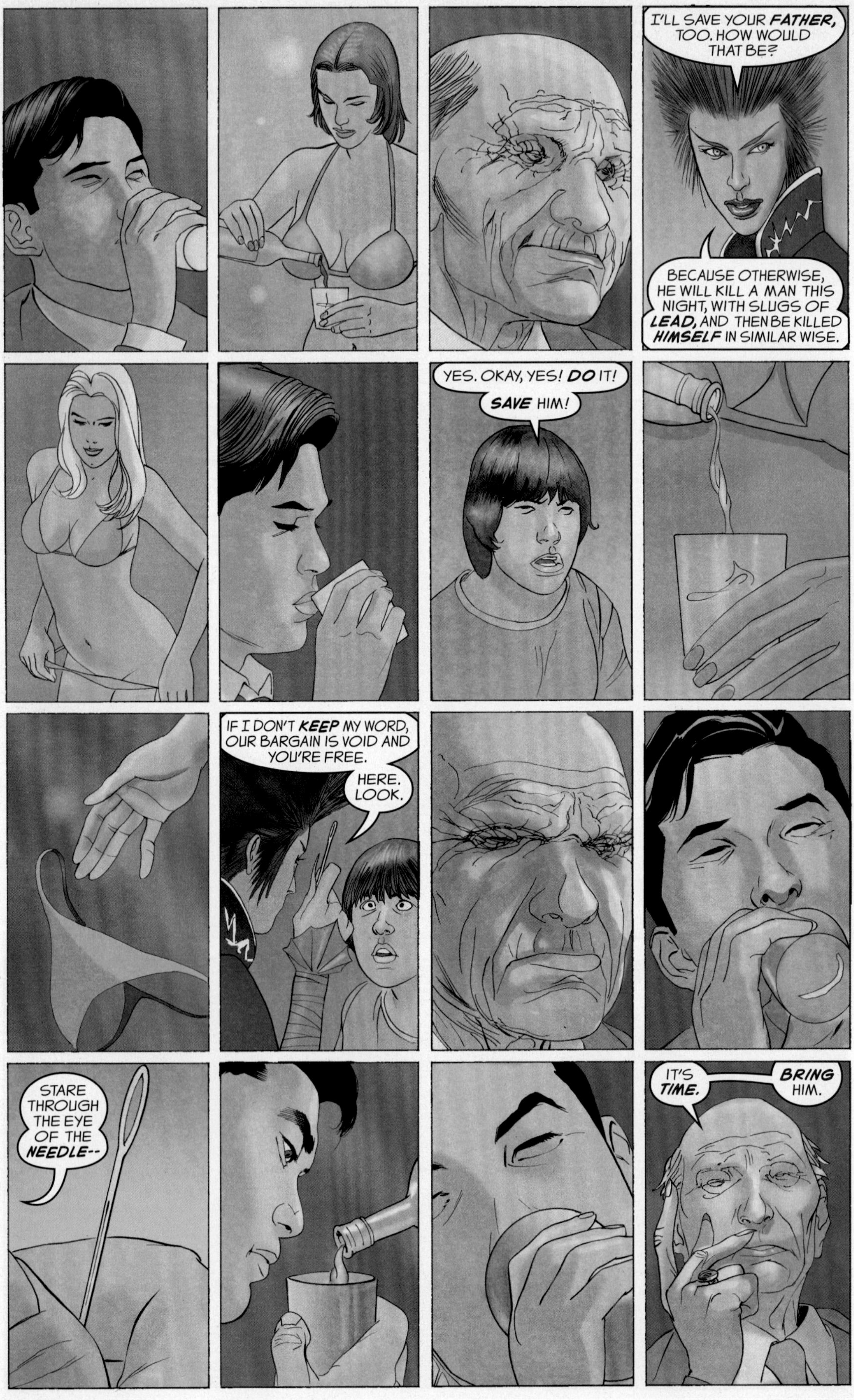

I'LL SAVE YOUR FATHER, TOO. HOW WOULD THAT BE?
BECAUSE OTHERWISE, HE WILL KILL A MAN THIS NIGHT, WITH SLUGS OF LEAD, AND THEN BE KILLED HIMSELF IN SIMILAR WISE.
YES. OKAY, YES! DO IT!
SAVE HIM!
IF I DON'T KEEP MY WORD, OUR BARGAIN IS VOID AND YOU'RE FREE.
HERE. LOOK.
STARE THROUGH THE EYE OF THE NEEDLE--
IT'S TIME.
BRING HIM.

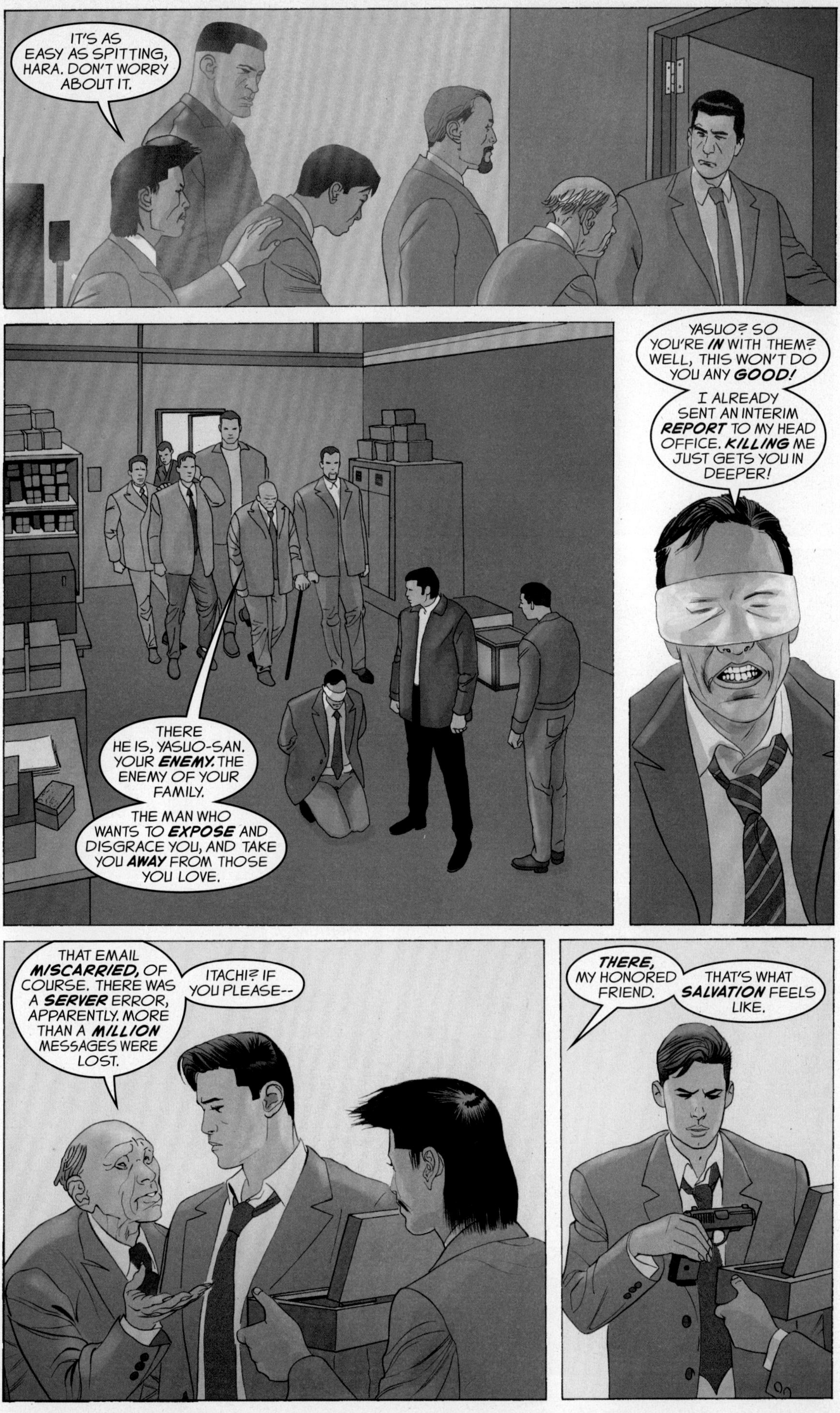
IT'S AS EASY AS SPITTING, HARA. DON'T WORRY ABOUT IT.
THERE HE IS, YASUO-SAN. YOUR ENEMY. THE ENEMY OF YOUR FAMILY.
THE MAN WHO WANTS TO EXPOSE AND DISGRACE YOU, AND TAKE YOU AWAY FROM THOSE YOU LOVE.
YASUO? SO YOU'RE IN WITH THEM? WELL, THIS WON'T DO YOU ANY GOOD!
I ALREADY SENT AN INTERIM REPORT TO MY HEAD OFFICE. KILLING ME JUST GETS YOU IN DEEPER!
THAT EMAIL MISCARRIED, OF COURSE. THERE WAS A SERVER ERROR, APPARENTLY. MORE THAN A MILLION MESSAGES WERE LOST.
ITACHI? IF YOU PLEASE--
THERE, MY HONORED FRIEND.
THAT'S WHAT SALVATION FEELS LIKE.

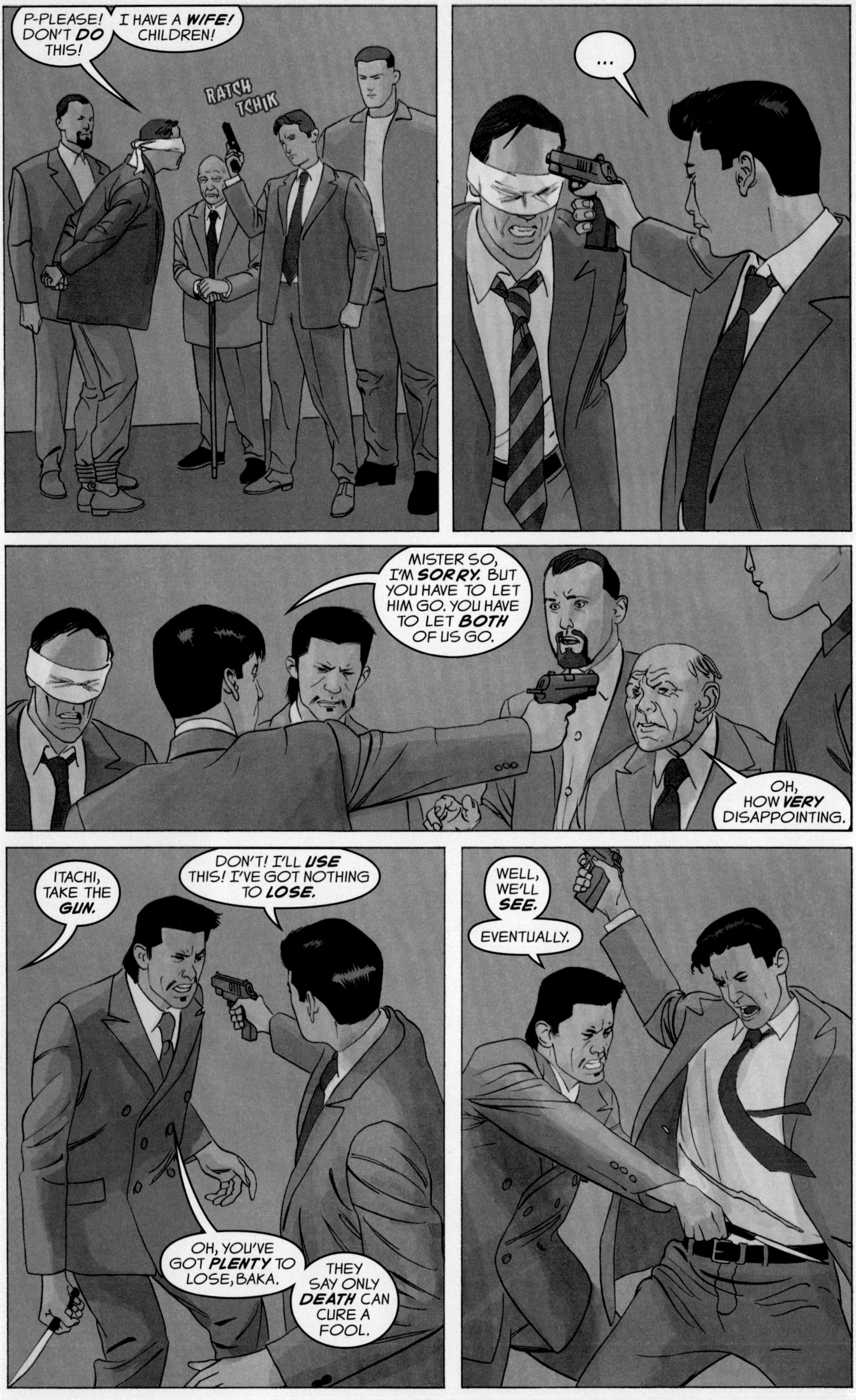
P-PLEASE! DON'T DO THIS!
I HAVE A WIFE! CHILDREN!
RATCH TCHIK
...
MISTER SO, I'M SORRY. BUT YOU HAVE TO LET HIM GO. YOU HAVE TO LET BOTH OF US GO.
OH, HOW VERY DISAPPOINTING.
ITACHI, TAKE THE GUN.
DON'T! I'LL USE THIS! I'VE GOT NOTHING TO LOSE.
OH, YOU'VE GOT PLENTY TO LOSE, BAKA.
THEY SAY ONLY DEATH CAN CURE A FOOL.
WELL, WE'LL SEE.
EVENTUALLY.

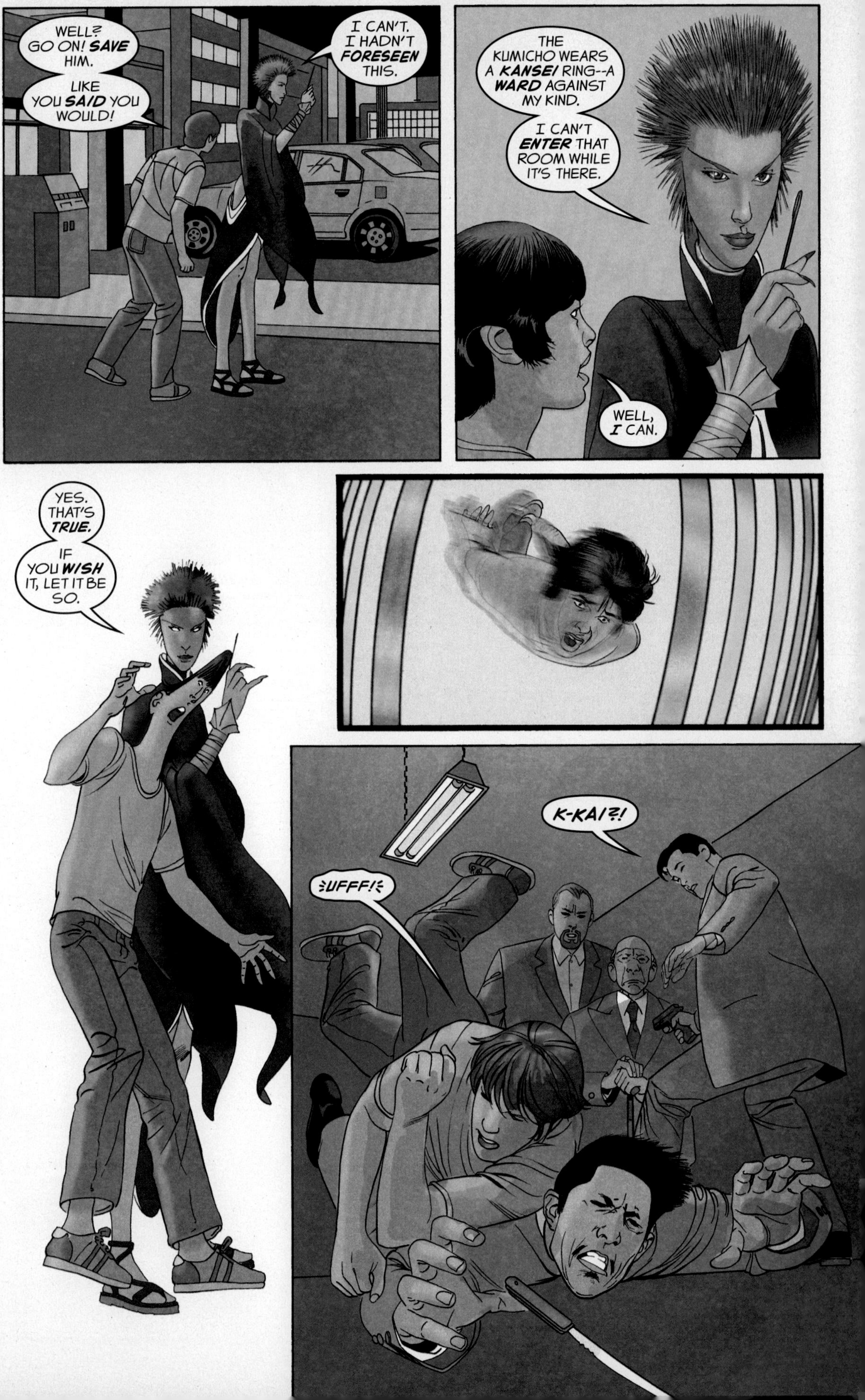
WELL? GO ON! SAVE HIM.
LIKE YOU SAID YOU WOULD!
I CAN'T. I HADN'T FORESEEN THIS.
THE KUMICHO WEARS A KANSEI RING--A WARD AGAINST MY KIND.
I CAN'T ENTER THAT ROOM WHILE IT'S THERE.
WELL, I CAN.
YES. THAT'S TRUE.
IF YOU WISH IT, LET IT BE SO.
K-KAI?!
UFFF!

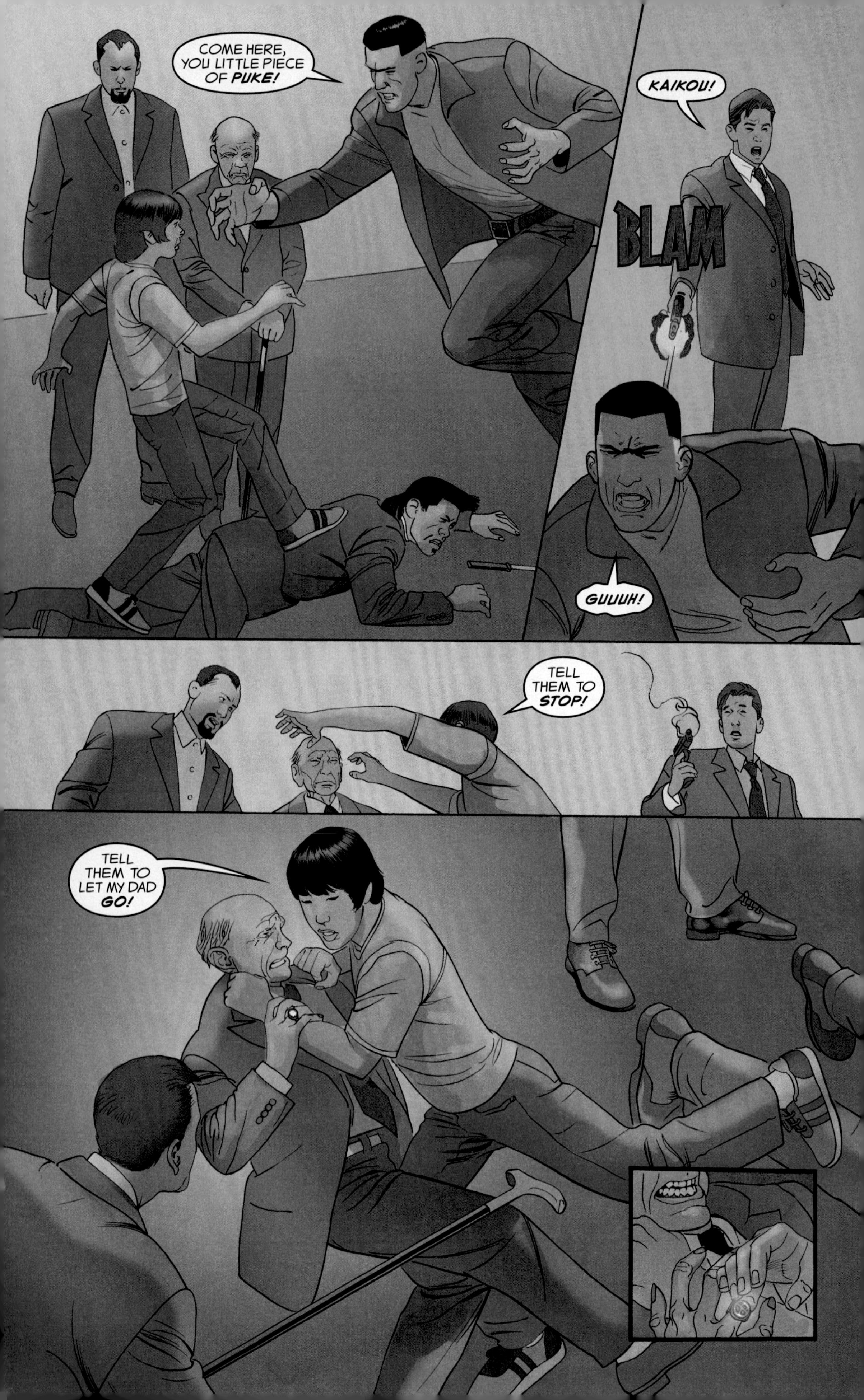
COME HERE, YOU LITTLE PIECE OF PUKE!
KAIKOU!
BLAM
GUUUH!
TELL THEM TO STOP!
TELL THEM TO LET MY DAD GO!

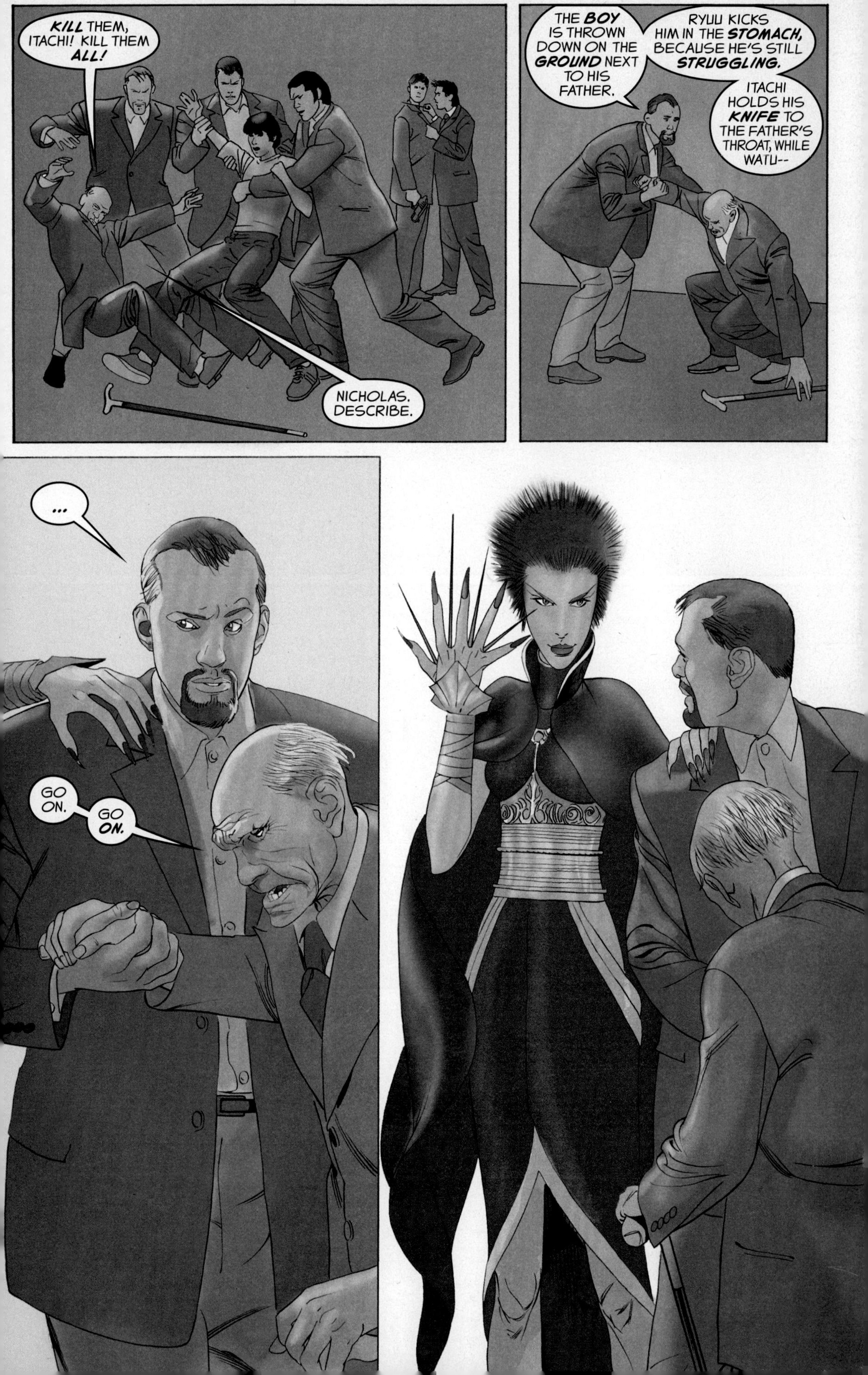

KILL THEM, ITACHI! KILL THEM ALL!
NICHOLAS. DESCRIBE.
THE BOY IS THROWN DOWN ON THE GROUND NEXT TO HIS FATHER.
RYUU KICKS HIM IN THE STOMACH, BECAUSE HE'S STILL STRUGGLING.
ITACHI HOLDS HIS KNIFE TO THE FATHER'S THROAT, WHILE WATU--
...
GO ON.
GO ON.

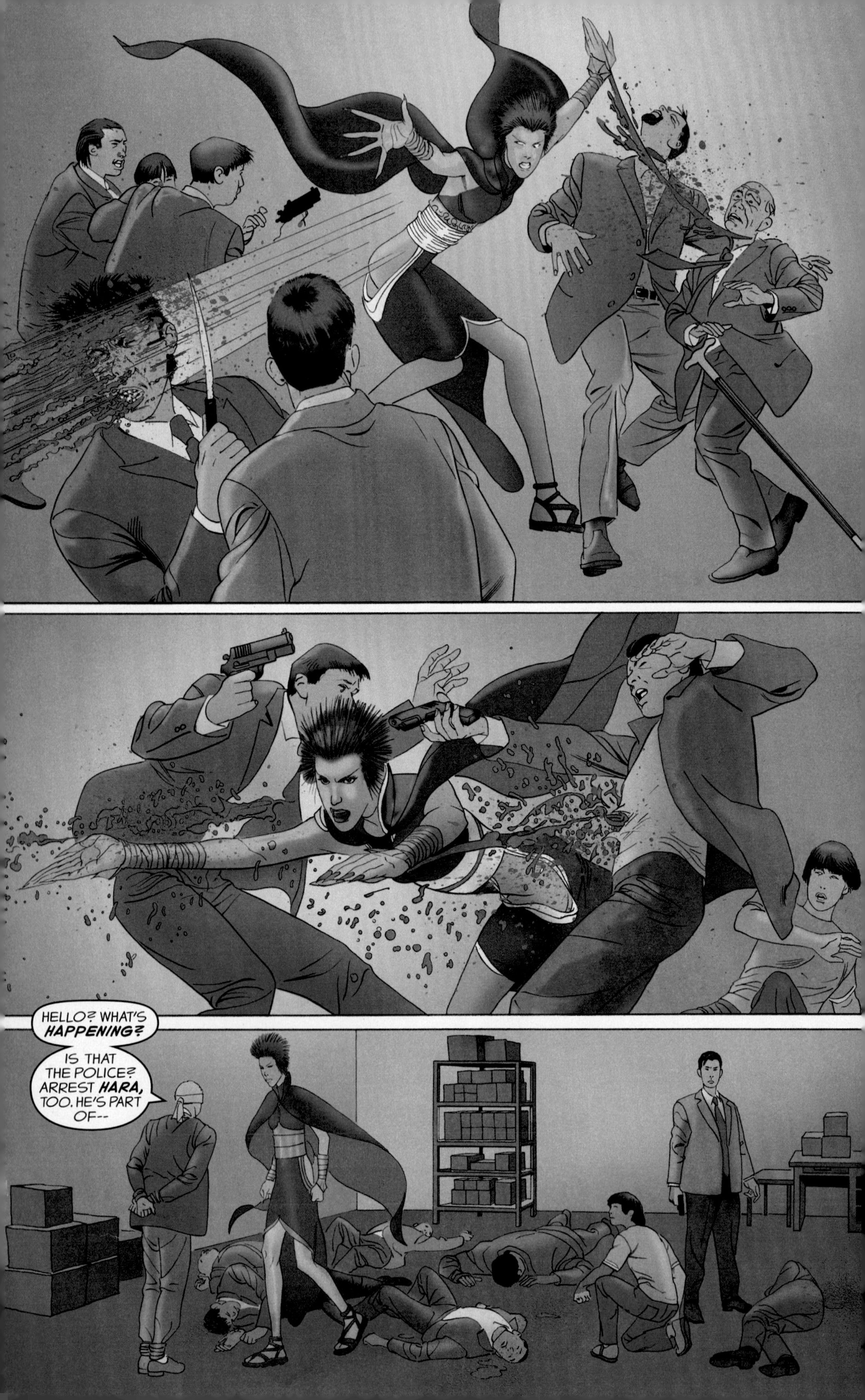
HELLO? WHAT'S HAPPENING?
IS THAT THE POLICE? ARREST HARA, TOO. HE'S PART OF--

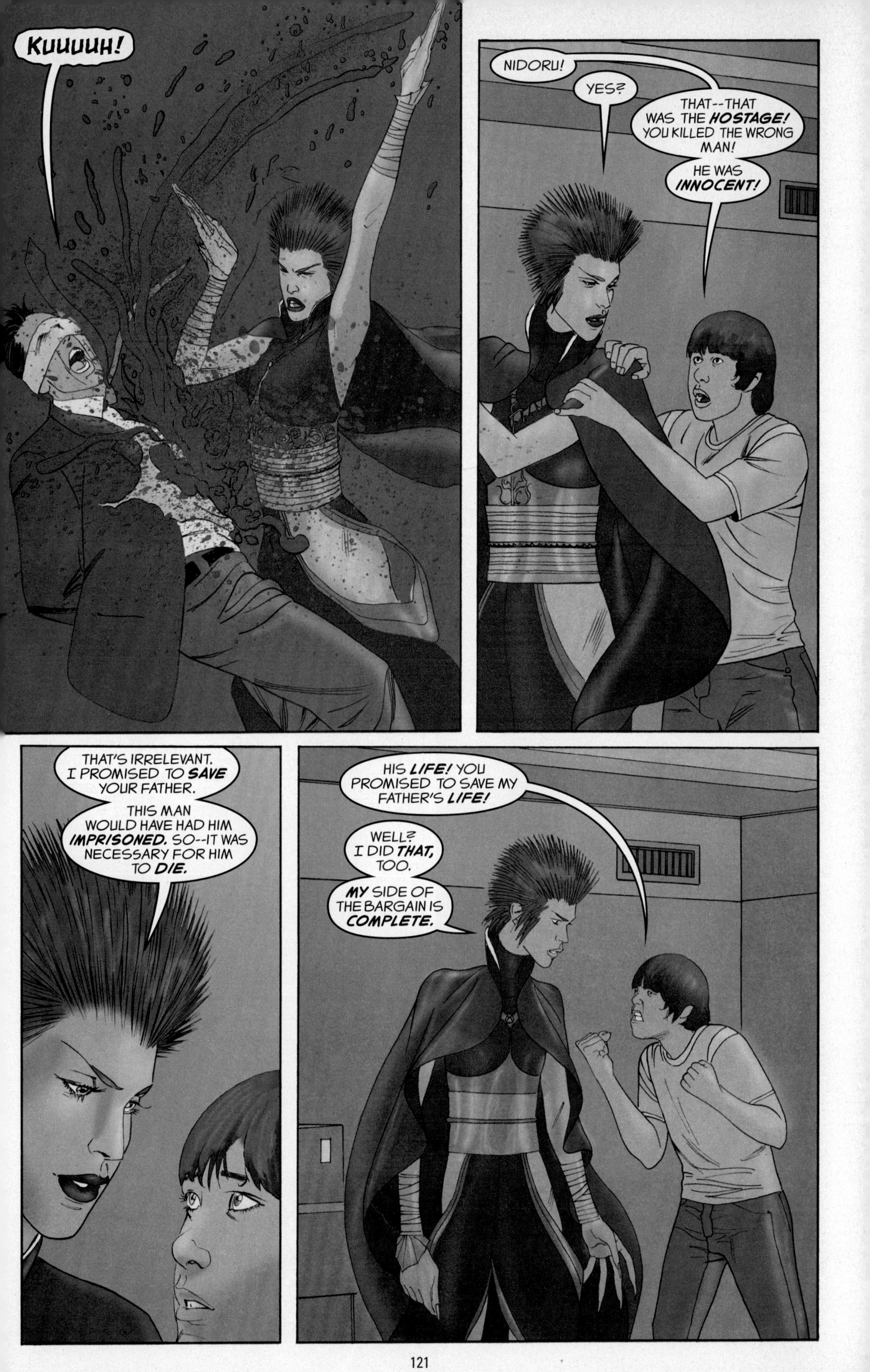
KUUUUH!
NIDORU!
YES?
THAT--THAT WAS THE HOSTAGE! YOU KILLED THE WRONG MAN!
HE WAS INNOCENT!
THAT'S IRRELEVANT. I PROMISED TO SAVE YOUR FATHER.
THIS MAN WOULD HAVE HAD HIM IMPRISONED. SO--IT WAS NECESSARY FOR HIM TO DIE.
HIS LIFE! YOU PROMISED TO SAVE MY FATHER'S LIFE!
WELL? I DID THAT, TOO.
MY SIDE OF THE BARGAIN IS COMPLETE.

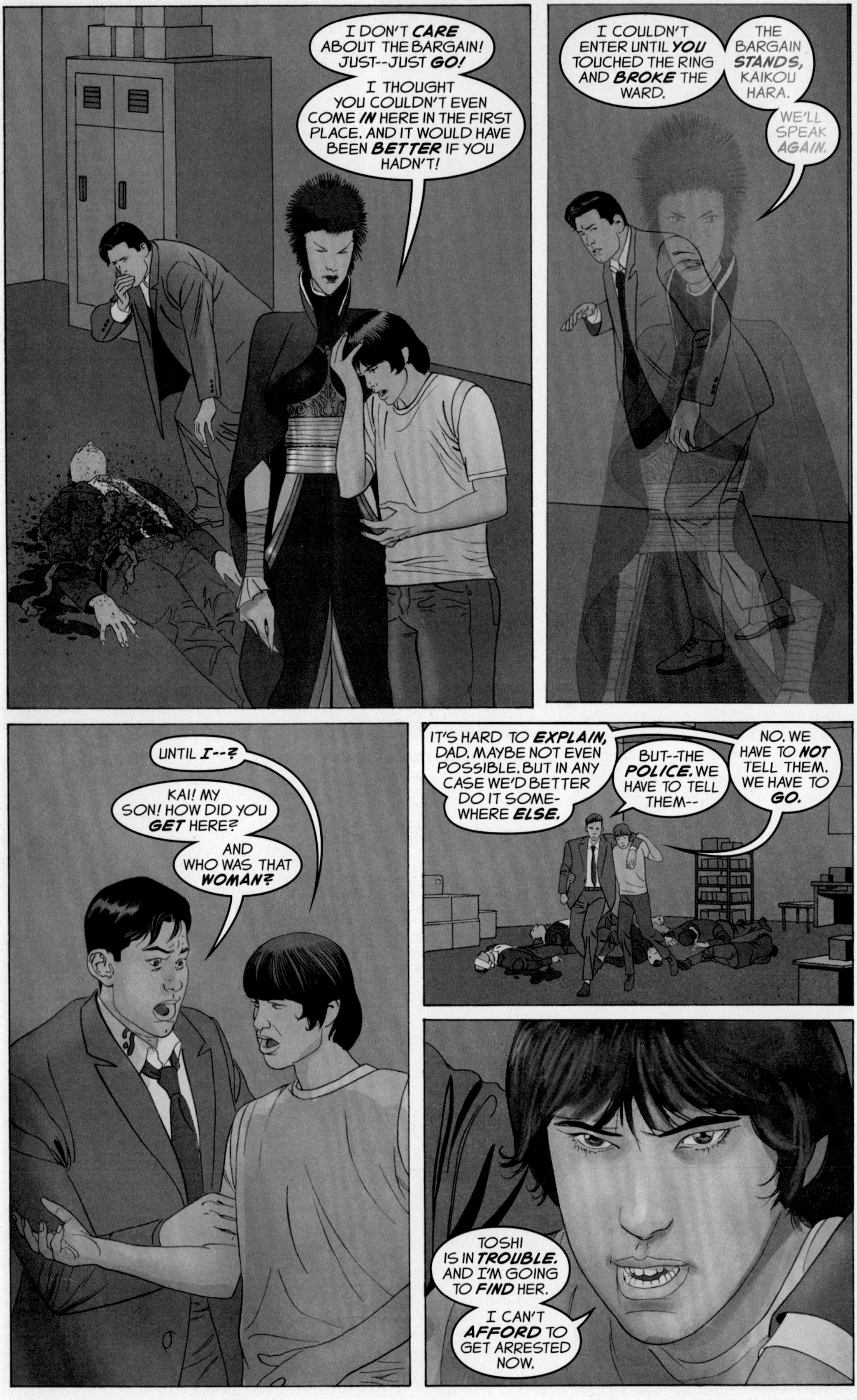

I DON'T CARE ABOUT THE BARGAIN! JUST--JUST GO!
I THOUGHT YOU COULDN'T EVEN COME IN HERE IN THE FIRST PLACE. AND IT WOULD HAVE BEEN BETTER IF YOU HADN'T!
I COULDN'T ENTER UNTIL YOU TOUCHED THE RING AND BROKE THE WARD.
THE BARGAIN STANDS, KAIKOU HARA.
WE'LL SPEAK AGAIN.
UNTIL I--?
KAI! MY SON! HOW DID YOU GET HERE?
AND WHO WAS THAT WOMAN?
IT'S HARD TO EXPLAIN, DAD. MAYBE NOT EVEN POSSIBLE. BUT IN ANY CASE WE'D BETTER DO IT SOMEWHERE ELSE.
BUT--THE POLICE. WE HAVE TO TELL THEM--
NO. WE HAVE TO NOT TELL THEM. WE HAVE TO GO.
TOSHI IS IN TROUBLE. AND I'M GOING TO FIND HER.
I CAN'T AFFORD TO GET ARRESTED NOW.

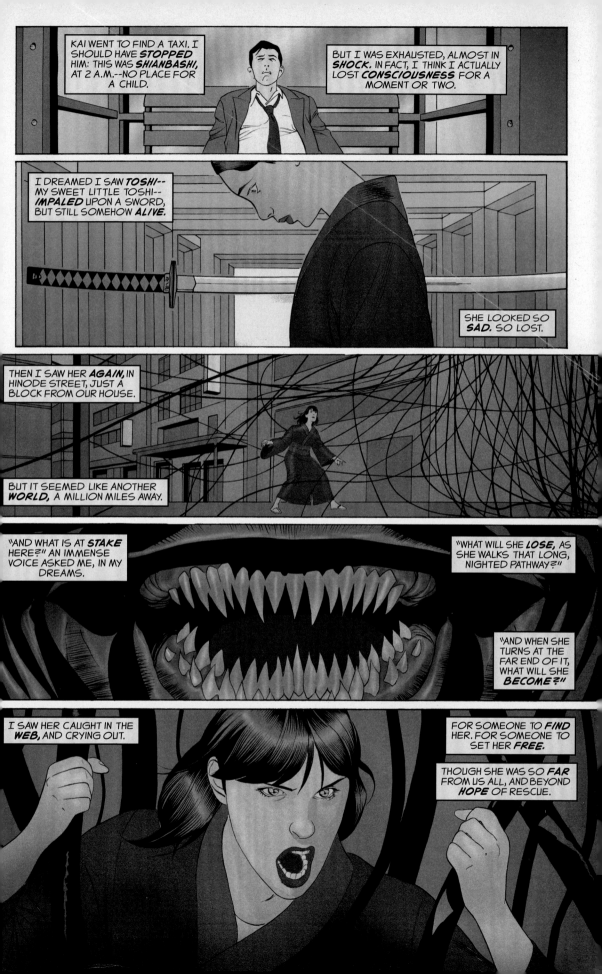

KAI WENT TO FIND A TAXI. I SHOULD HAVE **STOPPED** HIM: THIS WAS **SHIANBASHI,** AT 2 A.M.--NO PLACE FOR A CHILD.

BUT I WAS EXHAUSTED, ALMOST IN **SHOCK.** IN FACT, I THINK I ACTUALLY LOST **CONSCIOUSNESS** FOR A MOMENT OR TWO.

I DREAMED I SAW **TOSHI--** MY SWEET LITTLE TOSHI-- **IMPALED** UPON A SWORD, BUT STILL SOMEHOW **ALIVE.**

SHE LOOKED SO **SAD.** SO LOST.

THEN I SAW HER **AGAIN,** IN HINODE STREET, JUST A BLOCK FROM OUR HOUSE.

BUT IT SEEMED LIKE ANOTHER **WORLD,** A MILLION MILES AWAY.

"AND WHAT IS AT **STAKE** HERE?" AN IMMENSE VOICE ASKED ME, IN MY DREAMS.

"WHAT WILL SHE **LOSE,** AS SHE WALKS THAT LONG, NIGHTED PATHWAY?"

"AND WHEN SHE TURNS AT THE FAR END OF IT, WHAT WILL SHE **BECOME?"**

I SAW HER CAUGHT IN THE **WEB,** AND CRYING OUT.

FOR SOMEONE TO **FIND** HER. FOR SOMEONE TO SET HER **FREE.**

THOUGH SHE WAS SO **FAR** FROM US ALL, AND BEYOND **HOPE** OF RESCUE.

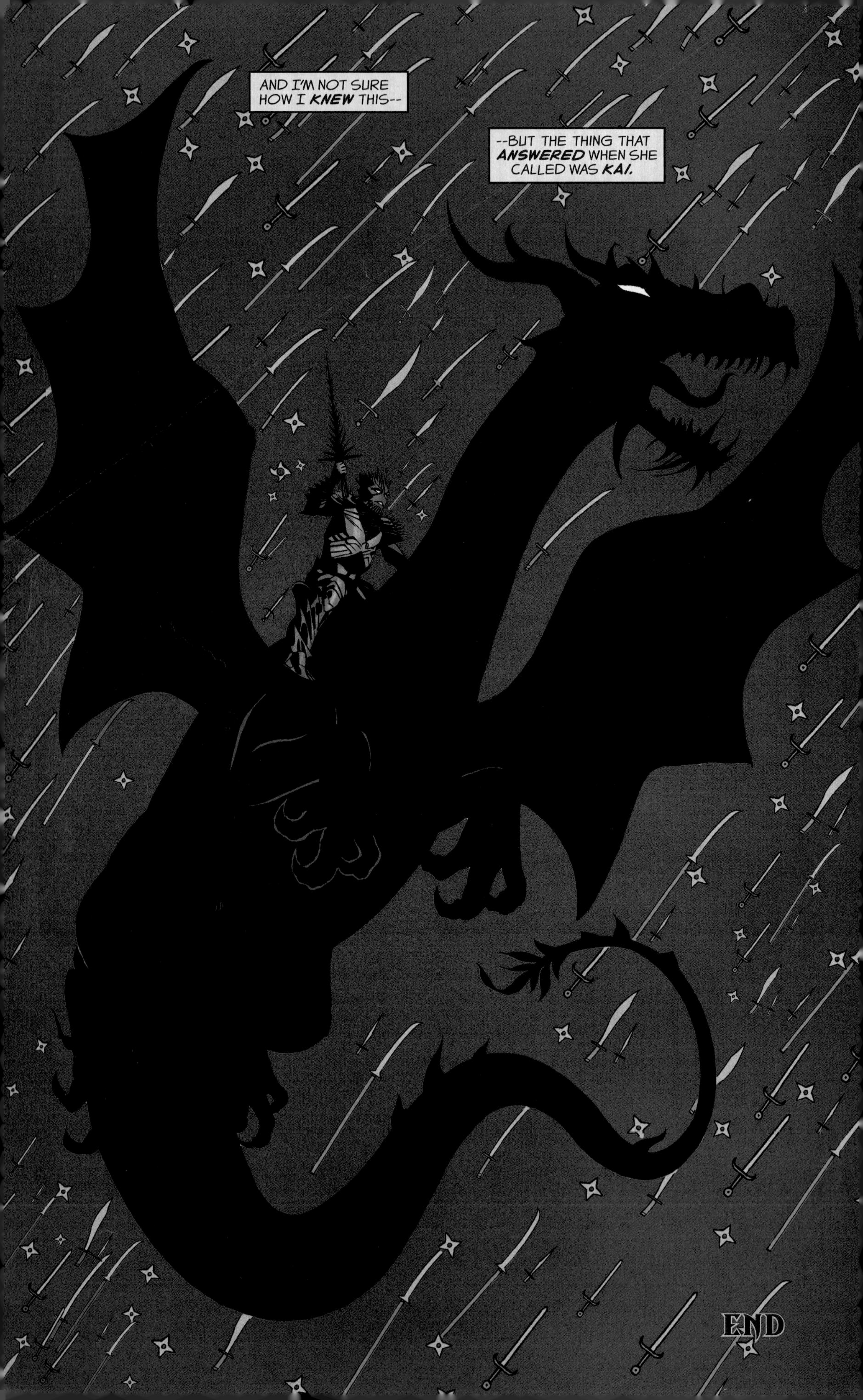
AND I'M NOT SURE HOW I **KNEW** THIS--
--BUT THE THING THAT **ANSWERED** WHEN SHE CALLED WAS **KAI.**
END

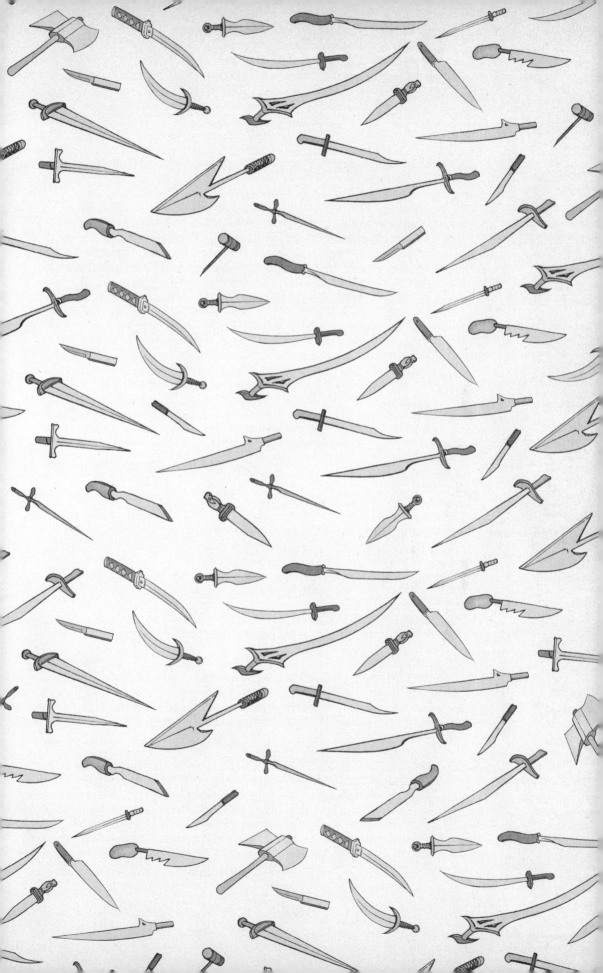

Afterword:

As CROSSING MIDNIGHT unfolds, it leans increasingly on the representation of two classes of supernatural entity drawn from Japanese folklore: the kami and the yokai. These beings have an important but elusive place within the shifting currents of Japanese culture both ancient and modern, and so it seemed appropriate to add some sleeve notes here when the space became available — especially since our own treatment of them is going to deviate from the traditional in some respects.

Broadly speaking, the kami are the spirits that live within ordinary objects or those that govern natural phenomena like thunder or earthquakes. The origin of the word isn't fully known, but it seems quite likely to have arisen from a root word meaning just that — ghosts or spirits. They're powerful supernatural entities, and in the Shinto faith they are sometimes worshipped, but they're emphatically not gods: a different word is used to describe the major deities.

It's hard to be more precise than that, because Japanese writers and cultural commentators use it themselves in a fairly loose and flexible way. In other words, there are no explicit rules for what can and can't be a kami. A particular place or a particular thing can have a kami of its own, and it's legitimate to show respect and make offerings to that kami in that place. Kami can also rule over classes of objects such as ploughs or bridges or ropes (our Aratsu presents himself as a kami of this type). But a revered ancestor can also be worshipped as a kami, and — notwithstanding what I said earlier about "god" being a different word — some Shinto priests make no distinction between the kami and the gods and goddesses of the Shinto pantheon: they're seen as being different instances of the same divine spark.

At rock bottom, we're looking here with the same powerful animistic belief that informs many other religions both in the East and here in the West.
When Wordsworth in *The Prelude* exclaims to "Ye Presences of Nature, in the sky/ Or on the earth! Ye Visions of the Hills / And Souls of lonely places!" he is invoking the kami, and he'd have been right at home with the concept.

The yokai are a different kettle of fish, and they have a more tortuous origin.
The word is often translated as "apparitions" or "demons," but for what it's worth I think you're on a better footing if you compare them with fairies and elves in Western folklore. There are many thousands of them, they all have their own names and their own unfathomable agendas, and they can range in temperament from compassionate and helpful to cruel and spiteful and motivelessly malignant.

It's impossible to exaggerate the wealth and sprawling extent of this folkloric tradition. If you're interested (and you probably wouldn't have read this far if you weren't at least a little curious), go online and type the word into Google. You'll find lists that run to screen after screen, covering just the yokai that have been written about and therefore have made it into the bestiaries and theories of modern anthropologists.

There's Akurojin-no-Hi — "the bad road fire monster" — who appears to lonely travellers at night as a flame dancing in the road ahead of them and will lead them astray or put a sickness on them if they let him get too close. There's Tamamo-no-Mae, who is variously a nine-tailed fox and a ravishingly beautiful and seductive woman; Ubume, the spirit of a woman who died in childbirth and now hovers around her own living child to protect it; Baku, who eats your nightmares, Zenfusho, who makes your kettle boil fast or makes it spill over if you piss him off, and literally thousands and thousands of others.

A Supernatural Bestiary

If all this sounds weird, bear in mind that just here in the UK, where I'm writing, the fairy tradition in folklore similarly includes a great many named individuals and types: the will o' the wisp, the light that leads travellers astray, is our version of Akurojin-no-Hi. And for Ubume and Zenfusho we've got Peg Powler, Jenny Greenteeth, Robin Goodfellow, and so on and so forth.

We're not talking about religion here, we're talking about a folk tradition that at its heart is quintessentially both pagan and rural: people living close to the land at a time when the dark was very dark and other human communities were a long journey away inevitably conceptualized and named the things that they feared or hoped for. The fairy tradition in Europe and the yokai in Japan both arose from this process.

And since we're talking about a folk tradition, the other thing that comes with the territory is that it was mostly oral: people weren't writing this stuff down, they were just living it. Tip your hat to Jenny Greenteeth as you go past the pond: throw a fish-tail into the water for Amikiri and he won't cut through your net the next time you catch a big one. You don't need to explain: anyone who sees you doing it will understand without being told.

So CROSSING MIDNIGHT sets out its shingle at a very busy and very confusing cultural crossroads — where formal religion meets rural superstition, where high culture meets low, and where badly informed Western dilettantes like me meet complex Eastern traditions that they barely understand but find pretty damn fascinating. That's good: that's very good. A crossroads is a fine place for us to be, because the story we're telling here is all about journeys and it's all about crossing from one state into another, whether objectively or internally.

As you'll see, the vision of the spirit world that we're setting out here is essentially a hierarchical one. That's an imposition on the material, in a sense, because we're creating an arbitrary order out of a glorious multiplicity, but we've got our own reasons for wanting to do that — not least, to avoid any accusations of whimsy.

Picking up on hints from some Shinto scholars, we've let our kami fall into two categories. The first and the highest, like Aratsu, are overlords of an entire class of objects — in Aratsu's case, knives, or more broadly everything that has an edge or a point. Beneath him, there are a great many lesser kami who are the spirits of particular knives or sharp objects, Nidoru being one.

Standing aside from this rigid hierarchy are the yokai. For the most part, they owe allegiance to no one: they do their own thing, follow their own (usually quite narrow) agenda, and deal with the humans they meet according to their own lights, graciously or viciously. They are, in a way, the demons and monsters to the kami's gods. The early story arcs in CROSSING MIDNIGHT are free of yokai, but they become vitally important later on as the interlocking quests of the Hara twins kick into gear — as they approach the crossroads, the point of transition, from their own separate quarters, with their own very different trajectories.

Perhaps inevitably, crossroads have a kami of their own. His name is Chimata, and if you want to keep him sweet, all you have to do is to put a smooth pebble down on the ground at the point where two roads meet, and say a prayer.

Now if only Kaikou and Toshi Hara had known that...

MIKE CAREY . London, April 21st 2007

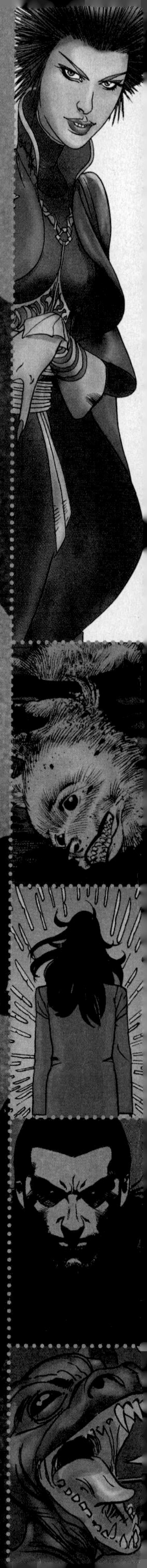

THE IMMORTAL CHARACTERS OF POPULAR
FAIRY TALES HAVE BEEN DRIVEN FROM THEIR
HOMELANDS AND NOW LIVE HIDDEN AMONG US,
TRYING TO COPE WITH LIFE IN 21ST-CENTURY
MANHATTAN IN THESE COLLECTIONS FROM
WRITER BILL WILLINGHAM AND VERTIGO:

FABLES

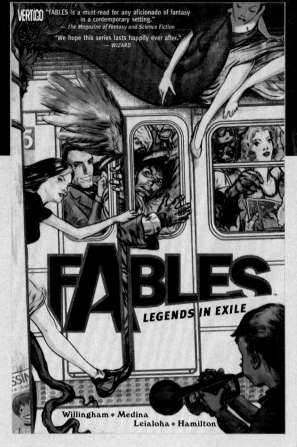

VOLUME 1:
LEGENDS IN EXILE

ALSO AVAILABLE:
VOL. 2: ANIMAL FARM
VOL. 3: STORYBOOK LOVE
VOL. 4: MARCH OF THE
    WOODEN SOLDIERS
VOL. 5: THE MEAN SEASONS
VOL. 6: HOMELANDS

"[A] WONDERFULLY TWISTED CONCEPT."
— *THE WASHINGTON POST*

"GREAT FUN."
— *BOOKLIST*

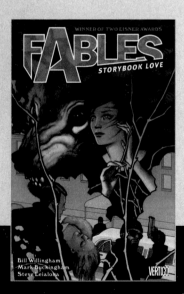

ALL TITLES ARE SUGGESTED FOR MATURE READERS.

SEARCH THE GRAPHIC NOVELS SECTION OF
www.VERTIGOCOMICS.com
FOR ART AND INFORMATION ON ALL OF OUR BOOKS!